THE
MAYAN
MISSION

THE
MAYAN
MISSION

Another Mission. Another Country.
Another Action-Packed Adventure.

*1,000 New *SAT
Vocabulary Words*

Karen B. Chapman

For general information on our other products and services or to obtain technical support please contact our Customer Care Department within the U.S. at (800) 762-2974, outside the U.S. at (317) 572-3993 or fax (317) 572-4002.

Wiley also publishes its books in a variety of electronic formats. Some content that appears in print may not be available in electronic books. For more information about Wiley products, please visit our web site at www.wiley.com.

Library of Congress Control Number: 2005926048

ISBN-13: 978-0-7645-9820-3
ISBN-10: 0-7645-9820-1

Printed in the United States of America

10 9 8 7 6 5 4 3 2 1

Book design by Kathie Rickard
Cover design by José Almaguer
Book production by Wiley Publishing, Inc. Composition Services

Table of Contents

About the Author

Karen B. Chapman, Ph.D., grew up in upstate New York and graduated from Cornell University with a B.S. in Biology. She received a Ph.D. in Molecular Biology and Genetics from John Hopkins University School of Medicine and went on to complete postdoctoral fellowships at both the Pasteur Institute in Paris and Harvard Medical School. Currently, she resides in Northern California with her husband and four young children.

1

A Pejorative Label

Alexa's eyes opened slowly and began to take in her surroundings in the dimness of the early morning light. Everything looked so familiar—the desk littered with stacks of magazines, the old rocking chair strewn with clothes, the threadbare[1] rug, and the Avril Lavigne poster tacked to the wall, its edges badly frayed.

Reaching up to the window above her bed, Alexa raised the shade and yawned widely as the bright rays of sunshine flooded her room. But instead of getting up, she nestled her head back in her pillow and lay there languidly[2] as she thought about the fact that she was home again, after her summer adventure in the Caribbean was abruptly curtailed[3]. As much as she loved her family and cherished her home in Ithaca, New York, she couldn't help but feel ambivalent[4] about being back. When she closed her eyes, she saw a white sandy beach, a spectacular expanse of clear blue water with dolphins cavorting[5] playfully on the surface, and of course, she saw José.

---

[1] **Threadbare:** frayed, worn, or shabby
[2] **Languid:** sluggish; lacking energy
[3] **Curtail:** to cut short; reduce
[4] **Ambivalent:** having a mixture of opposite feelings
[5] **Cavort:** to bound or prance about in a playful, boisterous, or sprightly manner

They had met earlier that summer at a Marine Biology station off the coast of Central America and immediately became fast friends, despite their disparate[6] backgrounds. He was really the first boy in her life who she could actually call a boyfriend. Of course there was Justin, her date for the junior prom. But he wasn't really a boyfriend. They didn't decide to go to the prom together out of romance. It was more of a pragmatic[7] decision—they both needed dates for the prom, so they decided to go together. Through a deal brokered by their friends, they jumped through the hoops of the junior prom—flowers, pictures, and a limousine rented with a group of friends. Alexa cringed whenever she thought about the awkward way that prom night had ended. They didn't kiss. Instead, they sort of bumbled through a weird, awkward handshake on her front porch. The whole episode was so painfully embarrassing that Alexa was left wishing that she had gone to the prom with a group of girl-friends instead.

José was different. They had met on the beach and their special friendship developed so naturally and so quickly. Alexa couldn't believe that for the first time, someone she liked actually liked her, too. He was cute and smart and interesting. It was like a dream come true. But every-thing came screeching to a halt when Alexa returned home in the middle of the summer and José stayed on his native island in the Caribbean Sea. Now they were separated by over a thousand miles. Somehow, the dis-tance did nothing to abate[8] her feelings. The knowledge that she might not see him again didn't cause her affection for him to wane[9]. It simply made her heart heavy as she climbed out of bed and got ready to go down-stairs for breakfast.

---

[6] **Disparate:** fundamentally different or dissimilar
[7] **Pragmatic:** practical, matter-of-fact
[8] **Abate:** to reduce; lessen
[9] **Wane:** to gradually decrease

"Good morning," Alexa's mom Helen chirped. "How did you sleep? I bet it felt good to be back in your own bed."

"Uh, yeah, I guess so," Alexa replied unenthusiastically, grabbing a banana from the fruit bowl. In her mind, she remembered the banana trees of the tropical island, and how José had once shimmied up the tree to fetch her a perfectly ripe, perfectly yellow banana. Alexa looked at the banana in her hand and decisively removed the shiny blue supermarket sticker. She peeled the skin and took a bite, but somehow it just didn't taste right. It wasn't quite the same as the banana plucked right off the tree.

Helen looked up from her newspaper. "You know, since you have some time on your hands, you might want to think about cracking open some of those SAT study guides I bought for you," she suggested cautiously.

Alexa set the banana on the counter and avoided her mother's probing gaze. Unconsciously, she pressed her lips together tightly, an expression that reflected the angst that she felt every time her mother brought up the SATs. She didn't even want to dignify her mother's suggestion with a response. She was so sick of all that trite advice about planning for the future. Alexa didn't need to be reminded of the fact that she had scored poorly on the SATs. That disappointing number was lurking everywhere—every time she closed her eyes she saw it and felt it. It was like a pejorative[10] label that she didn't want to own or acknowledge. Of course, Alexa knew that she had to take the test over in the fall. But she certainly didn't want to think about that now. It was summertime.

"Your father wants you to stop by his office this morning," Helen remarked casually. "I think that he has an idea to propose to you—something interesting for you to do with the rest of your summer."

---

[10] **Pejorative:** disparaging; belittling

"Really?" Alexa asked, brightening up at the shift in the conversation. "But there's only six weeks left of the summer until school starts."

"Six weeks is a long time to laze around the house, wallowing[11] in misery," Helen cautioned. "You've been acting despondent[12] ever since we got back, and I'm starting to get concerned. I know that you miss your friend José, but you'll feel better when you get back to work and try to accomplish something meaningful...trust me. That's why I was suggesting that you take the time now to study for the SATs. It makes all the sense in the world for you to use some of the time that you have now to study, before school starts up again and things get busy." Helen sighed, exasperated at this ongoing conversation that went nowhere. "But since you don't seem too eager to follow my advice, I think that you might want to hear what your father has in mind for you to occupy your time. It's not so onerous[13]...I think you'll be pleasantly surprised."

"What is it? What's Dad's plan?" Alexa asked eagerly.

"He wanted to tell you himself. Why don't you go see him after breakfast?"

"I'm going right now," Alexa declared, turning to grab her backpack out of the hall closet.

"Alexa!" Helen called out.

"What?" she replied, poking her head back into the kitchen.

"That's a meager[14] breakfast," Helen remarked, pointing to the half-eaten banana on the countertop. "I just made these healthy muffins—why don't you eat one? You're going to become emaciated[15] if you don't eat! You've hardly eaten anything the last few days—ever since we arrived back home."

---

[11] **Wallow:** indolent or clumsy rolling around, as if in water, snow, or mud: *pigs wallowing in the mud*
[12] **Despondent:** extreme discouragement, dejection, or depression
[13] **Onerous:** oppressive or troublesome; burdensome
[14] **Meager:** deficient in quantity or amount; scanty
[15] **Emaciate:** to become extremely thin, especially as a result of starvation

"Don't worry," Alexa replied, attempting to allay[16] her mother's concerns. "I'm going to stop at the Big Squeeze to get a smoothie on my way to Dad's office. It's filled with vitamins."

Her mother gave her a reproving[17] glance.

"OK, I'll take one with me," she said, taking a muffin in an effort to appease[18] her mother. In reality, she wasn't very hungry. Somehow, nothing looked palatable[19]. Maybe it had something to do with her heavy heart, she thought silently as she wrapped the warm brown muffin in a paper towel and popped it into her backpack.

"Don't forget to eat it," Helen warned.

"I won't," Alexa replied, giving her mother a reassuring smile. "Bye, Mom!" she called out, slinging the backpack over her shoulder.

Alexa ventured out the door and into the bright morning sunshine for the short walk to the Cornell University campus, where her father worked as a professor of molecular biology. She couldn't stop thinking about what kind of plan he had to propose. Alexa quickened her pace as her curiosity began to grow.

Passing by the Big Squeeze, Alexa scanned the crowd. The popular smoothie bar was a big hangout for high school students, especially during the hot summer months when the cool, frosty drinks held an irresistible allure. Alexa and her best friend Laurie liked to go there every day. But today the crowd was sparse, and when Alexa perused[20] the occupied tables and the short line at the counter, she didn't see Laurie anywhere. Even though Alexa hated to hang out at the Big Squeeze alone, she decided to go ahead and order a strawberry smoothie. Her throat felt really parched[21].

---

[16] **Allay:** reduce in intensity or severity; alleviate, relieve
[17] **Reprove:** to convey disapproval of
[18] **Appease:** to bring peace or quiet to; soothe
[19] **Palatable:** acceptable or agreeable to eat
[20] **Peruse:** to examine with attention and in detail
[21] **Parched:** dry; thirsty

Alexa popped a straw into the icy drink, eager to assuage[22] her thirst. Tugging at the thick, cold smoothie that was so reluctant to climb up the straw, she made her way out into the courtyard to find a seat.

"Hey, Alexa!" a male voice called out.

Alexa turned abruptly, her smooth brown hair swinging over her shoulder, searching the crowd for the source of the voice. When she realized who it was, she was absolutely flabbergasted[23]. It was Doug, the popular star of the varsity lacrosse team. The same Doug who rode in her carpool every day and yet still managed to pretend that she didn't exist. The same Doug who always acted indifferent[24] whenever their paths crossed in the hallways of Ithaca High School. Alexa stood there, motionless, too shocked to speak.

"Hey, how's your summer going? I haven't seen you around lately," he remarked casually, walking right up to her as if it were the most normal thing in the world. In his hand was the ever-present lacrosse stick, which he adroitly[25] maneuvered as he talked, bouncing the ball off of the pavement and catching it in the net with quick, skillful flicks of his wrist.

"Uh, yeah, I was away for the beginning of the summer," Alexa managed, still stupefied[26] by the fact that Doug had initiated a conversation. After years of acting aloof[27], why was he being so amicable[28] all of a sudden?

---

[22] **Assuage:** to put an end to by satisfying; quench, appease
[23] **Flabbergast:** to overwhelm with shock or astonishment; dumbfound
[24] **Indifferent:** having no marked feeling, interest, or concern
[25] **Adroit:** quick, skillful, or adept in action or thought; dexterous
[26] **Stupefy:** to amaze; astonish
[27] **Aloof:** emotionally distant, reserved, or remote
[28] **Amicable:** friendly

"Where did you go? You look so tanned," he remarked approvingly.

"Uh...down south...uh, an island in the Caribbean off the coast of Central America," she replied.

"Wow, that sounds really cool," he enthused.

"Yeah, it was," Alexa replied. She wished that she could think of something clever to say...something funny or irreverent[29]. But instead she felt utterly inarticulate[30], unable to put together a coherent[31] sentence.

Doug bounced the ball several times in rapid succession, then caught it and twirled the stick in an adept[32] display of virtuoso[33] lacrosse skills. "Do you want to get something to drink?" he asked nonchalantly[34], without taking his eyes off the ball.

"I have something to drink," Alexa replied, holding up her smoothie.

"Oh, yeah," he chuckled, flashing the winsome[35] grin that got him voted "nicest smile" in the school yearbook two years in a row. "But that's just fruit juice. What you really need is some wheatgrass juice," he asserted[36]. "It's really good for you—it's loaded with vitamins and antioxidants. Don't go anywhere," he commanded. "I'll be right back." Without giving her the opportunity to say no, Doug raced to the counter to procure[37] two portions of wheatgrass juice. With a triumphant grin, he returned with two small white paper cups and handed one to her.

Alexa eyed the opaque green liquid suspiciously. It looked like what it was...liquid grass. The thought of drinking the repulsive[38] juice

---

[29] **Irreverent:** critical of what is generally accepted or respected; satirical: *irreverent humor*
[30] **Inarticulate:** unable to speak clearly
[31] **Coherent:** marked by an orderly and logical relation of parts: *a coherent argument*
[32] **Adept:** very skilled
[33] **Virtuoso:** exhibiting the fine skill, masterful technique, and ability similar to that of a master musician
[34] **Nonchalant:** seeming to be coolly indifferent or unconcerned
[35] **Winsome:** charming, often in a childlike or naive way
[36] **Assert:** to state positively; affirm
[37] **Procure:** to get by special effort; obtain
[38] **Repulsive:** causing aversion or repugnance; disgusting

was horrifying. It looked and smelled utterly repugnant[39]. But how could she say no?

In a swift motion, Doug tossed his head back and swallowed the juice in one enthusiastic gulp. "Mmm..." he hummed, as if he had just enjoyed a savory[40] treat.

Alexa took another look at the viscous[41] green soup. She didn't relish[42] the thought of drinking it.

"C'mon, try it! It's good," he cajoled[43], smiling persuasively.

Bravely, she put the cup to her lips and took a big sip. As soon as the pungent[44] juice hit her tongue, she felt her stomach turn. Quickly, she swallowed it, in a desperate attempt to get the vile liquid off of her tongue. Once it went down her throat and into her empty stomach, she shuddered with revulsion. Immediately, she took a sip of her strawberry smoothie in an attempt to get the acrid[45] taste of wheatgrass out of her mouth.

Doug was laughing uncontrollably. "It's not that bad!" he chuckled. "I drink this all the time, especially when I'm training."

"Maybe it's an acquired taste," Alexa remarked. "One that I haven't acquired yet." She studied his expression, trying to figure out if he was laughing *with* her or *at* her. Did he buy her this drink to make fun of her? Her face flushed with embarrassment.

"Well, if it's an acquired taste, then I'll buy you another one tomorrow, so that you can acquire it," he said, his eyes twinkling.

"OK," Alexa agreed, feeling a little bit better. His offer seemed genuine. All of a sudden Doug seemed sincerely interested in fostering[46] a

---

[39] **Repugnant:** causing disgust or aversion; offensive
[40] **Savory:** appetizing to the taste or smell
[41] **Viscous:** having a high resistance to flow; thick and sticky, syrupy
[42] **Relish:** to take keen pleasure in
[43] **Cajole:** to repeatedly urge with gentle appeals, teasing, or flattery; wheedle
[44] **Pungent:** affecting the organs of taste or smell with a sharp, acrid, or irritating sensation
[45] **Acrid:** unpleasantly sharp or bitter to the taste or smell
[46] **Foster:** to promote the growth and development of; nurture, cultivate

friendship, although she couldn't fathom[47] why he had had this precipitous change of heart. He had managed to ignore her completely for an entire year, and now he was acting so affable[48] and congenial[49].

"OK, then, same time, same place, tomorrow," he declared, tossing the ball to one of his buddies, who were huddled in a group on the sidewalk. "See ya," he called out to her as he ran to join his friends.

Alexa waved goodbye and started to head outside, still astounded and a bit suspicious of Doug's atypical[50] behavior. But despite her lingering doubts and a little voice in the back of her mind telling her to be more circumspect[51] about Doug's sudden interest, she decided she would go by the Big Squeeze again tomorrow morning.

Alexa scanned the crowd one last time for Laurie, but she was nowhere to be found. She couldn't wait to pick up the phone and call her friend. They had a lot to talk about now.

Giving up on Laurie, Alexa walked briskly over the bridge that led to the Cornell campus and then slowed her pace when she reached the sun-drenched quad, a rectangular grassy area circumscribed[52] by a ring of academic buildings. Dozens of summer students were scattered on the grass, lounging, reading, or talking with friends while they basked in the sunshine. A few dogs also dotted the scene, enjoying the good weather and spectacular scenery along with their owners.

Alexa chuckled at the sight of the dogs frolicking on the quad. Despite the rules about keeping dogs properly restrained on campus, the canine species seemed to enjoy a special status at the university that was attributed to an old tale about a generous benefactor[53] with a penchant[54]

---

[47] **Fathom:** to understand the meaning or nature of; comprehend
[48] **Affable:** pleasant and easy to talk to
[49] **Congenial:** friendly and sociable; having a pleasant disposition
[50] **Atypical:** not conforming to type; unusual or irregular
[51] **Circumspect:** careful to consider all possible consequences; prudent, cautious
[52] **Circumscribe:** to draw a line around or surround by a boundary
[53] **Benefactor:** one who gives aid, especially financial aid
[54] **Penchant:** a strong liking or inclination

for dogs. According to the story, the wealthy philanthropist[55] made his sizable donation to the university contingent on a curious mandate[56]: that dogs would be allowed to run free on campus. Every time Alexa heard this story, she couldn't figure out if it was really true or if it was an apocryphal[57] legend. But it didn't seem to matter, because for many years the dogs did have an exalted[58] status and free rein on campus, until finally the university imposed a leash law, requiring owners to properly restrain their pets at all times.

Whether they were abiding[59] by the rules or not, Alexa loved seeing the dogs happily romping in the grass. Somehow it added to the carefree ambiance on the quad that was so inviting. It was a teasing glimpse of college life that Alexa couldn't wait to be a part of. Some students were sitting in groups, talking and laughing, while others were sitting by themselves, studying in the sunshine. Surveying the scene, Alexa was tempted to sit down on the grass, crack open a book, and join them. But her insatiable[60] curiosity compelled her to continue on to her father's office. What could he possibly have planned for her?

Alexa quickly made her way up to the third floor of the tall brick building that housed the molecular biology laboratories. The sign on the closed door said "Professor McCurry." She knocked softly.

"Come in," a gruff voice answered.

Alexa opened the door and poked her head in. "Hi, Dad."

"Good morning," he replied cheerfully, his face breaking into a warm smile. "C'mon in," he beckoned, pushing his chair back from the computer screen. Alexa's father was an esteemed[61] professor of molecular

---

[55] **Philanthropist:** a person who makes charitable donations with the intent of increasing the well-being of humankind

[56] **Mandate:** an authoritative command or instruction

[57] **Apocryphal:** of doubtful authenticity

[58] **Exalt:** to raise in rank, power; elevate

[59] **Abide:** to conform to; comply with

[60] **Insatiable:** incapable of being satisfied

[61] **Esteem:** to regard with respect

biology, highly respected by his colleagues for his astute[62] observations. His students were consistently amazed with his prescient[63] ability to predict the outcome of their experiments before they completed them. Among his friends, Professor McCurry was also renowned[64] for his collection of antique gadgets. His predilection[65] for old devices was evident to anyone who visited his office—the shelves were filled with a plethora[66] of vacuum tubes, Tesla coils, Crooke's tubes, transformers, and Van de Graff generators. If anyone asked a question about the antiquated[67] devices, Professor McCurry was thrilled to give them a demonstration and tell all about them. He was an erudite[68] scholar of the history of science, able to recall the inventor of even the most arcane[69] devices.

On the highest shelf of the bookcase in his office, Professor McCurry kept a collection of antediluvian[70] computers, all of which he had used at some point in the past. But as time went on and he continually upgraded his computer system, he was loath to toss out the outdated hardware. "There are files on there that I might need some day," he would say. But the ancient computers were never touched and the thick layer of dust that coated them was never disturbed. When people saw his office, they often commented that Professor McCurry was an archetypal[71] scientist.

But to Alexa, he was just Dad.

"I have a special surprise for you," he teased. "Did your mother tell you what it was?" he asked.

"No, she said that you were going to tell me. What is it?" Alexa asked. "Is it some job here on campus?"

---

[62] **Astute:** having shrewdness and discernment

[63] **Prescient:** foreknowledge of events

[64] **Renown:** a state of being widely acclaimed and highly honored; famous

[65] **Predilection:** a partiality or disposition in favor of something; a preference

[66] **Plethora:** an overabundance or excess

[67] **Antiquated:** too old to be useful or fashionable; outdated

[68] **Erudite:** having or displaying deep, extensive knowledge

[69] **Arcane:** known or understood by only a few; *arcane economic theories*

[70] **Antediluvian:** extremely old and antiquated

[71] **Archetypal:** an ideal example of a type

Her father shook his head, his eyes twinkling with merriment, as if he was about to bestow a great prize upon her.

"What is it?" Alexa pleaded.

"When you got back from Central America a few days ago, didn't you say something about how you weren't quite ready to come home yet and you really wanted to go back?"

"Yeah," Alexa agreed cautiously.

"And you know that Nadine is an archeologist, right?"

"Uh, yeah," Alexa answered reluctantly. She really didn't like talking about Nadine. She preferred to pretend that she didn't exist. Right after her parents' divorce was finalized, her father had introduced her to Nadine, his new girlfriend. Despite the fact that Nadine seemed eager to foster a friendship with her, Alexa coolly kept her distance.

"Well, Nadine is working on the excavation[72] of a Mayan ruin. You're familiar with the ancient Maya, aren't you?"

Alexa shook her head. "It sounds vaguely familiar, but I can't remember anything specific."

"They were a great civilization who inhabited Central America long before the arrival of the Europeans. You did learn about them in school, didn't you?"

"Not that I remember."

Professor McCurry clucked his tongue, showing his disappointment at this gross omission in her education. "There are some amazing ruins of ancient Mayan temples and cities scattered throughout the jungles of Central America. Some of these sites have been razed[73] and

---

[72] **Excavation:** the act of exposing or uncovering by digging
[73] **Raze:** to demolish or tear down to the ground

pillaged[74] by greedy treasure seekers, but others have been left untouched for more than a thousand years. They are yet to be explored!" He shook his head in wonder. "It's an archeologist's paradise."

Alexa's jaw dropped. "Did you say *Central* America?" she managed to ask. Her heart started to race with hope and anticipation. José lived in Central America!

"Yes, it's in Central America. Isn't that where you said you wanted to go? The site that they're working on is in Guatemala. Now I know that you just came back from that part of the world, but I can assure you that this would be a completely different experience. This is an actual archeological excavation site in the middle of the jungle."

Alexa felt a tingle of excitement shoot down her spine. She had expected her father to propose some tedious[75] job here on campus like filing papers or some such banal[76] task. But he had surprised her. Excavating an ancient Mayan ruin in Central America sounded incredibly interesting. And the thought that she would be in the same vicinity as José was like icing on the cake. Maybe they could see each other! Mentally, Alexa tried to calculate how far away he would be. "Can you show me on the map? Would you be going too?" Questions tumbled out of her mouth.

He chuckled at her enthusiasm. "Yes, but only for a day or two. I can travel there with you, but I can't stay there the whole time. I've got a collaboration set up at the university in Belize City, so I will be staying in Belize while you're at the dig in Guatemala—it's not too far away. So, if you want to take this opportunity, you would be on your own for several weeks at the dig. There would be plenty of adults there to watch over

---

[74] **Pillage:** to rob of goods by force or take as spoils; plunder
[75] **Tedious:** tiresome by reason of dullness, length, or slowness; boring
[76] **Banal:** lacking originality, freshness, or novelty

you—Nadine will be there, but we still need to have a serious discussion about whether you are ready for this level of independence." Professor McCurry looked at her questioningly, as if he were gauging her response.

"I'm ready!" Alexa exclaimed. "I'm seventeen now, and I'm going off to college in a year anyway."

He smiled when he saw the eager enthusiasm in her eyes. "You know, this is really an amazing opportunity for someone your age. Usually these digs are staffed by graduate students and a few very lucky undergraduates. Apparently, two of the students had to go home in the middle of the summer for personal reasons, and that opened up two spots." He stood up from his chair and reached up to the bookshelf above his computer to pull down a thick paperback volume entitled *The Ancient Maya: Treasures From a Lost Civilization*. "Here, you can get started with this. There's a map right in there."

Alexa took the book from his outstretched hand. The cover had a picture of a Mayan temple, a tall pyramid rising high above the jungle thicket.

Alexa's father glanced at his watch. "You know, I've got a faculty meeting at ten-thirty, but it shouldn't take longer than an hour. Why don't we have an early lunch together and I can tell you more about this trip. You can take that book down to the quad and read for a little while. I'll come find you when I'm done, and we can head over to the Big Red Barn for a sandwich."

"Sounds good," Alexa smiled, accepting his offer with alacrity[77]. She couldn't wait to dive into the book.

---

[77] **Alacrity:** promptness in response; cheerful readiness

Deciding that the elevator was a waste of precious time, she raced down three flights of stairs and out onto quad. Alexa picked out a shady spot under an oak tree and sat down, resting her back against the trunk. Eagerly, she thumbed through the pages looking for a map. There! Guatemala and Belize...it was only a few hundred miles from the tiny island off the coast of Nicaragua that José called home. Alexa's heart raced at the possibility of seeing José again. It was all so exciting.

Curiously, she began flipping through the pages of the book, looking at the fascinating photos. Who were these people and why did their civilization end, leaving the jungle adorned[78] with their seductive temples? Alexa was captivated[79] with the beckoning images of ancient stone pyramids and the aura of mystery that enveloped them. She was utterly enthralled[80] by the stunning photographs of huge stone monuments rising up above the jungle thicket. Without a doubt, she felt that her life was about to take an interesting turn.

Alexa reached for her backpack and rummaged around inside. Her hand grasped the object she was seeking. Triumphantly, she pulled out the brown muffin, chock-full of grated carrots, dried fruit, and whole-wheat flour, lovingly baked by her mom. All of a sudden, she was ravenous[81].

---

[78] **Adorn:** to lend beauty to, enhance or decorate
[79] **Captivate:** to attract and hold by beauty, charm or excellence
[80] **Enthrall:** to hold spellbound; captivate
[81] **Ravenous:** extremely hungry

2

Felicitous News

Alexa sat down at a picnic table across from her father, bursting with questions. He had adumbrated[82] this exciting plan in the vaguest of terms, leaving Alexa wondering about the specifics. "When do we leave?" she asked, eager for him to elaborate[83] on the details. "And where, exactly, are we going? Will I be working on the dig, doing real archeology?"

Alexa's father chuckled at her enthusiasm. "Hold your horses, there! I haven't even had a bite of my sandwich and you're accosting[84] me with a slew of questions," he complained good-naturedly.

"I'm sorry, but I just want to hear more," Alexa apologized, even though she could tell that her father was actually very pleased with her enthusiasm.

"I know I've said it before, but I just want you to really understand what a great opportunity this is," he said, popping open the top of his Diet Coke. "Yes, you will actually be able to work on the dig and learn how archeology is done. You'll be able to see firsthand what it's like to be an archeologist working in the field and all that it entails[85]. Of course,

---

[82] **Adumbrate:** to give a sketchy outline of
[83] **Elaborate:** to express at greater length or in greater detail
[84] **Accost:** to approach and speak to boldly or aggressively, as with a demand or request
[85] **Entail:** to have, impose, or require as a necessary accompaniment or consequence

you won't be compensated[86], but you will be able to help out and learn. It's basically a volunteer position."

"That's OK," Alexa said quickly. "It's not like I was expecting to make a copious[87] amount of money during summer break anyway. I love the sound of this job—it sounds so adventurous! I don't have aspirations[88] of being an archeologist when I'm older—I really want to be a marine biologist, but it definitely sounds more interesting than the jobs that my friends have this summer. I'm so happy that you were able to get this opportunity for me. It's a real coup[89]!"

"Actually, one of your friends will be going too. Remember how I said that there were two spots?"

"Who's going? Did you say it's someone I know...a friend of mine? Who is it?" Alexa asked quickly, her curiosity skyrocketing.

"I'm trying to remember his name..." Professor McCurry took a sip of Diet Coke, his forehead wrinkled in thought. "His father Nicholas is in the archeology department...what *is* his name?" he mused, frustrated with his faulty memory.

"It's a boy? Someone I know from school?" Alexa prodded, desperately curious.

"Well, yes, of course you know him...he's in our carpool. Doug! That's his name!" Professor McCurry exclaimed triumphantly.

"Doug? Doug is going too?" she asked, stunned at this development. She wasn't necessarily opposed to the idea, but silently, she wondered if Doug already knew about this and maybe that's why he'd acted so amiable[90] this morning. Maybe he knew that they were going to be

---

[86] **Compensate:** to make satisfactory payment or reparation to

[87] **Copious:** large in quantity; abundant

[88] **Aspiration:** a strong desire or ambition to achieve

[89] **Coup:** a brilliant, sudden, and usually highly successful stroke or act; a triumph

[90] **Amiable:** friendly, sociable

spending the rest of the summer together and he wanted to start off on the right foot.

"Yes, your friend Doug is going too. I just spoke to his father this morning. They're going to be on the same flight that we are. We're leaving really early Saturday morning. We'll be flying into Belize City and then catching a smaller plane for the half-hour flight to Santa Elena in the northern part of Guatemala. Then we'll be catching a ride to Tikal National Park, about 45 minutes away. I'm going to be staying there for a few days with you and then I'll be heading back to Belize."

"Wow, Saturday...that's soon. That's only three days from now."

"Yes, I know it's soon...are you OK with that?" he asked.

"Sure!" she replied enthusiastically. "I'm ready to go anytime," she added to emphasize the point that she truly was amenable[91] to this exciting plan.

"You know, I have to warn you about the accommodations. Just so you know now, you won't be staying in a commodious[92] suite at a deluxe cosmopolitan[93] hotel when you're at the dig. You'll probably be in a tent. The accommodations will be simple and utilitarian[94] at best. There probably won't be any hot showers...there may not be running water at all—or toilets, for that matter. You'll have to do without a lot of the amenities[95] that you're accustomed to at home."

"But where will I plug in my straightening iron?" Alexa joked, referring to the device that she used religiously every day to straighten the waves in her shoulder-length brown hair.

Professor McCurry burst out laughing. He could see that she was kidding and he thoroughly enjoyed a sense of humor.

---

[91] **Amenable:** readily brought to yield or cooperate; willing
[92] **Commodious:** roomy, spacious
[93] **Cosmopolitan:** having wide international sophistication
[94] **Utilitarian:** having utility, often to the exclusion of other values; practical
[95] **Amenities:** something that confers material or physical comfort

"Seriously, it's not a problem. I've been camping lots of times," she offered, making every effort to be accommodating[96]. There was no question in her mind that she was willing to abjure[97] luxury and conveniences in order to take advantage of this opportunity.

Alexa took a big bite of her ham sandwich, eager to satiate[98] her hunger. Her mind was racing as she thought about the upcoming weeks. Without a doubt, things were going to get interesting.

∽ ∾

The next morning, Alexa rifled through her closet, searching for clothes to pack. Even though they weren't departing for a couple more days, she wanted to take the time to pack carefully. With the phone pressed tightly to her ear, she searched the farthest reaches of her closet while she listened to her father talk about the details of their upcoming trip. Decidedly, she plucked a sweater off the shelf and then turned to toss it on top of the growing pile of clothes in her big suitcase.

"Since our flight departs at six forty-five Saturday morning from Syracuse, we'll be leaving here by three-thirty, just to be on the safe side," he said. "It will probably take us about an hour and a half to drive to the airport and I think that it would be prudent[99] to give ourselves a little extra time, just in case we run into traffic."

"But there won't be any traffic at that hour," Alexa pointed out.

"You never know what you might run into...better safe than sorry," he said. "Oh, and by the way, you'll need to pack light—just your sleeping bag and a small suitcase or backpack. We don't want to be encumbered[100]

---

[96] **Accommodate:** to adapt oneself, become adjusted
[97] **Abjure:** to give up or abstain from
[98] **Satiate:** to satisfy a need or desire fully or to excess
[99] **Prudent:** marked by wisdom in handling practical affairs; exercising good judgment or common sense
[100] **Encumber:** to put a heavy load on; burden

with a lot of stuff. It's just not practical to lug around big, unwieldy[101] bags all of the way to this remote site in the jungle."

Alexa looked at the behemoth[102] suitcase that lay open on the floor of her bedroom. A huge pile of clothes, shoes, and accessories were piled in its capacious[103] cavity. "OK, Dad. But I'm going to have to go now, because I need to repack."

After saying goodbye to her father, Alexa looked at the big pile of clothes and sighed. The vast majority needed to go back in the closet. Although Alexa wanted to bring her big suitcase, she didn't want to contravene[104] direct orders from her dad.

Alexa spied her brand-new black leather camera case and picked it up to inspect the digital camera inside. She ran her fingers lovingly over the smooth gray surface of the new camera she had just received the night before. Usually, her mother was much too frugal[105] to indulge her with pricey electronic gadgets, so this gift had come as a surprise. Carefully, she placed the camera back in its case and gently set it in her backpack. She couldn't wait to fill it with memories.

After a half-hour of sorting through the pile of clothes, Alexa decided to take a brief respite[106] from packing and check her e-mail. She was fervently[107] hoping to receive an e-mail from José, but every time she checked her inbox, it was empty. Alexa remembered their tearful goodbye, when they had each promised to write diligently[108]. A full week had passed, during which Alexa sent five e-mails, but José had not yet reciprocated[109]. Even after Alexa wrote to tell José the exciting news that she

---

[101] **Unwieldy:** difficult to manage or carry because of size or shape

[102] **Behemoth:** something of enormous size or power

[103] **Capacious:** capable of containing a large quantity; spacious, roomy

[104] **Contravene:** to act or be counter to; violate

[105] **Frugal:** marked by economy in spending; thrifty, sparing

[106] **Respite:** a short interval of rest or relief

[107] **Fervent:** having great emotion or zeal

[108] **Diligent:** characterized by steady and earnest effort

[109] **Reciprocate:** to give in response or return

was going to Tikal, he still hadn't responded. Alexa felt disheartened[110] every time she logged on to the computer and saw her empty inbox. She had so hoped they could keep their friendship strong by exchanging e-mails. Even though it wasn't the same as a real face-to-face conversation, an epistolary[111] friendship was better than no friendship at all.

When she heard the telltale ding, that delightful noise that her computer emitted when e-mail arrived, her heart began to flutter. There it was—the letter she had been waiting and wishing for so ardently[112]. Eagerly, Alexa clicked on the coveted[113] e-mail to open it.

> **Time:** 10:05 A.M.
> **To:** Alexa McCurry
> **From:** José Consuales
> **Subject:** Great News!
>
> Dear Alexa,
>
> I am so sorry I have not been able to write. Do you remember that old computer in the town library that I used to access the Internet? Well, the archaic[114] machine was out of commission for a whole week...but finally I fixed it and all of your e-mails came through! I am so happy to receive your letters and I am absolutely ecstatic[115] that you are going to the great ancient Mayan city of Tikal. I have had so much good news in the past few days, but this is the best of all.
>
> So much has happened here in the days since you left. Do you remember how there was a lot of media attention focused on me after we freed the dolphin from captivity? I wasn't sure if the coverage was going to make me look good or bad. Technically,

---

[110] **Disheartened:** to cause to lose spirit or morale
[111] **Epistolary:** carried on by or composed of letters
[112] **Ardent:** characterized by strong enthusiasm or devotion; fervent
[113] **Covet:** to wish for longingly
[114] **Archaic:** characteristic of an earlier or more primitive time; antiquated
[115] **Ecstatic:** a state of intense joy or delight

freeing the dolphin was a crime. But when everyone found out about all of the extenuating[116] circumstances, I was vindicated[117] in most people's eyes. Amazingly, it appears that the notoriety[118] I gained actually worked in my favor. Someone heard my story on TV. They heard about my background and how I really wanted to go to college, but that I couldn't afford it. You are not going to believe this, but I have been offered a scholarship! I can use this money at any college I choose, even one in the United States!

This is a very special scholarship from a foundation that funds archeological expeditions of ancient Mayan ruins. Once a year, they also give away a scholarship to a person of Mayan descent. You see, although my father is Nicaraguan, my mother is from Guatemala. She is of Mayan descent, so I fit the bill for this scholarship. I was so surprised when I found out that I was going to receive this award. I didn't even apply for it—I had no idea it even existed. They just saw me on the TV and decided that I was going to be the one.

When they sent me the notification that I had been chosen for this scholarship, they also sent me a big brochure that describes the foundation and their activities. I devoured the whole thing from cover to cover. This is where I read that the archeologists who run this foundation are also working on an excavation in Tikal. Isn't that cool? Maybe there's some way I can talk them into letting me work there this summer. I will write to them right now and see if there is a possibility. Keep your fingers crossed for me.

José

---

[116] **Extenuating:** partially excusing or justifying

[117] **Vindicate:** to clear of blame or suspicion with supporting arguments or proof

[118] **Notoriety:** the state of being generally known and talked of, especially in an unfavorable way; ill fame

Alexa was bursting with excitement, elated[119] at this interesting development. It was so tantalizing to think that maybe José could go to Tikal too, and they could see each other. But the best part of his letter was the news that he was going to receive a scholarship. Alexa knew that José was an exemplary[120] student—he was smart, hardworking, and always completed his assignments fastidiously[121]. In addition, he was very ambitious and he set lofty goals for himself. He wanted to go to college in the United States, even though, by his standards, the cost was exorbitant[122]. He lived in a humble home in a small fishing village in Central America and had begun working at a young age to help support his family.

Alexa breathed a sigh of relief and contentment that José was going to have the opportunity to go to college. It simply didn't seem fair to her that such a deserving person couldn't go to college simply because he didn't have enough money. Alexa reflected on the very different lives she and José lived. While her family wasn't affluent by any means, paying for college tuition wasn't an issue. Her provident[123] parents had been saving diligently for years. In fact, for Alexa, going to college didn't feel like something that was optional. Her parents made her feel like she was expected to go—it was incumbent[124] upon her. But for José, given his impecunious[125] circumstances, paying for college tuition would have been a formidable[126] challenge. Alexa was thrilled that he was going to be able to achieve his dream.

Alexa immediately fired off a reply e-mail, encouraging José to write to the foundation immediately and try to find a way to go to Tikal. As soon as she pressed Send Alexa sat back in her chair and waited. She

---

[119] **Elate:** to fill with joy or pride
[120] **Exemplary:** deserving imitation because of excellence
[121] **Fastidious:** displaying careful, meticulous attention to detail
[122] **Exorbitant:** exceeding all bounds of what is customary or fair: *exorbitant prices*
[123] **Provident:** providing carefully for the future
[124] **Incumbent:** imposed as an obligation or duty; obligatory
[125] **Impecunious:** lacking money; penniless
[126] **Formidable:** difficult to undertake or surmount

knew it wasn't rational[127] to sit and wait for José's reply. It might take days. But somehow she felt connected to him through the computer and she didn't want to get up. She was so preoccupied with her daydreams that she completely forgot she had promised to meet Doug at the Big Squeeze. Alexa started surfing the Internet, gazing at websites with photographs of the ancient ruins of Tikal. It looked so romantic.

ᔶ   ᔷ

The night before their departure, Alexa felt both excited and nervous as she finished her last-minute preparations for the trip. Knowing she was going to be groggy when her father came to pick her up 3:30 A.M., Alexa had her sleeping bag and backpack packed and ready to go down by the front door. Then she carefully set out the clothes that she planned to wear on the trip. Alexa looked at the clock on her computer screen: 7:47 P.M.

"Alexa?" her mom called out from downstairs. "You should really try to go to bed early tonight," she advised. "Your father is coming to pick you up awfully early in the morning."

"I know," she replied. As much as it made sense to go to bed early, she knew that there was no way she could fall asleep before 9:00 P.M. Alexa looked at the blank screen of the computer. The last few days, she had developed a propensity[128] for checking her e-mail all the time. "One last time," she said out loud, logging on to her e-mail.

When she saw her computer downloading a new message, she felt her heart lurch. Then her computer emitted that lovely dinging sound that signaled a new e-mail. When she saw that the sender was José, Alexa felt a sense of ineffable[129] happiness. Quickly, she scanned the contents.

---

[127] **Rational:** based on reason; logical
[128] **Propensity:** an innate inclination or tendency; predilection
[129] **Ineffable:** incapable of being expressed; indescribable

"Yippee!" Alexa shrieked when she finished reading the short missive[130].

"What's going on?" Alexa's mother called out from the kitchen, alarmed at the sound of her high-pitched cry. "Are you OK?"

"Don't worry, Mom," Alexa responded. "Everything's fine. Actually, it's great!" Alexa sat back in her chair with a big smile on her face, thrilled with the felicitous[131] news. José was going to Tikal. Alexa reveled[132] in the knowledge that she would soon see him. It seemed too good to be true.

Alexa clicked Reply and started typing rapidly, her face flushed with a euphoric[133] glow. They had a lot of planning to do.

---

[130] **Missive:** a written message; a letter
[131] **Felicitous:** marked by good fortune or happiness
[132] **Revel:** to take intense pleasure, delight, or satisfaction
[133] **Euphoric:** exaggerated feeling of great happiness, elation, or well-being

3

An Interminable Journey

"Good morning!" Professor McCurry chirped, opening the trunk of the car.

"It's not quite morning yet," Alexa retorted, glancing at her watch. It was precisely 3:30 A.M. "It's still the middle of the night," she complained, plopping her backpack and sleeping bag into the trunk.

"Were you able to get any sleep?" he asked, slamming the trunk closed.

"No," she replied succinctly. "I still can't believe that we're leaving this early in the morning."

"There's no room for grumpy teenagers on the airplane to Tikal," he teased. "Where's the ebullient[134] daughter I was talking to last night? The one who was chomping at the bit to go on an adventure? Is she still lying supine[135] on the bed or wishing that she was?"

---

[134] **Ebullient:** zestfully enthusiastic
[135] **Supine:** lying on the back or having the face upward

"Very funny," she retorted sarcastically as she buckled herself into the passenger's seat. "I just haven't woken up yet."

"Somehow I have a feeling that you're going to wake up soon," he said, pulling out of the dark driveway.

"Hey, why are you turning this way? Don't you want to get on the highway?"

"We have a couple of people to pick up. Don't you remember? Doug and his father are coming with us. Doug's father Nicholas is in the archeology department with Nadine. His specialty is the Aztecs and he and Nadine are working on a new book together about the ancient civilizations of Central America and Mexico."

"Oh!" Alexa gasped when she heard Doug's name mentioned. Suddenly, she realized that she completely forgot about his invitation to meet at the Big Squeeze for a second round of wheatgrass juice. She had been so distracted with José's e-mail that the "date" had slipped her mind.

"What's wrong?"

"It's nothing...I just forgot something."

"What did you forget? Do we need to turn around and go back to the house?"

"Oh no, it's not like that. It's nothing really," Alexa replied.

"Good, because we're running short on time. We're also stopping to pick up Nadine."

"Nadine?" Alexa repeated. "She's coming with us? I thought that she was already there."

"Well, she was there earlier this summer, but she came back here for a brief hiatus[136] from her work. It just so happens that she needs to go

---

[136] **Hiatus:** a gap or interruption; a break

back to Tikal at the same time that we are headed there. So it's serendip-itous[137] timing, because now we can all travel together."

Alexa shrugged impassively[138] and looked out the window. She didn't want to show her father how she really felt about his relationship with this woman. The pain that she felt from her parents' recent divorce was still fresh. The knowledge that her father had begun a new relation-ship only served to exacerbate[139] the uneasy feeling that she had about her new familial situation.

But Alexa didn't have time to ruminate[140] about it now. The car meandered through the darkened suburban streets and pulled into Doug's driveway, where Doug and his father, Nicholas, were waiting in the garage. Alexa hopped out of the passenger's seat and nestled herself into the corner in the backseat while Professor McCurry helped the men put their bags in the trunk. Each of them carried just a single backpack and a sleeping bag. Alexa had to suppress a giggle when she realized Doug was without the ubiquitous[141] lacrosse stick. He also looked uncharacter-istically disheveled, as if he had just rolled out of bed and didn't have time to run a comb through his unkempt[142] hair.

"Doug, why don't you climb in the backseat with Alexa and your father can sit up here with me," Professor McCurry directed.

Silently, Doug climbed into the seat next to Alexa and grunted a laconic[143] greeting before focusing his gaze on the scenery out the window.

Alexa turned away from Doug and looked out her own window. Apparently, the genial[144] behavior he displayed the other day at the Big

---

[137] **Serendipitous:** finding valuable or agreeable things not sought for: *serendipitous discoveries*

[138] **Impassive:** devoid of emotion; expressionless

[139] **Exacerbate:** to increase the severity of; aggravate

[140] **Ruminate:** to reflect on over and over again

[141] **Ubiquitous:** being or seeming to be everywhere at the same time; omnipresent

[142] **Unkempt:** deficient in order or neatness

[143] **Laconic:** using few words; terse or concise

[144] **Genial:** having a pleasant or friendly disposition or manner

Squeeze was just an anomaly[145], she thought, because now it was back to usual. He was completely ignoring her. For a brief moment, Alexa considered apologizing to him for not showing up at the Big Squeeze, as she had promised. But the thought of bringing up this awkward topic of conversation was too daunting[146].

Within minutes, the car pulled up to Nadine's apartment complex and Professor McCurry hopped out of the car and ran up the steps.

"So, Alexa," Doug's father turned in his seat to address her, "are you looking forward to this adventure?" he asked, making an effort to be cordial[147].

"Yes, I am...but it's hard to show my enthusiasm at three-thirty in the morning," Alexa joked.

"I agree," Nicholas chuckled.

Professor McCurry came down the stairs, struggling with Nadine's huge suitcase. Alexa cracked a smile at the sight. Apparently, he hadn't given Nadine the same lecture about packing light so that they could traipse[148] through the jungle, unfettered[149] by heavy baggage.

Nadine bounded down the steps of the apartment complex, managing to look perky despite the early hour. Her long brown hair was pulled back into a neat ponytail and her eyes sparkled with enthusiasm.

"Hi, everybody!" she said cheerfully, sticking her head into the open window of the car.

"Good morning, Nadine," Nicholas replied warmly. "Can't wait to see Tikal, after hearing you rave about it for years. Why don't you take my seat here in the front?"

---

[145] **Anomaly:** deviation from the common rule; irregularity
[146] **Daunting:** having the effect of lessening courage or discouraging through fear
[147] **Cordial:** warm and sincere; friendly
[148] **Traipse:** to walk or tramp about
[149] **Unfettered:** free of shackles, chains, or other restrictions

"No, that's OK," she said quickly, "stay right where you are." Nadine glanced in the backseat, assessing the seating arrangements. "I can sit right here in the back, next to Alexa. Is that OK with you?" she asked Alexa.

"Sure," Alexa replied unenthusiastically. She looked over at Doug, who was still staring out the window. Now she was going to have to move over and sit uncomfortably close to Doug, in order to make room for Nadine in the back seat. It was going to be painfully awkward. Alexa heard the trunk slam and her father hopped into the driver's seat. There was no avoiding it. Alexa scooted over on the vinyl seat and Nadine settled in next to her.

Before the car even pulled out of the driveway, Nadine started talking, her gregarious[150] personality and boundless enthusiasm permeating[151] the car. "Boy, you guys sure are in for a treat!" she exclaimed to Alexa and Doug. "Tikal is one of the most awe-inspiring places I've ever seen."

"Maybe this would be a good opportunity to tell them about it," Professor McCurry suggested. "We have a ninety-minute drive to the airport ahead of us. Hey, kids, listen up, because you have one of the most highly respected scholars of the ancient Maya about to enlighten[152] you," he said proudly. "Nadine wrote a tome[153] on the subject—a huge book on the ancient Maya. So go ahead, Nadine, launch into one of your eloquent[154] lectures," he said, goading[155] her to talk. "But keep it simple for the teenagers. If you delve into abstruse[156] theories or concepts, they're likely to tune out."

"Don't worry, I've never had anyone fall asleep during *my* lectures," Nadine said. "How about you?" she teased Professor McCurry.

---

[150] **Gregarious:** marked by seeking and enjoying the company of others; sociable
[151] **Permeate:** to spread or diffuse throughout; pervade
[152] **Enlighten:** to give information or knowledge to; illuminate, inform, or instruct
[153] **Tome:** a book, especially a large or scholarly one
[154] **Eloquent:** marked by persuasive, fluent speech: *an eloquent speaker*
[155] **Goad:** to urge or prod, as if with a pointed stick
[156] **Abstruse:** hard to understand; incomprehensible

Everyone in the car burst out laughing as Professor McCurry assumed a sheepish expression. "I'm not going to answer that," he replied. "I'm still waiting to hear your scintillating[157] lecture about the Maya."

"OK," she relented, "I'd love to tell you a little bit about the ancient Maya."

Alexa and Doug looked over at Nadine, waiting for her to begin.

"The Maya were an indigenous[158] people, native to the Americas. In other words, they were here before the European explorers, such as Columbus and Cortez, sailed to the New World. They had a thriving civilization that encompassed[159] a large area from Southern Mexico to Central America. What was so special about the Maya is what they managed to achieve. They were an advanced culture with knowledge of mathematics, astronomy, and architecture. They actually developed their own calendar and written language—you'll see some fine examples of Mayan hieroglyphs at Tikal. The Mayan civilization flourished during the classic period from 200 A.D. to 800 A.D. Contemporaneously[160], Europe was wallowing in the Dark Ages. It's really amazing what the Maya managed to achieve so long ago and under such adverse[161] conditions—the city of Tikal is smack-dab in the middle of a jungle! But what's really going to knock your socks off is the colossal[162] temples that they built." Nadine's face glowed with effervescent[163] enthusiasm. "Wait until you see these grand temples that are over a thousand years old. The ancient Maya managed to construct these incredible structures without the use of metal tools or even the wheel."

---

[157] **Scintillating:** animated and brilliant: *scintillating conversation*

[158] **Indigenous:** having originated in a particular area or environment; native

[159] **Encompass:** to constitute or include

[160] **Contemporaneously:** occurring during the same time period

[161] **Adverse:** contrary or against one's interests; difficult or unfavorable: *adverse criticism*

[162] **Colossal:** of a size, extent, or bulk that elicits astonishment; immense

[163] **Effervesce:** exhibiting liveliness, high spirits, or exhilaration

Alexa studied Nadine as she talked about the Maya. Her zeal[164] for her work was infectious.

"Tikal was a big city in its heyday, around 750 A.D.," Nadine continued. "It's been referred to as the 'New York City' of the Mayan civilization. Not a bad analogy[165], because Tikal was a center for trade and commerce during that era. But when you have an understanding of the history of that era, the grandiose[166] ruins of Tikal have a haunting quality about them."

"Haunting?" Doug spoke up for the first time. "The ruins are haunted with ghosts?"

"No, no," Nadine laughed. "I wasn't referring to ghosts. What I'm talking about is the fact that the great city of Tikal, a resplendent[167] jewel of civilization in the jungle...well, it was completely abandoned by the Mayan people and no one really knows why. This enormous Mayan city lay absolutely empty and unknown to the rest of the world for over one thousand years. The jungle literally[168] grew right over the buildings, obfuscating[169] them from view. This is why you sometimes hear the Maya referred to as a 'Lost Civilization.' The first real expedition to Tikal was in 1848...and boy, did they ever get a surprise!"

Alexa's brow furrowed in thought. It was hard to listen to the tumultuous history of the Mayan civilization without thinking about José and the fact that he was of Mayan descent. "What happened to the Mayan people?" Alexa asked, her voice fraught[170] with concern.

---

[164] **Zeal:** enthusiastic devotion to a goal and tireless diligence in its pursuit
[165] **Analogy:** a comparison based on similarities between things that are otherwise dissimilar
[166] **Grandiose:** uncommonly large and impressive in scope or intent; grand
[167] **Resplendent:** splendid or dazzling in appearance; brilliant
[168] **Literally:** in a literal or strict sense
[169] **Obfuscate:** to render indistinct, obscure, or difficult to see; to hide by covering
[170] **Fraught:** filled with a specified element; charged: *a situation fraught with danger*

"The Mayan people still exist," Nadine explained. "In fact there are still millions of people of Mayan descent living throughout Southern Mexico, Guatemala, and Honduras. Some of these people are still living a traditional lifestyle, while others have adapted a more modern way of life. But the ancient Mayan cities such as Tikal, Uxmal, Palenque, and Chichen Itzá...they were all abandoned about a thousand years ago. The Mayan people themselves didn't disappear, but their civilization did. This is why the ruins of Tikal have an enigmatic[171] quality to them. We're still trying to figure out the story behind them."

"If they had a written language, wouldn't they have recorded some of the important events? Didn't they write books about their own history?" Doug asked, perplexed[172] with the mystery Nadine outlined.

"Excellent question!" Nadine exclaimed. "But unfortunately, the answer is rather tragic. Yes, the ancient Maya did write thousands of books that are called codices. They were written on fig bark..." Nadine paused, her tone becoming uncharacteristically melancholy. "But sadly, all but four of these books were burned by the Spanish conquistadors back in the sixteenth century. This grievous[173] act was so thorough that only four books remain. It was a gross iniquity[174] with tragic consequences," she commented somberly. "Despite the fact that this culture developed a written language and painstakingly recorded their history, the sad reality is that there are only a small number of extant[175] manuscripts from the ancient Maya."

In the front seat, Nicholas shook his head in disgust. "Book burning has to be one of the most ignominious[176] acts that was perpetrated by the early settlers."

---

[171] **Enigmatic:** resembling an enigma (something puzzling, ambiguous, or inexplicable); mysterious

[172] **Perplex:** to confuse or trouble with uncertainty or doubt

[173] **Grievous:** characterized by severe pain, suffering, or sorrow: *a grievous loss*

[174] **Iniquity:** a wicked act or thing; a sin or gross injustice

[175] **Extant:** still in existence; not destroyed, lost, or extinct

[176] **Ignominious:** deserving of shame or infamy; despicable

Nadine nodded her head in agreement. "Ostensibly[177], they were attempting to help the indigenous peoples by bringing them Christianity. They were proselytizing[178] their religion. They wanted the Maya to abandon their own beliefs and convert to Christianity. The burning of the Mayan books was actually supervised by Friar Diego de Landa of the Catholic Church. In his own memoir, he wrote that the Mayan books were 'superstitious and lies of the devil.' So he simply burned the books. But from a different perspective, one might call this sad episode in history a travesty[179] of mores[180]. The Spanish conquistadors basically expunged[181] the culture, religion, and cumulative knowledge that the Maya had recorded in thousands of books." Nadine shook her head sadly. Then she focused her intense gaze on the two teenagers sitting beside her, as if she wanted to hear their opinion on the topic. "So the question is, were they missionaries[182] or mercenaries[183]?"

"That's a loaded question," Professor McCurry commented with a rueful chuckle.

"Sounds like a good topic for an essay question on a final exam," Nicholas chimed in.

"Uh, what do you mean?" Alexa asked.

"Well, a missionary is someone who tries to persuade other people to subscribe to his or her religion. A mercenary is someone who is hired as a soldier in a foreign army—basically it's someone who is paid to wage war. So the question was, were the Spanish conquistadors missionaries or mercenaries? Were they waging war or saving souls by forcibly imposing their religion on the Mayan people and burning their books?"

---

[177] **Ostensibly:** to all outward appearances; plausible rather than demonstrably true: *the ostensible purpose of the war*

[178] **Proselytize:** to induce someone to join one's religion, cause, or party

[179] **Travesty:** a debased, distorted, or grotesque imitation; parody: *a travesty of justice*

[180] **Mores:** moral attitudes

[181] **Expunge:** to strike out, obliterate, erase, or destroy

[182] **Missionary:** one who is sent on a mission, particularly to do religious work in a foreign country

[183] **Mercenary:** one who serves merely for wages, especially a soldier hired into a foreign service

"Um, well, I think it depends on your point of view," Alexa replied.

"Now that's what I call a diplomatic answer!" Professor McCurry exclaimed.

"I wasn't trying to sit on the fence," Alexa replied defensively. "I think the burning of all those books—it sounds so tragic. It's tragic because it's irrevocable[184]. Here we are one thousand years later wondering what was in those books, but we'll never know. They're gone." Alexa couldn't help but think of José when she listened to the stories of the ancient Maya and their hardships. "So how did we learn all of these things about the ancient Maya if there are only four books left?"

"Some of the history of the Maya was carved into stone monuments called stalae. You'll see those when we get there. The Mayan written language was a unique form of picture writing called hieroglyphs. Of course, the Mayan hieroglyphs are completely different from the Egyptian hieroglyphs that you may be familiar with from school."

"How can you tell what the pictures are supposed to mean?" Doug asked.

"With a lot of hard work," Nadine said, smiling widely. "That's what I do for a living—it's my vocation[185]." Nadine's voice became even more enthusiastic and her gestures more animated[186] as she talked about her specialty. "But I can't take all the credit for what we know about the Maya today. Do you realize we didn't even begin to decipher the Mayan hieroglyphs until the 1960s? It was actually quite difficult to break the Maya code. The task seemed insuperable[187], until a key manuscript was found

---

[184] **Irrevocable:** impossible to retract or revoke
[185] **Vocation:** a regular occupation, especially one for which a person is particularly suited or qualified
[186] **Animated:** lively, spirited, or zestful
[187] **Insuperable:** impossible to overcome; insurmountable

and researchers started making headway. Today we've deciphered many of the Mayan hieroglyphs, but there's still a lot of work to do."

"Well, if there's work to be done, Alexa and Doug are ready, willing, and able...right, guys?" Professor McCurry glanced in the rearview mirror, watching the teenagers' response.

"Oh, yes, Doug has been chomping at the bit! He can't wait to get to work," Nicholas joked sarcastically.

Alexa felt a stab of empathy[188] for Doug. Apparently he did not want to be going on this expedition with his father. Alexa glanced over at Doug, who rolled his eyes in mock protest. Then his eyes met Alexa's sympathetic gaze, and he gave her a brief smile—a tacit[189] signal that he appreciated her gesture.

"Well, I hope you're all ready to dig, because we don't have any room in our camp for laggards[190] or lethargic[191] student volunteers," Nadine warned. "There's so much work to be done that it's imperative[192] everybody pulls their own weight. A lazy worker at the camp is actually a liability[193], because the group still has to haul in the food and water for this person who is not helping. So believe me, everyone will be working."

"What are we going to be doing, exactly?" Alexa asked.

"We're working at a new site, deep within Tikal National Park. We'll all be camping out right at the dig, although for our first night there, we'll be staying at a hotel right in the heart of Tikal, near all of the big temples. So you'll have a day to see the touristy stuff, then the next day we'll set out for the dig."

---

[188] **Empathy:** direct identification with and understanding of another person's situation or feelings
[189] **Tacit:** expressed without words or speech
[190] **Laggard:** one who lags or lingers
[191] **Lethargic:** lacking alertness or activity; sluggish
[192] **Imperative:** not to be avoided or evaded; necessary: *an imperative duty*
[193] **Liability:** something that holds one back or acts as a disadvantage; drawback

"What are we going to be working on?" Doug asked curiously.

"Well, did you realize that there are hundreds of buildings at Tikal that have yet to be excavated?" Nadine asked. "They are still hidden in the dense jungle. When the city was abandoned by the ancient Maya over one thousand years ago, the jungle just grew right over these buildings, hiding them quite efficaciously[194]. There are lots of discoveries yet to be made."

Professor McCurry merged onto the highway and the conversation lulled as the car started gaining speed on the nearly empty roadway. The drive to the airport was quick and Alexa had to suppress the urge to groan out loud when they arrived at the Syracuse Airport at 4:40 A.M., before the airport even opened. Professor McCurry was a meticulous[195] traveler who liked to arrive everywhere early. He always had all of the details, such as the tickets and hotel reservations, taken care of well in advance. He liked to plan ahead, in order to circumvent[196] any last-minute difficulties. Alexa resisted the temptation to point out that they could have left an hour later and gotten a little more sleep. She knew her father would not appreciate any caustic[197] remarks about his punctilious[198] travel habits. So she kept quiet as they all congregated[199] outside of the locked doors of the terminal.

"Say, why don't I get a picture of the whole group standing right here?" Professor McCurry suggested. "Alexa, why don't you pull out that new camera of yours and I'll snap a picture. I'm telling you, when you're older, you'll appreciate having these pictures so that you can look back nostalgically[200] at the adventures of your youth."

---

[194] **Efficacious:** having the power to produce a desired effect
[195] **Meticulous:** extremely concerned with details
[196] **Circumvent:** to manage to avoid or get around; bypass
[197] **Caustic:** marked by incisive sarcasm; cutting
[198] **Punctilious:** strictly attentive to minute details of form in action or conduct; meticulous
[199] **Congregate:** to come together in a group or crowd
[200] **Nostalgic:** a bittersweet longing for things of the past

Alexa rolled her eyes, but dutifully pulled out the camera and handed it over.

Professor McCurry backed up a few paces. "Closer together now...smile...say cheese!" he directed before snapping the picture. "Good job," he commended them, handing the camera back to Alexa.

Alexa couldn't resist taking a look at the digital image in the camera's window. Everyone in the picture was obediently smiling for the camera except for Doug, whose buffoonery[201] made Alexa laugh out loud when she saw the picture. Unbeknownst to her, he had held two fingers up behind her head, simulating[202] rabbit ears. He had acted like a clown and she was his target, but was he laughing with her or at her? She still couldn't be certain.

Alexa looked up, trying to catch his eye, but Doug was staring off in the distance, ignoring her again.

When the airport doors were finally opened, they were the first ones in line to check in, and then they were the first ones to go through the security checkpoint. Alexa could see from the satisfied grin on her father's face that he was very pleased to have successfully avoided the chaos[203] that inevitably envelops the terminal when it becomes inundated[204] with crowds of travelers.

"OK, here's everyone's boarding pass," Professor McCurry declared, doling out the tickets. "I think it's about a four-hour flight to Miami...Alexa, I've got you sitting next to Doug, so that you guys can chat on the way there. Nadine, Nicholas, and I will be sitting in the row in front of you."

---

[201] **Buffoonery:** ridiculous, joking, or clowning behavior
[202] **Simulate:** to take on the appearance of; imitate
[203] **Chaos:** a condition of great disorder or confusion
[204] **Inundate:** to overwhelm, as if with a flood of water: *the museum was inundated with visitors*

"Thanks, Dad," Alexa said politely, although inside she was balking[205] at the thought of sitting next to Doug for such a long flight, particularly when he was being so painfully quiet. The uneasy silence between them was going to make the journey seem interminable[206]. But what could she do about it now? She realized that she had to capitulate[207] to her father's plan. Dutifully, Alexa took the boarding pass from her father. With a long trip ahead, she hoped that she would eventually become inured[208] to the discomfort of the awkward seating arrangements.

"I'm going to go check out the magazines at the bookstore over there," Alexa announced to her father.

"OK, but don't linger too long...I don't want you to be late for the boarding call," he said, his expression clouded with anxiety.

"Don't worry, Dad. I'm wearing a watch, and I know I have to adhere[209] to the schedule."

Professor McCurry shook his head, looking dubious[210].

"I'll be right back," she promised, in an effort to alleviate[211] his anxiety. She could see that he was considerably disgruntled[212] at the mere thought of being late for the boarding call. But she couldn't stand the thought of just sitting there at the gate doing nothing, so she set off for the bookstore.

Alexa sifted through the eclectic[213] collection of books on the "sale" table and then turned her attention to the rack of magazines that lined

---

[205] **Balk:** to stop short and refuse to proceed

[206] **Interminable:** seeming to never end; endless

[207] **Capitulate:** to cease resisting; acquiesce

[208] **Inure:** to habituate to something undesirable, especially by prolonged exposure; accustom

[209] **Adhere:** to carry out without deviation

[210] **Dubious:** unsettled in opinion; doubtful

[211] **Alleviate:** to relieve or make more bearable: *aspirin alleviated the pain*

[212] **Disgruntle:** to make ill-humored or discontented

[213] **Eclectic:** made up of a variety of different elements or sources: *eclectic taste in fashion*

the wall. A different celebrity graced the cover of each magazine and bold headlines promised that sordid secrets about the famous stars would be divulged[214] inside. Alexa walked right by the magazines. She didn't have a proclivity[215] for gossip. In fact, she detested the tabloid newspapers that published scathing[216] articles about movie stars, attempting to defile[217] their reputations. Some of the "secrets" the magazines disclosed[218] were so outrageous it seemed to Alexa that they probably were not fact, but instead mere speculation[219]. The shocking headlines of the tabloid publications strained her credulity[220].

Alexa headed to the travel section of the bookstore. She browsed the extensive selection of travel guides that reflected the myriad[221] destinations of the modern-day traveler. Curiously, she pulled down a book on Guatemala and began flipping through it. Inside, there was a diagram that depicted a chronological[222] timeline of the ancient Maya, detailing a history that stretched back thousands of years. Alexa flipped through the pictures and became lost in the text that described the Mayan ruins. It was fascinating.

"Alexa!"

Startled, Alexa looked up from her book to see Doug at the foot of the aisle.

"It's time to go! C'mon, you need to hurry," he said. "Your dad is really getting antsy. They've already started boarding our plane."

---

[214] **Divulge:** to make known or public something that was previously secret; reveal

[215] **Proclivity:** a natural propensity or inclination, especially a strong inherent inclination toward something objectionable

[216] **Scathing:** harshly critical or injurious: *a scathing review*

[217] **Defile:** to corrupt the purity or perfection of; sully, dishonor: *defiling the flag*

[218] **Disclose:** to make known something that was previously secret; divulge

[219] **Speculation:** a conclusion based on insufficient evidence; conjecture

[220] **Credulity:** willingness to believe, especially on slight or uncertain evidence

[221] **Myriad:** a large, indefinite number; innumerable: *myriad fish in the sea*

[222] **Chronological:** arranged in order of time of occurrence

"Do I have time to buy this?" she asked, holding up the book.

Doug shrugged. "They just started boarding, so yeah, probably you have time to buy it. But your dad is looking really impatient."

"I know he doesn't like to be late. But I really want to buy this—it'll just be a minute," she said, hurrying toward the checkout.

"I'll wait for you," he said, standing near the cash register.

As soon as the book was paid for, the two of them started racing back to the gate, weaving their way through the crowds of people. The terminal, which had been empty 20 minutes earlier, had filled up incrementally[223] after several flights arrived and passengers streamed into the terminal. When Alexa saw the look on her father's face, she began to regret her actions. Alexa gave him an apologetic smile, but Professor McCurry was implacable[224].

"Alexa, you said you were only going to be a minute, but you were gone forever! We almost missed our plane," he said sternly, ushering her toward the line of people waiting to board.

Alexa wanted to roll her eyes to show her disdain[225] for such hyperbole[226]—she wasn't gone forever, just 20 minutes. But she knew her father would see such a gesture as impudent[227] and disrespectful. So instead she apologized contritely[228] while dutifully taking her place in line. "I'm sorry, Dad. It's just that I found this book on Mayan ruins and I needed to buy it. I'm sorry if I made you worry." Alexa gave her father another apologetic smile, in an attempt to convince him that her penitence[229] was real.

---

[223] **Increment:** the process of increasing in number, size, or value

[224] **Implacable:** impossible to placate or appease

[225] **Disdain:** a feeling or show of contempt and aloofness; scorn

[226] **Hyperbole:** extravagant exaggeration; as in *I ate a ton of food*

[227] **Impudent:** marked by offensive or cocky boldness; impertinent

[228] **Contrite:** feeling regret and sorrow for one's sins or offenses; penitent

[229] **Penitence:** the quality or state of being penitent; having sorrow or regret for wrongdoing

Professor McCurry's face softened. "Well, that looks like a good book, but you need to realize that airplanes don't wait for individuals browsing in bookstores," he admonished[230] her. "If we missed this plane, we would also miss our connection in Miami and our whole itinerary would be thrown out the window."

Alexa rifled through her backpack for her boarding pass while her father waited impatiently. Meanwhile, Doug pulled his boarding pass out of his back pocket, handed it to the attendant, and started down the ramp, but then turned to give Alexa an anxious glance as she searched for the elusive[231] ticket. Finally, she pulled the ticket out of the depths of her stuffed backpack and quickly stepped forward to hand it to the attendant.

After stowing her backpack under the seat in front of her, Alexa breathed a sigh of relief when she finally settled into her seat, her new book on her lap. Doug, already seated at the window seat with his seatbelt fastened, trained his gaze outside, where workers scurried about in the early morning light, loading baggage and directing other planes. Alexa glanced at her watch. It was going to be a long flight, especially with such a nontalkative seatmate. In an effort to palliate[232] the boredom, Alexa began flipping through the pages of her new book, immersing herself in the tantalizing descriptions of Mayan ruins. She barely even noticed when the airplane took off and began its ascent.

"Hey, isn't that a picture of one of the temples at Tikal?" Doug asked.

Alexa looked up, startled to realize that Doug had been reading over her shoulder. "Yes, it's a picture of Temple IV."

---

[230] **Admonish:** to gently express warning or disapproval
[231] **Elusive:** tending to evade grasp or pursuit
[232] **Palliate:** to make less intense or severe; mitigate

"I can't wait to see it," he said. "It's supposed to be a great place to watch the sunrise."

Alexa nodded in agreement. "That's what it says in the guidebook."

"Do you want to?" he asked timidly. "Go to see the sunrise, I mean? Do you want to climb to the top of Temple IV to watch the sunrise?"

"Yes, of course," Alexa answered, not sure if he was asking her to go *with* him to watch the sunrise, or if he was merely inquiring in a general sense if this was something that she wanted to do.

"Good. Nadine said we're staying at the Hotel Jaguar tonight, so we'll be within walking distance of the major sights. I have an alarm on my watch, so I can set it for five-thirty and we can be to the temple by six to watch the sunrise. Sound good?"

"Uh...OK," Alexa mumbled, nonplussed[233] by this development. He was asking *her* to go with *him*. Tomorrow morning. For the second time in one week, Doug had surprised her.

When the flight attendant came by with earphones for the movie, Alexa and Doug both opted to watch it. After the movie, the conversation between them started to flow as they traded funny stories about past family vacations. Alexa was surprised when they started making their descent into Miami. The time had passed by so quickly.

"Let's check the monitor for our connection to Belize City," Professor McCurry urged the group as soon as they disembarked from the airplane and entered the terminal.

---

[233] **Nonplus:** to put at a loss as to what to say or do; bewilder

"Our flight arrived here on time, so we shouldn't have any trouble making the connection," Nicholas said assuredly as they all walked over to the television monitors that displayed the schedule of departures.

"Oh, no!" Professor McCurry exclaimed, his eyes squinting at the monitor as he reread the schedule. "Our flight to Belize City is delayed for two hours. We're going to miss our connecting flight to Guatemala." He shook his head in despair and then his expression turned angry. "Now our whole schedule is thrown off and we're going to be stuck in Belize City," he ranted[234]. "These airline companies drive me crazy—they're always changing the schedule to increase their passenger load and plump up their profit margins," he said, railing[235] against the airlines for putting them in such a predicament.

"I doubt that something like that is going on," Alexa said, refuting[236] her father's theory. "I bet that something was wrong with the airplane and they needed time to fix it."

"Oh, I don't believe that for a minute," he retorted. "With big corporations, everything is about the profit margin. It's never about the needs of the individual," he said firmly, concluding his rebuttal[237]. "And now we're going to be stuck in Belize City, because we're going to miss our flight to Guatemala."

Alexa decided not to argue any further. She didn't want to incite her father to launch into a polemic[238] about the pervasive[239] role of big corporations in American society. He could go on for hours ranting about industry-funded lobby[240] groups and the immense sway they wielded in politics. Alexa had heard his opinionated lecture on the subject many times already and she didn't want to hear it again.

---

[234] **Rant:** to speak or write in a angry or violent manner
[235] **Rail:** to express objections or scold in bitter, harsh, or abusive language
[236] **Refute:** to deny the accuracy or truth of: *he refuted the allegations*
[237] **Rebuttal:** the act of refuting by offering a contrary argument
[238] **Polemic:** a controversial argument, especially one attacking a specific opinion
[239] **Pervasive:** having the quality of being diffused or permeated throughout: *a pervasive odor*
[240] **Lobby:** a group of persons engaged in trying to influence legislators in favor of a specific cause

∽ ∾

After a three-hour wait in the Miami Airport, the flight to Belize City finally departed. But by the time they landed in Belize at 7:00 P.M., their flight to Flores, Guatemala, had long since left. They were stuck.

"I'll go see what our options are," Nadine offered. "My Spanish is fluent."

The rest of the group watched as Nadine ventured up to the counter to talk with the airline attendant. When she came back to the group, her demeanor was uncharacteristically morose[241]. "Well, we definitely missed the last flight of the day to Flores, so there's no question that we're staying here tonight. But the big problem is that all of the flights to Flores for the rest of the week are booked."

"So they're just going to leave us stranded here?" Professor McCurry asked.

"You have to understand that this is just a small local airline company and the airplanes are also very small. We're a group of five people...this is not so easy to arrange at the last minute like this," Nadine replied.

"Isn't there another airport near Tikal?" Nicholas asked hopefully. "What's the name of that town...Santa Elena!" he cried triumphantly.

Nadine nodded. "Yes, in theory, that would work, but that would be expensive. It's a different airline that flies there and we would have to purchase all new tickets. Unfortunately, we're on a tight budget and my boss on this dig is the most parsimonious[242] person I've ever met. So let's just drop that idea or any other idea that involves extravagant expenditures,"

---

[241] **Morose:** sullenly melancholy; gloomy
[242] **Parsimonious:** excessively frugal or sparing

Nadine said firmly. "Our other option is to hire a driver to take us there. I've never done this drive. The roads between here and Tikal might be rough...it definitely won't be a newly paved divided highway," she warned.

"But I think that's better then waiting here endlessly," Professor McCurry argued.

"I agree," Nicholas chimed in. "How bad can it be to drive there?"

"OK," Nadine reluctantly agreed. "I'll go make the arrangements."

A few minutes later, she returned with a triumphant grin. "It's all set," she said. "Tonight we'll stay at the hotel here near the airport, and tomorrow morning a van will be waiting for us outside the hotel. It should only take us a few hours to drive to Tikal, so we should be there by lunchtime."

"You know, this actually might work out better than taking the plane. We'll have a chance to see the countryside. I'm looking forward to it," Professor McCurry said, his mood improving dramatically.

4

Hardy Survivors

After an uneventful evening at the airport hotel, Alexa felt a tingle of anticipation as she and the rest of the group waited on the curb for the van to pick them up. The morning sun bathed the drab gray exterior of the hotel in a cheerful golden hue. Everyone was in high spirits after their restful night in the hotel and a sense of adventure permeated the air as they waited to embark on the final leg of their journey.

A ramshackle old van, rusting around the edges and sloppily painted a garish[243] shade of bright green, pulled up to the curb. Alexa looked at the well-worn tires and the broken windshield wiper that stuck straight out instead of resting obediently on the windshield. The van looked like it was at least 20 years old—a relic from a bygone era. Two men hopped out and asked them a question in Spanish. Alexa had no idea what they were saying.

Everyone turned to Nadine. As the only one in the group who spoke fluent Spanish, she was the designated interlocutor[244]. Nadine immediately became embroiled in a heated conversation with the men,

---

[243] **Garish:** excessively vivid or flashy; gaudy: *garish eye makeup*
[244] **Interlocutor:** one who takes part in dialogue or conversation, often in an official capacity

her face flushed with emotion as she pointed at the van. Finally, she turned back to the group. "This is our van," she said, sounding defeated.

"Can't we get a different one?" Alexa asked.

"This is not a propitious[245] sign," Nicholas muttered under his breath, shaking his head in disapproval as he looked at the old van.

"No, there's nothing else available right now," Nadine answered. "We can refuse to go with them, but we'll be taking our chances that we'll find something else. And that may not be so easy. I've already checked into the bus schedule. There are tour buses that go to Tikal, but they're all booked right now—it's high season for tourism."

"Is this a reputable[246] company?" Professor McCurry asked skeptically.

"Actually, it's not a company," she answered. "These men here are just individuals who offer to drive people places for a fee. It's a nominal[247] fee, I might add—just a pittance[248]."

"Let's hope so," Professor McCurry said, raising his eyebrows to emphasize his point. He hesitated for a moment as he stared at the old van. "Well..." he began slowly, "I vote we take it. It's not that long of a drive and at least we'll get there today. I can't stand the thought of sitting around here, trying to figure out how to get to Tikal at some point in the nebulous[249] future. I vote we go now."

Nicholas nodded reluctantly. "OK," he agreed. "Then let's load up the baggage."

The driver and his cohort smiled widely when they got the affirmative nod from Nadine. Immediately, they scrambled to load the bags in the back of the van.

---

[245] **Propitious:** presenting favorable circumstances; auspicious
[246] **Reputable:** having a good reputation; honorable
[247] **Nominal:** insignificantly small; trifling
[248] **Pittance:** a meager wage or monetary payment; a small amount
[249] **Nebulous:** indistinct, vague

Alexa felt a prickle of apprehension in the pit of her stomach as she stepped into the rickety old vehicle. The adults settled into the first two rows of seats, while Alexa and Doug were relegated[250] to the far back.

"Hey, at least we won't be constrained[251] by seat belts," Doug joked, holding up the broken buckle. He looked as if he was enjoying the adventure. "You can have the window seat," he offered. "I sat by the window on the airplane."

"Thanks," Alexa said sincerely, touched by his magnanimous[252] gesture.

As soon as the passengers settled into their seats, the van took off with a jerk and made its way outside the confines of the city, where the quality of the road quickly deteriorated. The ride became bumpy and uncomfortable as the driver negotiated the roadway, rife[253] with potholes.

Alexa kept her gaze focused on the passing scenery. They meandered through a quaint[254] little town with a beautiful Spanish-style church in the central square and a farmer's market, bustling with activity. But the next town wasn't nearly as attractive. The small, makeshift houses looked as if they would tumble down in a strong breeze. Alexa felt a rush of empathy when she saw an indigent[255] young mother sitting on a street corner, holding her infant. It was clear from her tattered clothes that she was living in privation[256].

As the van continued west, the towns became farther and farther apart, the road conditions became increasingly treacherous and their progress slowed to a crawl.

---

[250] **Relegate:** to assign to an obscure place, position, or condition
[251] **Constrain:** to secure, confine, or keep within close bounds
[252] **Magnanimous:** courageously noble and generous in spirit
[253] **Rife:** abundant or numerous
[254] **Quaint:** charmingly odd or unusual, especially in an old-fashioned way
[255] **Indigent:** experiencing want or need; poor, impoverished
[256] **Privation:** a state of extreme poverty

"Now I know how popcorn feels when the popper gets hot," Doug joked, as their vehicle bounced through the abundant potholes and gullies in the road.

Alexa wanted to agree. It was stiflingly hot in the van and the continual bouncing up and down was starting to wear on her nerves. But before she had a chance to come up with a funny retort, the van suddenly lurched to the side and careened off of the road and down into a gully, coming to a sudden stop that caused all of the passengers to pitch forward in their seats.

For a moment, no one said a word. They sat still in a stunned silence. Then, a flurry of Spanish broke out from the driver's seat.

"Alexa, Doug, are you OK?" Professor McCurry called out.

"I'm OK, Dad," Alexa replied.

"Me too," Doug added.

"What the heck happened?" Nicholas asked, once they had ascertained[257] that no one had been injured in the accident.

"They said something happened to the steering, but they don't know what," Nadine translated.

"Oh, great!" Professor McCurry groaned. "Now we're hapless[258] victims of misfortune, stuck in the middle of nowhere!"

"Oh, c'mon...we're not hapless victims, we're hardy[259] survivors," Nadine said with forced cheerfulness. "The intrepid[260] traveler does not give up when the going gets rough," she continued, holding her finger in the air as she delivered her edict[261].

---

[257] **Ascertain:** to find out or learn with certainty; discover

[258] **Hapless:** having no luck; unfortunate

[259] **Hardy:** capable of withstanding unfavorable conditions; sturdy, robust, and healthy

[260] **Intrepid:** characterized by resolute fearlessness, courage, and endurance: *an intrepid explorer*

[261] **Edict:** an order or decree issued by an authority

"Well, we might as well get out of this van. It looks like we're not going anywhere in a hurry," Nicholas said.

"We'll be lucky if we ever get out of here," Doug muttered to Alexa as they climbed out of the van.

Alexa took a look around. It was a desolate[262] area, devoid of any sign of civilization. A few sparsely scattered trees dotted the sun-parched field that flanked the empty roadway. There wasn't a single house, store, gas station, or even a passing car in sight.

"Are we stuck here?" Alexa asked Nadine, a hint of panic starting to creep into her thoughts.

"Don't worry," Nadine reassured the group cheerfully. "This sort of thing happens all the time. They'll fix the van, then we'll be on our way. We may get there late, but don't worry, we'll get there."

Alexa looked over at the driver and his cohort, who were bustling about under the open hood of the van. "Maybe we should try to walk to the nearest gas station," she suggested. "How far away is the nearest sign of civilization?"

"I'll check," Nadine offered, walking over to the driver to confer with him in Spanish. "It's about four miles away," she translated. "But the driver says he can fix the van, no problem. And it would be really hot to walk that distance at this time of day. The sun is nearing its zenith[263]. Why don't we sit in the shade for a little while and let them fix the van."

---

[262] **Desolate:** devoid of inhabitants; deserted
[263] **Zenith:** the highest point above the observer's horizon attained by a celestial body

"Sounds good," Alexa readily agreed. Even though they had only been standing there for a few moments, she could already feel the top of her head getting hot from the intense tropical sunshine.

They all headed over to the center of the field to congregate under the umbrage[264] of a solitary tree. From this shady vantage point they watched the driver and his cohort disassemble the steering column, piece by piece, in the blazing late-morning sun. Soon an argument broke out between the two men. The assistant pointed off in the distance, as if he wanted to dispatch[265] a messenger to the nearest town. He adapted an aggressive pose and wagged his finger in the driver's face, as if he were threatening him. But the driver argued dogmatically[266], pointing to the disassembled steering column that lay on the ground. Despite the threats from his cohort and the hot sun beating down upon him, the driver was not going to concede[267] the argument under duress[268].

"This doesn't look good," Alexa moaned. She was growing increasingly restive[269] in the face of the seemingly hopeless situation. "It looks like they can't even agree if the problem is fixable. And we've already been waiting for an hour and a half."

"Don't worry," Nadine said. "Everything's going to be all right."

Alexa rolled her eyes. She really didn't want to hear such meaningless platitudes[270]. She wanted to know exactly how and when they were going to get out of this quagmire[271].

---

[264] **Umbrage:** Shadow or shade (can also be used to indicate resentment or offense: *she took umbrage at his insult*)

[265] **Dispatch:** the act of sending off, as to a specific destination

[266] **Dogmatic:** characterized by an authoritative, arrogant assertion of unproved principles

[267] **Concede:** to make a concession; yield

[268] **Duress:** constraint by threat; coercion: *confessed under duress*

[269] **Restive:** a feeling of impatience or uneasiness, usually as a result of external restriction or coercion

[270] **Platitude:** a banal or trite statement; cliché

[271] **Quagmire:** a difficult or precarious position; a predicament

"It looks like the driver has won this argument," Doug commented, pointing to the drama that was continuing to unfold before them. Having dissuaded[272] his assistant from leaving, the driver resumed the assembly of the steering column while the passengers continued to watch with a mixture of fascination and anxiety.

Within 20 minutes, the various parts of the car had been reassembled and the driver looked over at his passengers triumphantly, holding his thumb up in the air as if to celebrate his prowess[273] as a mechanic.

"Do you think it's fixed?" Alexa asked skeptically. "They didn't even test it yet. Is it really a smart idea for us to get back in that van when we don't even know if the steering works?" Alexa couldn't help but be wary[274].

"Let me go see what's going on," Nadine offered, getting up to walk over to the van. After conferring with the driver and his cohort for a minute, she returned to the group, along with the two men. "They said it's fixed and ready to go!" she exclaimed. "They really deserve plaudits[275] for their persistence. I'm going to tell them how much we appreciate their skill and effort." Nadine turned to the men and lauded[276] them effusively.

The two men smiled at her lavish[277] praise.

"They're just going to take a little break before we leave. They want a bit of a reprieve[278] from the sun," Nadine explained as the driver and his assistant sat down in the shade next to Alexa and got out a canteen and paper sack of food. The driver unscrewed the cap of the canteen and prepared to take a well-deserved drink. But first, he offered the food and water to his passengers.

---

[272] **Dissuade:** to deter someone from a course of action by persuasion
[273] **Prowess:** extraordinary ability, superior skill
[274] **Wary:** cautious, on guard, watchful
[275] **Plaudits:** enthusiastic approval or praise
[276] **Laud:** to praise, extol
[277] **Lavish:** to give in abundance; very generous
[278] **Reprieve:** temporary relief, as from danger or pain

Alexa wondered if the water was really potable[279]. As thirsty as she was, she really didn't want to get sick from contaminated water. She was also very hungry, but she was even more concerned about the food. Would it be rancid[280] after sitting outside on such a hot day? The putrid[281] odor that emanated from the paper sack suggested that it had turned bad. Alexa refused his generous offer as politely as she could, using a mixture of English, Spanish, and sign language.

Then she turned to her father and repeated her question. "Are we really going to get back on that broken-down van?"

Before he answered, Professor McCurry looked to Nadine and Nicholas, as if to ask their opinions on the matter. Both were vigorously nodding their heads.

"Let's just go and get out of here," Doug said, voicing the sentiment of the group. Everyone was eager to get to their destination.

"Normally, I wouldn't condone[282] such a thing," Professor McCurry said to Alexa. "You really shouldn't take any chances with vehicular safety. But we're faced with a conundrum[283] here. The consensus[284] among the group is that we go," he shrugged, as if to say that the decision was out of his hands.

Alexa was surprised her father was being so compliant[285] with the wishes of the group. Usually he was quick to form a cogent[286] argument that supported his own opinion.

The driver and his cohort motioned for them to get up and head back toward the van. It was time to go. But first, they needed to get the van out of the gully.

---

[279] **Potable:** suitable for drinking

[280] **Rancid:** having a foul smell or taste

[281] **Putrid:** being in a state of putrefaction; rotten

[282] **Condone:** to forgive, excuse, or overlook

[283] **Conundrum:** a difficult or insoluble problem; a dilemma

[284] **Consensus:** an opinion reached by a group as a whole

[285] **Compliant:** willing to carry out the orders or wishes of another

[286] **Cogent:** appealing to the intellect or powers of reasoning; valid and persuasive: *a cogent analysis*

"They want everyone to help," Nadine said. "If we all push, it should be easy."

The driver climbed into his seat and put the van in reverse while everyone else positioned themselves to push from the front. When the driver gave them a signal with his hand, they all pushed, attempting to extricate[287] the vehicle from the ditch. Despite their combined effort, the rear wheels of the van spun in place, digging deeper into the sandy soil.

The driver hopped out of the van and said something in Spanish before heading to the back of the van to retrieve an item from the trunk.

"He has an idea," Nadine explained.

"What is it?" Alexa asked, eager to hear what sort of innovative[288] idea the driver was proposing.

"He's going to put some boards under the rear wheels to give them a little traction," Nadine replied.

"That should work," Professor McCurry said. "We almost had it out anyway."

Sure enough, the driver's ingenious[289] idea worked like a charm and the van practically leapt out of the ditch.

Alexa settled back into her window seat, wincing at the searing heat of the shiny vinyl upholstery. As soon as they started on their way, a refreshing breeze from the open window cooled them off. At the next town, they stopped to eat at a local restaurant. The food was simple but surprisingly delicious, and everyone's mood improved measurably. After stopping at a small store to pick up bottled water, they settled back into

---

[287] **Extricate:** to release from entanglement or difficulty
[288] **Innovative:** marked by the act of introducing something new, such as a creation or invention
[289] **Ingenious:** marked by inventive skill, imagination, or cunning; clever

the van for the final leg of their journey. Their progress was still slow and bumpy, but not nearly as aggravating. Everyone felt a sense of relief that they were on their way again.

Alexa chatted easily with Doug as they watched the passing scenery and swigged water from big plastic bottles. They had been through so much together already that sense of camaraderie[290] had developed. The social hierarchy[291] of Ithaca High School seemed like a distant memory.

By the time they arrived at the entrance of Tikal National Park, it was dark. Officially, the park was closed for the evening, but Nadine hopped out of the van and had a cursory[292] discussion with the attendant at the booth. Smiling widely, the attendant waved them into the park, a wildlife preserve covering 25 square miles of tropical rainforest.

Despite the fact that she couldn't see a thing, Alexa felt a keen sense of anticipation bubbling up inside her. The long and difficult journey had not dampened her enthusiasm in the slightest. It had only served to heighten her excitement for this very moment, when she would set foot on the land of the ancient Maya for the very first time. Alexa gazed out into the darkness, trying to discern[293] something about her surroundings. But all she could see was blackness. She couldn't stop wondering if José had made it here as well. Was he somewhere out there in the darkness of this park?

The van pulled up to the Hotel Jaguar, which consisted of an inviting group of bungalows nestled in the rainforest. Alexa's spirits rose even higher when she saw the accommodations. Her father had warned her that they would not be staying at an exclusive[294] five-star resort, but this hotel looked great to her eyes.

---

[290] Camaraderie: lighthearted rapport and goodwill between friends
[291] Hierarchy: a group of people categorized according to rank, ability, or status
[292] Cursory: performed hastily and without attention to detail
[293] Discern: to perceive with the eyes or intellect; detect
[294] Exclusive: tending to exclude most from entry, membership, or participation: *an exclusive nightclub*

"Why don't I go in and see if there's room at the inn," Nadine offered when the van came to a stop. "Our reservations were actually for last night, not tonight."

Professor McCurry groaned. He abhorred[295] last-minute difficulties when he traveled.

Nadine returned quickly, the dour[296] expression on her face signaling that she had not been successful. "Sorry, folks," she said, climbing back into the van. "There's no room at the inn."

"Where will we stay?" Alexa asked.

"I was able to get us a *cabaña*. It's kind of like a little cabin."

"That sounds nice," Alexa said hopefully.

"It'll be fine," Nadine replied. "At least we won't have to worry about pitching a tent tonight. But I'm just warning you that it's more like camping than staying in a hotel. We'll all be sharing one room and we'll each have a cot—we'll have to get out our sleeping bags. Oh, and I almost forgot, there's no bathroom or running water. So we'll have to use the public facilities at the campground. OK?" she questioned, looking at Alexa.

"I'm fine with it," Alexa reassured her. Truthfully, she wouldn't have minded if they had to sleep outside with no roof over their heads. She was just so excited to finally be here. She couldn't wait to wake up and have it be tomorrow so that she could finally see the spectacular sights in person. And, of course, she couldn't wait to see José.

---

[295] **Abhor:** to regard with loathing or horror; detest
[296] **Dour:** silently ill-humored or gloomy

5

Poised on the Precipice

"**A**lexa," a voice whispered in her ear. "It's time to wake up!"

Alexa rubbed her eyes, groggy from sleep. The cabin was still dark and she was nestled snugly in her warm sleeping bag. Doug was standing over her, a flashlight and map in his hands.

"C'mon," he coaxed. "We have to hurry if we want to catch the sunrise from the top of the temple."

Alexa was bewildered for a moment, but then the memory of her promise popped into her mind. Two days ago when they were sitting on the airplane to Miami, she had promised Doug that she would go with him to the top of Temple IV to watch the sunrise.

"You still want to go, don't you?" he asked.

"Of course," she replied, grabbing a sweatshirt from the top of her backpack and quickly pulling it on over her rumpled t-shirt. The previous night, when Alexa realized that they were all going to sleep in the same room, she had decided that she was going to climb into her sleeping bag fully clothed in jeans and a t-shirt. The alternative—wearing her pajamas in front of everyone—seemed unimaginably embarrassing. "I'll be ready in a second," she said, fumbling with the laces on her sneakers. "But first I'll need to make a quick stop at the ladies room." Alexa rummaged around in the side pocket of her bag, searching for her hairbrush, but she couldn't find it.

"We need to hurry, or else we're going to miss it!" Doug warned her.

"OK, I'm coming," Alexa assured him, deciding to forego the hair-brush. There wasn't time for vanity. Instead, she grabbed her camera, attached the Velcro strap to her belt, and the two of them slipped out of the cabaña before the adults woke. "I've got to stop here," Alexa pointed to the public restrooms that were clustered in the center of the campground.

"OK, but make it quick. We've got a twenty-minute walk in front of us."

"I'll be right out," Alexa assured him as she slipped into the bath-room and scrutinized[297] the facilities in the dim light provided by a single bare light bulb hanging from the ceiling. Mercifully, the restrooms were kept scrupulously[298] clean by the staff and the building smelled like antiseptic[299]. Alexa didn't waste any time in front of the mirror, but quickly finished her business and went back outside to join Doug, who beckoned her with his flashlight.

---

[297] **Scrutinize:** to examine closely and minutely
[298] **Scrupulously:** conscientious and exact; painstaking, meticulous
[299] **Antiseptic:** a substance that inhibits the growth and reproduction of disease-causing microorganisms

"If we walk really quickly, we might be able to make it there before the sun comes up," he said as they started off on the trail toward the *Gran Plaza*, the center of the ancient city.

They made rapid progress on the well-trodden path, which meandered through the rainforest. Alexa was acutely[300] aware of the dim jungle on either side of them. A variety of animal sounds emanated from the murky darkness. "What was that noise?" she asked nervously, unable to contain her growing trepidation[301].

"Don't worry," Doug said. "It's nothing."

Alexa sighed. He was probably right, but nevertheless, she didn't like the way he trivialized[302] her concerns. "It might have been a jaguar, you know. This jungle is filled with them."

"Hey, that would be great!" he laughed. "I'm dying to see one."

"Yeah, right," she said sarcastically. "I bet your bravery is just a façade[303]," Alexa teased. "If a jaguar jumped out of the jungle right now, you would be cowering[304] behind that tree over there. Kind of like the 'brave' lion in *The Wizard of Oz*. Remember how the lion pretended to be fearless at first, but then it turned out that he was a coward? *Dorothy* had to be the brave one."

Doug gasped, pretending to be gravely offended at her comment. "Hey, how dare you denigrate[305] my bravery," he retorted with mock indignation[306]. "Besides, as I recall, the lion actually turned out to be pretty brave in the last few scenes. He was going to the wizard seeking courage, but he actually had it all along."

---

[300] **Acute:** reacting readily to stimuli or impressions; keenly perceptive; sensitive

[301] **Trepidation:** a state of alarm, fear, apprehension, or dread

[302] **Trivialize:** to make appear trivial or insignificant

[303] **Façade:** a showy misrepresentation intended to conceal something unpleasant

[304] **Cower:** to cringe in fear

[305] **Denigrate:** to belittle, disparage, or minimize

[306] **Indignation:** a feeling of righteous anger aroused from something mean or unjust

Alexa burst out laughing. "I guess you're right about that, *Mr. Lion!*"

"And don't forget, we're going to be here for several weeks, so we'll see who is brave and who is not, *Dorothy*."

Alexa laughed. Truthfully, she was terrified of spiders and snakes. But she was not about to reveal her weakness to Doug.

After a few more minutes at a brisk pace, they stepped out of the dense jungle and into a cleared grassy area. Looming over them, in the dim twilight of the early morning, was the most awe-inspiring sight Alexa had ever seen. Rising out of the jungle like a colossus[307] was a huge pyramid of stone that reached up through the treetops toward the sky. "Oh, my gosh!" she exclaimed. "I can't even see the top!"

"It's absolutely incredible," Doug agreed. "But that's not the temple we're looking for," he said, consulting his map. "We need to keep going to reach Temple IV."

"I'm coming," Alexa replied, even though she was inclined[308] to stay right where she was and stare at the magnificent temple before them.

By the time they reached the enormous Temple IV, they were breathless with exertion. "C'mon, we have to hurry...the sun is coming up," he said, exhorting[309] her to move even faster through the tangle of vines at the base of the massive stone pyramid. "Here's the stairs. You can go first."

"Stairs? That looks more like a ladder," she said, looking at the steep wooden staircase that rested on the ancient stone structure. The staircase was obviously intended to help visitors climb the structure without damaging the ancient stonework, but the steps were so narrow and the ascent so steep that Alexa feared the climb. The top of the temple was completely

---

[307] **Colossus:** a huge statue (for example, the Statue of Liberty)
[308] **Inclined:** to be disposed to a certain preference or course of action
[309] **Exhort:** to urge strongly by argument, advice, or appeal

obscured by the morning mist, so it looked like the stairs headed straight up into the clouds. Alexa hesitated, remembering that there were really three things that truly frightened her...spiders, snakes, *and* heights. The thought of climbing hundreds of feet up the side of an ancient temple on a precarious wooden ladder was unnerving[310]. But she was even more afraid to admit this fear to Doug.

"Go ahead," he urged her. "I'll be right behind you."

Alexa took a deep breath and started climbing, even though she was trembling with fear. She could hear Doug below her, but she didn't want to turn around and look down. Instead, she kept her gaze focused on her goal above, the mist-covered pinnacle[311] of the temple, and she kept climbing. Higher and higher she climbed, to the top of one of the highest pre-Columbian structures known in the Americas, rising some 212 feet above the ground.

Alexa heard voices from above. Evidently, some people had managed to get up to the top earlier than they had. Finally, she reached the terrace, where a cluster of people were gathered, looking at the spectacular view. Alexa breathed a sigh of relief. A few seconds later, Doug was at her side and they both looked out over the treetops together. The confluence[312] of leaves and branches from a multitude of treetops formed the jungle canopy, which stretched out like a green canvas[313] below them. The early morning twilight was quiet and peaceful. A layer of mist gently rested on the treetops, like a diaphanous[314] white blanket over a sea of green leaves. The hint of early morning light hovering beneath the horizon lent an ethereal[315] beauty to the scene.

---

[310] **Unnerve:** to deprive of strength or vigor and the capacity to act
[311] **Pinnacle:** the highest point; the culmination; summit
[312] **Confluence:** the coming or flowing together at one place
[313] **Canvas:** a piece of such fabric on which a painting is executed
[314] **Diaphanous:** of such fine texture as to be transparent or translucent
[315] **Ethereal:** not of this world; heavenly

"We can go even higher, you know," Doug said, breaking the silence. "There's a ladder that goes all the way to the top. I'll show you. Let's go!" he said enthusiastically.

Alexa groaned. Actually, she had already noticed the iron ladder that lead straight up, but she was secretly hoping they could just stay there to watch the sunrise. But no such luck. Now she was going to have to summon every last bit of fortitude[316] she had to reach the top. Taking a deep breath to quell[317] the fear that was rising up in her throat, Alexa put her hands on the metal rungs and started up.

When she finally reached the top and sat down at the very top of the ancient stone temple, Alexa could feel her heart beating wildly. It wasn't just from the exertion of the climb or the fact that she was poised on the precipice[318] of a towering face of rock. The view was absolutely stunning. Doug sat down next to her and they both marveled at the scene spread out before them.

They looked out over the remote, uninhabited jungle. The only sign of the ancient civilization that flourished[319] in this spot was the tops of four temples that rose up out of the lush forest canopy.

Silently, they watched the scene change before their eyes. The dim twilight became increasingly brighter and the sky began to lighten with a golden orange glow. It was as if the jungle was nudged awake with these first few rays of sunshine. The birds, which were quiescent[320] in the darkness, awoke with the first rays of sunshine and broke the silence with a cacophony[321] of chirps, songs, and whistles.

---

[316] **Fortitude:** strength of mind that allows one to endure adversity with courage

[317] **Quell:** to pacify, quiet

[318] **Precipice:** a very steep or overhanging place

[319] **Flourish:** to grow well, thrive

[320] **Quiescent:** being quiet or at rest; inactive

[321] **Cacophony:** jarring, discordant sound; dissonance

"I can't believe how loud the birds are!" Alexa exclaimed over the inces-sant[322] noise of the vociferous[323] birds. "There must be a lot of them in the jungle. They are so boisterous[324]—it sounds like they're having a party."

"Yes, and I can't wait to be invited. Do you know there are toucans, parrots, and macaws in this jungle? There is even a resplendent quetzal...do you know what that is?" he asked.

"No," Alexa replied, shaking her head. "Is it a bird?"

"Oh, yes," Doug replied. "But not just any bird. The resplendent quetzal is supposed to be the most beautiful bird in the world—that's why they call it 'resplendent.' It's bright green and red with luminous[325] feathers. The ancient Mayans used to wear these feathers on their head-dresses. Very few people have the chance to see the quetzal in the wild. But I intend to while I'm here. You should, too—you should come bird-ing with me."

"What do you do when you go birding?" Alexa asked.

"You just look for birds and try to identify their species. It's really fun."

The two friends became quiet again, consumed with the sight of the dramatic sunrise. The morning sun peeked over the horizon and the sky turned a beautiful shade of pale blue. Right before their eyes, the sunlight melted the mist, revealing the details of the leafy treetops below. Not a single human voice was audible[326], only the sounds of nature. After trumpeting their morning songs, the birds quieted down into a period of restful repose[327].

---

[322] **Incessant:** continuing without interruption; unceasing

[323] **Vociferous:** marked by noisy and vehement outcry

[324] **Boisterous:** loud and lacking in restraint; rowdy

[325] **Luminous:** emitting or reflecting light

[326] **Audible:** that is heard or is able to be heard

[327] **Repose:** the act of resting

"It's so serene[328] and beautiful here," Alexa whispered quietly, so that she wouldn't disturb the tranquility[329] of the moment. They sat there in silence for another 10 minutes, just gazing at the spectacular scene and listening to the subtle sounds of nature. The temperature climbed with the rising sun and quickly burned off the chill of the early morning. All of a sudden, Alexa was cognizant[330] of the fact that she was sweating in the steamy heat and humidity. The sun was bearing down on them with an intensity that was beginning to become uncomfortable. The sunrise was over so quickly, Alexa thought silently. The magical golden-orange glow of the sunrise was beautiful, but ephemeral[331]. Now it was daytime. The sun was shining with a blinding strength, the sky was an intense shade of blue, and a new day had begun. The dreamy colors of the sunrise were evanescent[332], but Alexa hoped that the memory of that special moment would stay in her mind forever.

"Let's get a picture," Doug said, as if reading her mind.

"Good idea," she replied, pulling out the camera. Alexa snapped a few pictures of the jungle canopy spread out below them.

"Here, let me get a picture of you," he suggested, grabbing the camera from her hands. "Smile," he coaxed, snapping a picture. Then he held the camera out in front of the two of them and trained the lens on their faces. "Cheese!" he said as he simultaneously pulled her close to him and snapped a picture.

Alexa laughed and grabbed the camera back from him. Curiously, she toggled through the stored images and stole a glimpse of this impromptu photo. He was sitting close to her with his arm around her shoulders, a silly

---

[328] **Serene:** without disturbance; calm

[329] **Tranquility:** the quality or state of being tranquil (free from disturbance, agitation, or turmoil)

[330] **Cognizant:** fully informed; conscious, aware

[331] **Ephemeral:** lasting a very short time

[332] **Evanescent:** tending to vanish like vapor; fleeting

smile plastered on his face. It looked like they were boyfriend and girlfriend. Alexa giggled at the sight of it. The boy in the picture was so far removed from the aloof lacrosse star from Ithaca High.

"We really need to go now," Doug said, looking at his watch. "I promised my dad we wouldn't be late for breakfast, but I think we might be."

"OK," she said, reluctantly getting up from her perch. She could see that Doug was in a rush to get back to the camp. But actually, Alexa was terrified at the thought of getting on the ladder for the harrowing[333] descent down the steep face of the temple. She approached the ladder and looked down. Just glancing at the treacherous drop to the ground far below made her dizzy.

"Did you know this temple was built back in 470 A.D.?" Doug remarked as he started descending backward down the stairs.

Alexa barely nodded in response as she looked at the ladder that loomed in front of her.

"Tourists call it Temple IV, but it's really the Temple of the Two-Headed Snake, built over fifteen hundred years ago by King Yaxkin Caan Chac. That's what it says in my guidebook."

"Temple of the Two-Headed Snake? *Great,*" she muttered sarcastically. "That's all I need right now. The image of a two-headed snake to comfort me when I'm trying to get down."

"Hmmm..." Doug said, smiling mischievously he raised his eyebrows in a high arch. "Is Dorothy afraid of heights?" he taunted.

---

[333] **Harrowing:** extremely distressing; agonizing

Alexa could feel her whole body sweating profusely[334] as she looked at the challenge before her. Truthfully, she was terrified. But she was determined to put on a brave face. "I'm fine," she said tentatively.

"Hey," he said, his voice taking on a note of concern, "just follow me. I'll be right underneath you. You can't fall. I'll catch you," he added tenderly. "Just follow me," he coaxed, taking a few steps down the ladder.

Alexa felt comforted by his words of assurance. The kind words of support strengthened her resolve[335] to face her challenge. Timorously[336], she started descending, focusing on one step at a time. When they got to the terrace level, halfway down the temple, Alexa realized that the most difficult part of the descent was still before her. The ladder had been relatively easy, because she didn't have to look down. She just stared straight at the face of the temple and descended rung by rung without looking down at the distant ground below. But the steep wooden staircase that led to the ground would have to be negotiated head on. She was going to have to go straight down, watching her every step, the treacherous drop always looming in her peripheral vision.

"I'll hold your hand," Doug offered sympathetically when he saw the look of terror on her face. "You can't fall—I'm right here," he said, grasping her hand firmly.

Alexa squeezed his hand tightly and tried to take a few steps down. But her body was so rigid with fear that her steps were ungainly[337].

"I've got you. You can't fall. You're doing fine," he coaxed.

---

[334] **Profuse:** produced or growing in great abundance
[335] **Resolve:** to make a firm decision about
[336] **Timorous:** full of apprehensiveness; timid, fearful
[337] **Ungainly:** lacking grace or ease of movement; clumsy

Alexa started moving faster. His encouraging words were like a salve[338] for her anxiety. They were almost to the bottom when Alexa saw something that shocked her...and thrilled her.

It was José. He was standing on the ground below, along with two other gentlemen. He looked up at her curiously, a forlorn[339] expression clouding his face when he noticed her holding Doug's hand.

"José!" Alexa shrieked. Excitedly, she waved vigorously with her free hand and called out a salutation[340]. "Hello, José! I can't believe you're here!" In the excitement of the moment, Alexa impetuously[341] hurried down the rest of the stairs without watching her footing on the narrow wooden steps, slick with dew. Her foot slipped off of the slippery surface and she felt herself falling forward.

Doug immediately strengthened his grip on her hand to keep her from plummeting to the bottom. Then, in a single agile[342] maneuver honed by years of lacrosse practice, he pivoted on one foot to face her and grasped her other arm with his free hand. But his attempt to forestall[343] her fall was not successful. Her downward momentum was simply too great. They both went tumbling down to the grassy field below, landing together in a jumbled pile.

"Are you OK?" Doug asked in a muffled voice.

Alexa was dazed from the fall and it took her a moment to realize that she had landed right on top of Doug. Immediately, she rolled off to the side and sat up. "I'm OK," she answered. "I think you broke my fall."

---

[338] **Salve:** something that soothes or heals; a balm
[339] **Forlorn:** appearing sad or lonely because deserted or abandoned
[340] **Salutation:** a polite expression or gesture of greeting
[341] **Impetuous:** characterized by haste and lack of thought; impulsive and passionate
[342] **Agile:** characterized by quickness, lightness, and ease of movement; nimble
[343] **Forestall:** to delay or prevent by taking precautionary measures beforehand

"Alexa!" José cried, running over to see her. "Are you OK?" he asked.

"I'm fine, but it's Doug that I'm worried about."

"Oh, I'm OK. Just a cut on my shin," he replied, pointing to a small laceration[344] on his leg that was beginning to bleed. "But it's nothing."

Alexa looked at José and his big brown eyes looked into hers. All of a sudden she was bashful[345]. She was painfully aware of the fact that she had not even bothered to run a brush through her hair that morning and now she was sticky with sweat and covered with dirt. She felt a tinge of regret. Why did she forsake[346] vanity today of all days? This was not how she had envisioned her reunion with José.

But even more distressing was the fact that José looked dejected by the sight of her holding Doug's hand. His typically sanguine[347] demeanor was replaced with a look of genuine sadness. He didn't realize that the hand-holding was truly an innocent, innocuous[348] thing. It certainly didn't reflect an amorous[349] relationship with Doug. But Alexa could plainly see that José had construed[350] their hand-holding as a sign of romance.

She desperately wanted to find some way to exonerate[351] herself. But how was she going to convince José that she was really enamored[352] with him, not Doug? She knew that attempting to talk about such a delicate matter now, in front of Doug, would be too difficult. It would have to wait for a more private moment. José's companions, both dressed in khaki-colored, safari-style outfits, were walking toward them.

---

[344] **Laceration:** a jagged cut or wound

[345] **Bashful:** shy, self-conscious, and awkward

[346] **Forsake:** to give up

[347] **Sanguine:** cheerfully confident, optimistic

[348] **Innocuous:** having no adverse effect; harmless

[349] **Amorous:** indicative of love or sexual desire

[350] **Construe:** to explain the meaning of; interpret

[351] **Exonerate:** to free from blame

[352] **Enamor:** to inspire with love; captivate

"You kids sure took a tumble," the older man remarked with a thick British accent. He adjusted his wide-brimmed sunhat over his gray hair as he looked at Alexa and Doug still lying on the ground.

Alexa gave him a brave smile. "We're not hurt," she reassured him, as she stood up, brushing dirt off the seat of her pants.

"Oh, you young folks are amazing," the gray-haired man said admiringly. "If that had been one of us wizened[353] old men falling down those steps, we would have broken a bone or two. Wouldn't we have, Grady?"

"Hey, speak for yourself, Rothschild," the younger man retorted, chuckling at his companion's self-deprecating[354] humor. "I may have a few wrinkles, but I'm not wizened yet!" He smiled widely as he gave Rothschild a genial clap on the back. Grady's thinning hair suggested he was in his mid-forties, but he looked to be in terrific shape. The well-defined muscles undulating[355] under his thin tan t-shirt suggested that he exercised rigorously and didn't let his muscles atrophy[356] from leading a sedentary[357] lifestyle. His swarthy[358] complexion was that of someone who had spent many hours in the sun.

"Alexa, this is Mr. Grady and Mr. Rothschild," José said. "They're from the foundation, the one that's giving me the scholarship."

"Oh, hello," Alexa said awkwardly, wiping the dirt off her hand before shaking hands. "And this is Doug Whittiker. He's one of my classmates back home and he's here with his father. His father and my father and Nadine, we all came here together. Our car broke down on the way

---

[353] **Wizened:** shriveled, withered, dried up
[354] **Deprecate:** to belittle, depreciate
[355] **Undulate:** to rise and fall in volume or pitch as if in waves
[356] **Atrophy:** decrease in size or wasting away of a body part or tissue
[357] **Sedentary:** characterized by a lack of physical activity and a lot of sitting
[358] **Swarthy:** having a dark complexion or color

here, and then this morning we decided to climb to the top of the temple to watch the sunrise," Alexa mumbled, her trembling hands revealing just how flustered she was in the awkward situation. She was trying to find a way of explaining to José that Doug was not her boyfriend, but instead she rambled on and on. "We're working on an archeological dig here in Tikal."

"Ah, yes," Rothschild said. "I know of this excavation. You're working on the newly discovered settlement area in the thick of the jungle in the northern quadrant of the park, aren't you? There's a consortium[359] of archeologists from several different universities working on that dig, isn't there?"

"Yes, I think so," she replied. "I think there are archeologists from both Guatemala and the United States working on the excavation. But I haven't been there yet. We just arrived in Tikal and we're hiking out to the site later today."

"Well, well, well...aren't you lucky, José!" Rothschild exclaimed, looking at him with a twinkle in his eye. "When José wrote to us that he wanted to come to Tikal, I was puzzled. But now it all makes sense," he said with an amused grin as he looked from Alexa to José. "Now I know why he wanted to come to Tikal before he received his well-deserved commendation[360]. As it turns out, I was able to get José a volunteer position on our excavation team, and we are working on a different site just several hundred yards away. So you two kids can see each other quite often," he smiled satisfactorily, looking pleased with his own munificence[361].

---

[359] **Consortium:** a cooperative arrangement among groups or institutions

[360] **Commendation:** something, especially an official award, that commends (expresses approval or praise)

[361] **Munificence:** showing great generosity

Alexa felt her spirits rise as she heard this exciting news.

But José, who was usually exuberant and talkative, was uncharacteristically taciturn[362]. Alexa couldn't wait to talk with him alone and clear the air. This was not at all how she had envisioned their reunion. Over and over again, she replayed her dream scenario in her mind...they would lock eyes from a distance, he would come rushing toward her, they would fall together in a tight embrace, and then, maybe share a romantic kiss. In her dream, she looked beautiful and he couldn't take his eyes off of her.

But the harsh reality was that she had just rolled out of bed in the morning without so much as running a brush through her hair, she was hot and sticky, and now she had just fallen into the dirt. But the worst part of it was that now he didn't even want to look in her eyes. She couldn't wait to clear up the misunderstanding.

"Actually, we are hiking out to the dig later today, too," Rothschild continued. "But right now, we were just giving José a brief tour of the major sites. So, what do you think so far, young man?"

"It's incredible," José said succinctly[363].

"Did you know that José's antecedents[364] were native to the Mayan highlands?" Rothschild asked Alexa. "This young man here is of Mayan descent! His ancestors constructed these acclaimed[365] temples and built a great civilization," he exclaimed approvingly.

"Well, I can hardly take credit for this," José said humbly, looking as if he felt uncomfortable receiving accolades[366] for something he didn't do.

---

[362] **Taciturn:** temperamentally disinclined to talk; uncommunicative

[363] **Succinct:** characterized by clear, precise expression in few words; concise and terse

[364] **Antecedents:** one's ancestors or something that goes before or precedes

[365] **Acclaim:** to praise enthusiastically and often publicly; applaud

[366] **Accolade:** an expression of approval; praise

"These temples were built more than a thousand years ago by anony-mous[367] Mayan workers. We will never know the names of the people who struggled under difficult circumstances to put one stone upon another. Only the names of the nobility[368] are etched into stone for us to read centuries later. The monarchs[369] will be recorded in the textbooks for us all to regard with reverence[370], but it is really the working class that built these magnificent temples."

"My boy, aren't you the precocious[371] one!" Rothschild exclaimed proudly. "I've never heard such a sophisticated sentiment[372] coming from the mouth of such a youngster. Yes, it's true that the Mayan kings had a glorified status in their society and they ruled with an iron fist. By today's standards, you might even say they were despots[373]. But what you have to understand is that back in those days, the people worshipped their kings—they were seen as having divine[374] powers. That is why they built these magnificent temples for them. So don't let the idolatrous[375] practices of the Mayan society mar[376] your view of their civilization, because it was a great one. They made great strides in architecture and astronomy, and they developed a written language."

---

[367] **Anonymous:** name unknown

[368] **Nobility:** a privileged class holding hereditary titles such as dukes, duchesses, earls, countesses, etc.

[369] **Monarch:** one who reigns over a state or territory, usually for life and by hereditary right

[370] **Reverence:** a feeling of profound respect and awe; veneration

[371] **Precocious:** characterized by early development or maturity

[372] **Sentiment:** a thought or attitude, especially one based primarily on emotion rather than reason

[373] **Despot:** a person who wields power oppressively; a tyrant

[374] **Divine:** God-like, having the nature of a deity; superhuman

[375] **Idolatrous:** given to blind or excessive devotion to something

[376] **Mar:** to impair or spoil

"I certainly wasn't trying to denounce[377] the great civilization of the ancient Maya," José said with a charming smile, "I was merely trying to point out the inequity[378]."

"Your comments are duly appreciated, my boy," Rothschild said, putting his arm around José's shoulders like a proud parent. "Thank you for edifying[379] us with that observation. You certainly are attuned[380] to the subtleties of the history here. I am very pleased with our choice for the recipient of the foundation's scholarship. You are a fine young man."

Alexa looked over at José, who was blushing modestly from all of the compliments. She gave him a sympathetic smile. Alexa knew him well enough to know that he was modest at heart, preferring to eschew[381] praise.

"Excuse me," Doug cleared his throat. "I don't mean to interrupt, but Alexa, we need to get back to the camp right away. We're supposed to be back there for breakfast and I promised my dad we wouldn't be late. And I know for a fact that your dad wouldn't want you to be late, either."

Mentioning how her dad didn't like to be late was all Doug needed to do to elicit[382] a response from Alexa. She knew she couldn't dither[383] in this awkward situation indefinitely. She desperately wanted to talk to José, but she knew that would have to wait. "Yes, you're right," she reluctantly agreed. "We should get going."

---

[377] **Denounce:** to condemn openly as evil or reprehensible
[378] **Inequity:** injustice; unfairness
[379] **Edify:** to instruct, inform, or enlighten
[380] **Attune:** to make aware or responsive
[381] **Eschew:** avoid, shun
[382] **Elicit:** to bring or draw out
[383] **Dither:** to act nervously indecisive

6

Resolving an Imbroglio

"**A**re you going back to the campsite?" Rothschild asked Alexa and Doug. "Because we're headed that way, too. We can all walk together," he suggested cheerfully.

"Sounds good," Alexa replied, hoping she would have a chance to talk to José on the hike back to the camp. They all set out single file on the narrow trail.

"We have to move José out of his cushy quarters at the Hotel Jaguar and out into the field with the rest of the archeological team," Rothschild said, as the trail widened up and they all walked together as a group. "Only one night of luxury for you, young man, and then from here on out, we're going to be roughing it. We lead an austere[384] lifestyle at the camp—there is nothing but the essentials: food, water, and a tent for shelter."

Grady laughed uproariously. "Except for the box of goodies that Rothschild has me carry in every week...it's filled with Swiss chocolates,

---

[384] **Austere:** severely simple or stark

English toffees, and several bottles of fine brandy," Grady teased. "Rothschild, you couldn't lead the lifestyle of an ascetic[385] if your life depended on it!"

"Shush, Grady!" Rothschild exclaimed with a rueful smile. "I've already told José that we will share abstemious[386] meals at the camp. We always eat and drink in moderation[387], don't we, Grady?"

"Oh yes, nothing but the bare essentials," Grady said sarcastically. "We never indulge in goodies."

Everyone broke out laughing, because they could tell from the innuendo[388] in Grady's tone of voice that he was implying just the opposite.

"You stayed at the Hotel Jaguar last night?" Alexa asked, turning to José. "That's where we were trying to stay, but it was all booked."

"Yes, I did stay there, and it was very nice. It was so kind of you to put me up there for a night," José thanked Rothschild. "But don't worry about me roughing it at a campsite in the jungle. I'm used to leading a very simple life."

"Ah, yes," Rothschild replied. "I know that your family was very poor and you didn't have many luxuries growing up. But despite these difficulties, you managed to succeed in your studies. That's one of the reasons why we chose you to be the recipient of the scholarship from our foundation. You will rise from penury[389] to the lofty ivory towers of academia, and the world will be yours."

José broke out in a big grin at the mention of the scholarship. Going to college had always been his lifelong dream.

"Check it out!" Doug exclaimed, pointing ahead. The path emptied into the grassy courtyard of the *Gran Plaza*.

---

[385] **Ascetic:** one who renounces material comforts and practices self-denial as a measure of personal and especially spiritual discipline.

[386] **Abstemious:** marked by restraint and moderation, especially as applied to eating and drinking

[387] **Moderation:** being within reasonable limits; not excessive or extreme

[388] **Innuendo:** an indirect or subtle implication (usually derogatory) in expression; an insinuation

[389] **Penury:** an oppressive lack of resources; severe poverty or destitution

Alexa gasped with wonder when she saw the spectacle before her. At the eastern and western ends of the plaza, two large ancient stone pyramids rose toward the sky. In the full light of day, the sight was absolutely stunning. They headed to the center of the courtyard, which was already dotted with tourists.

"These magnificent temples were built by the greatest of all Mayan rulers, King Hasaw Chan K'awil," Rothschild said in a booming voice, as if he were delivering a speech to a crowded lecture hall. He swaggered[390] forward and turned to face the group with a proud look on his face, as if he had assembled the remarkable structures himself.

"Wow!" Alexa exclaimed, taking in the amazing panorama.

"Totally cool!" Doug echoed.

Alexa glanced over at José, hoping that somehow they could share the excitement of this special moment. But he looked pensive[391] as he stood there listening to Rothschild lecture. He looked as if he was thinking about something disturbing, Alexa noticed. She couldn't wait to talk with him alone to unravel this imbroglio[392] and set the record straight.

"Right here we have Temple I and Temple II, dating back to circa 700 A.D.," Rothschild continued, pointing to the two imposing pyramids that stood at opposite ends of the plaza. "You youngsters might be interested to know that these two temples were built to honor King Hasaw and his wife, Lady Twelve Macaw. See how the two temples are facing each other from opposite ends of the plaza? Back when these were built, an image of Hasaw was on the top of this temple, and his wife's image was on the other temple. This way, they could look at each other for eternity.

---

[390] **Swagger:** to walk or conduct oneself with a proud, arrogant air; strut

[391] **Pensive:** deeply and often wistfully or dreamily thoughtful; often suggestive of melancholy thoughtfulness

[392] **Imbroglio:** a very embarrassing misunderstanding

That's the way Hasaw wanted it. How romantic," he sighed, giving Alexa and José a knowing look.

Alexa could feel her face flush with embarrassment. Was it really that obvious to everyone that she liked José? It seemed like it was obvious to everyone but José himself.

"Ah, yes...King Hasaw and his wife were in love," Rothschild said. "Hasaw was considered quite handsome in his day, a man of great pulchritude[393] by all accounts, although *you* might not think so," he said looking at Alexa.

"Why not? What did he look like?" she asked curiously.

"Well, back in the days of the ancient Maya, it was considered attractive to have a flat forehead. So, when children were mere infants, the Mayans used to press a flat board to their face to achieve this aesthetically[394] pleasing result."

"Aesthetically pleasing?" Alexa repeated incredulously. "It sounds like just the opposite. That's got to look terrible—and it sounds so torturous."

"Yuck!" Doug exclaimed.

"And that's not all," Rothschild continued enthusiastically, as if he was taking great delight in their shocked reactions. "His eyes were crossed! This was also considered beautiful to the Mayans, and to achieve this result, they dangled an object right in between the infant's eyes so their eyes focused on this target and became permanently crossed."

"No way!" Doug exclaimed. "But how could he see?"

"Not very well, I imagine," Rothschild answered. "But since crossed eyes and a flat forehead were considered the epitome[395] of beauty by the

---

[393] **Pulchritude:** great physical beauty and appeal
[394] **Aesthetic:** relating to beauty and the appreciation of beauty and good taste
[395] **Epitome:** a standard, typical, or representative example of a class or type

Mayans, that's what they aimed to achieve. To our eyes, these traits would appear to be ugly aberrations[396]. But not to them. Standards of beauty are very different from one culture to the next and they are constantly evolving with time. Take body weight, for example. In some cultures, corpulence[397] is considered attractive, whereas in our culture, it's an anathema[398]. No one wants to be fat."

Alexa couldn't take her eyes off the ancient structures that surrounded her. What is all of this over here?" she asked, pointing to the cluster of ancient ruins on the northern side of the plaza.

"This is the North Acropolis, which actually has a hundred different structures in this jumble of ancient ruins that you see here. The Mayans tended to build new buildings on top of the old ones, so some of these ruins are very complex, from an archeologist's point of view. Some of the structures date back to before the time of Christ," Rothschild said, his eyes sparkling with excitement.

José was quiet as he looked at his surroundings with profound respect. To Rothschild, the ancient Mayan ruins were fodder[399] for his considerable intellect. But to José, it was so much more. It was hallowed[400] ground, the site where his ancestors had lived and died.

Doug, who had wandered off to the side of the plaza, called out to the rest. "Hey, check this out," he beckoned them. "This is really cool!"

"This is the ball court," Rothschild explained, as they made their way over to join Doug, who was standing on a stone platform looking down at a small courtyard. The sides of the courtyard were flanked by stone walls that angled outward. "This is where the ancient Maya played

---

[396] **Aberration:** a departure from the normal or typical

[397] **Corpulence:** the condition of being excessively fat; obesity

[398] **Anathema:** someone or something intensely loathed or shunned

[399] **Fodder:** a consumable, such as feed for livestock, that is used to supply a heavy demand

[400] **Hallowed:** holy or sacred: *a hallowed cemetery*

ball. It was not a sport for the weak of heart. It was a very rough game, played with a large, heavy black rubber ball that the players were not allowed to touch with their hands or their feet. They wore special pads around their ribs to keep them from cracking when they were hit by the ball. The object was to keep the ball in motion, and let me just say, they took their sporting very seriously."

"Sounds like fun," Doug said enthusiastically, jumping down onto the stone ball court.

"Young man," Rothschild said, "you should know that back in the days of the ancient Maya, these games were not played for fun...they were played for life. The ancient Mayans were not pacifists[401]. There was great enmity[402] between the various city-states of the Mayan world and they were constantly at war with their neighbors. This war-like mentality extended to the games they played. The losing team was sacrificed. They were literally slain right on the spot."

"No way!" Doug exclaimed, looking both horrified and fascinated at the same time.

"Let me show you around," Rothschild said, climbing down off of the stone platform and to the surface of the ball court along with Doug. "Grady," he called out, "come show this young man how this ball game was played and what happened afterward," Rothschild smiled mischievously as he beckoned his colleague. He looked as if he enjoyed talking about the macabre[403] aspects of the ancient Mayan society.

Alexa stayed up on the stone platform above, next to José. Now that they had a moment alone, it seemed like the perfect time to talk to him.

---

[401] **Pacifism:** the belief that disputes (such as between countries) can and should be settled peacefully, without war or violence

[402] **Enmity:** mutual hatred or ill will

[403] **Macabre:** suggesting the horror of death; gruesome

But she had no idea how to begin. It was so difficult to say what she was really feeling...that meeting him earlier this summer had been the most exciting thing that had ever happened to her, and that she had missed him over the past several weeks when they'd been apart. And, despite the fact she had been holding Doug's hand earlier, they were *not* romantically involved. She desperately wanted to say all of these things in an attempt to mitigate[404] the damage that had been done to their relationship, but the task seemed daunting.

Alexa looked over at José, waiting for the right moment to say something. He was uncharacteristically quiet and serious as he studied the impressive height of Temple I.

Usually, José was jocular[405]. He was always telling a joke or doing some funny antics that made her laugh. Sometimes, he even joked when Alexa thought it was more appropriate to be serious. But his usual levity[406] was absent this morning, and Alexa missed the José she'd known so well.

"Uh, José?" Alexa asked timidly, trying to get his attention.

He turned to look at her, his big brown eyes focused on hers intently. His face was expressionless as he waited for her to speak.

"Umm...uh, there's something I think you should know," Alexa began. "Doug and I—I mean, Doug was just holding my hand to help me down from the temple. I'm afraid of heights. He offered to hold my hand going down and I took it because I needed to. There was no other way I could get down otherwise. I was terrified!"

"Really?" he asked cautiously. "He's not your boyfriend from back home?"

---

[404]**Mitigate:** to make less severe; alleviate
[405]**Jocular:** characterized by joking behavior and good humor
[406]**Levity:** lightness of manner or speech, especially when inappropriate; excessive frivolity

"No!" Alexa replied emphatically[407], looking directly into his eyes to reinforce her point.

José's entire demeanor metamorphosed[408] in an instant. The expression of grave concern melted into a joyful smile and his eyes sparkled with mirth[409] as he laughed at himself. "I thought...well, never mind what I thought! I'm so sorry that I thought that. I didn't even give you a proper hello."

Alexa fell into his open arms and the two friends embraced tightly. Alexa felt a huge sense of relief wash over her. Everything felt right between them, finally. Their reconciliation[410] was complete. José held her tight in a never-ending hug and whispered something in Spanish.

"What are you saying?" Alexa asked.

"Oh, I just wanted to tell you something," he said, smiling mischievously. He knew she couldn't understand what he had said.

"Just give me a hint," she pleaded.

José made a motion like he was zipping his lips closed. "My lips are sealed," he said. "For now, at least!"

Alexa burst into laughter. The zipping of the lips was something she had seen him do before. It was reminiscent[411] of the very first time they had met. He knew she would remember this and that it would make her laugh. Alexa felt a warm glow inside. This was the José she knew so well and cared about deeply.

"I'm glad we are here in Tikal together," he said.

"You are?" Alexa asked.

"Yes," he said. "Not only because I am so happy to see you, but also because I think that I'm going to need your help," he added seriously.

---

[407] **Emphatic:** expressed with emphasis; forceful and definite

[408] **Metamorphose:** to change into a wholly different form or appearance; transform

[409] **Mirth:** gladness and great merriment, especially as expressed by laughter

[410] **Reconciliation:** the act of reestablishing a close relationship

[411] **Reminiscent:** tending to recall or suggest something in the past

"What's going on?" Alexa asked worriedly as she pulled back from their long embrace.

"I have some suspicions..." he said, his voice trailing off as he looked down at Rothschild and Grady with narrowed eyes. "I'm not sure if these two people are who they say they are."

"They sure seem to know what they're talking about." Alexa looked down at Rothschild and Grady, who were busy lecturing Doug on the intricacies of the ancient Mayan ball game. To her eyes, the two men appeared to be redoubtable[412] scholars, knowledgeable and dedicated to their field of study.

José's face contorted in a pained expression. "Last night, I overheard a conversation that made me think something sinister may be going on...something utterly execrable[413]," he added, his brown eyes narrowing with contempt[414] as he looked at Grady and Rothschild.

"What did you hear?" Alexa asked.

"I can't tell you right now—here they come!" he whispered furtively[415]. "Don't tell anyone what I just told you."

"I won't," she assured him, making a motion like she was zipping her lips.

But José didn't laugh at their little private joke this time. He looked serious, as if he was contemplating a weighty issue.

What is going on? Alexa wondered silently. What could José have overheard that would cause him to turn against Grady and Rothschild and become so disaffected[416]?

But she knew the answer would have to wait. Doug was rapidly approaching, pointing to his watch with an anxious expression.

---

[412] **Redoubtable:** worthy of respect or honor; illustrious, eminent

[413] **Execrable:** detestable, very bad: *execrable crimes*

[414] **Contempt:** the act of despising, hating

[415] **Furtive:** characterized by stealth or secrecy; surreptitious

[416] **Disaffected:** resentful and rebellious, especially against authority

"Alexa, we really have to hot-foot it back to the campsite," he said. "We're late for breakfast and I know for sure your dad is not going to like it."

"I know, I know," she reluctantly agreed. She desperately wanted to stay and talk to José, but she also wanted to avoid being rebuked[417] by her father for being late. "If we're seriously late, we'll never hear the end of it. We'd better go."

"And we'd better go fast," Doug repeated, beseeching[418] her to leave immediately.

Alexa looked at José, as if to silently ask, when will I see you again?

Without a single word, José understood the question that she was communicating with a single glance. They knew each other so well that sometimes words were superfluous[419]. "I'll come visit your campsite the first chance I get," he said.

"But how will you find it?" she asked.

"Don't worry," he said, flashing a bright smile, "I'll find it."

---

[417] **Rebuke:** to scold or criticize sharply; reprimand
[418] **Beseech:** to beg for urgently; implore
[419] **Superfluous:** beyond what is required or sufficient

7

Empirical Evidence

"**A**lexa, it's time to wake up."

Alexa felt a hand on her shoulder, gently nudging her. "What time is it?" she asked Nadine, who was standing over her, prodding her awake. Alexa looked at her surroundings in the semi-darkness of the early morning. The girls' tent housed the eight female members of the archeological team, and last night they had all slept in a row on the nylon floor of the tent. Their sleeping bags, each a different color, were lined up side by side, nestled next to each other like crayons in a box. But now, all of the sleeping bags were rolled up tightly and neatly stowed away, their owners already up and about.

"It's about five-thirty," Nadine replied. "Remember how I warned you that we start early? We need to get a lot of work done before the sun gets too hot."

"I'm coming," Alexa said with all of the enthusiasm she could muster in her somnolent[420] state. She always had a hard time waking up in the morning. "Boy, I slept like a rock," she commented with a note of surprise in her voice. "When I first saw the tent, I wasn't so sure I'd be able to sleep so well. It was so crowded in here. And we went to bed so early—I thought I'd be awake all night. But as soon as you turned out the lantern, I fell right asleep."

"Me too," Nadine replied with a smile. "I think the fresh air has a great soporific[421] effect, don't you? I always sleep better when I'm camping than when I'm back home in my nice bedroom. I'm glad that you're all rested, because it's breakfast time."

Alexa rummaged around in her backpack for a clean t-shirt and a pair of pants. Spying her brush, she quickly ran it through her hair before pulling her smooth brown tresses back in a simple ponytail. A shower was out of the question. Last night, after they arrived at the dig, Nadine had explained the situation to her. There was no running water at the camp, so the workers took turns making the hour-long hike back to the main campground, where there was a public shower. Since this was a time-consuming endeavor[422], and a seemingly extravagant waste of precious work hours that could better be spent making important discoveries at the dig, all of the workers tried to restrict their showers to once a week.

Alexa was dismayed with the lack of showers, but she was determined to endure this hardship with equanimity[423]. She didn't want to start off on the wrong foot by complaining loudly and clamoring[424] for the luxury of a hot shower. But the worst part of their accommodations, the part that she had trouble accepting, was the fact that there were no

---

[420] **Somnolent:** drowsy, sleepy

[421] **Soporific:** tending to induce sleep

[422] **Endeavor:** an activity directed toward a specific goal

[423] **Equanimity:** evenness of mind especially under stress; composure

[424] **Clamor:** to make loud, insistent demands or complaints

toilets. There was not even an outhouse. They were just supposed to go off into the woods to take care of their personal needs.

Alexa thought that this was absolutely appalling[425]. Even though she had been camping several times with her family while growing up, they had always gone to a designated campsite, where there were public bathrooms and toilets that flushed. In actuality, she was a neophyte[426] when it came to genuine wilderness camping.

"Don't worry, you'll get used to it," Nadine had told her when she explained the situation. Nadine herself appeared to be impervious[427] to the hardships of camping in the jungle.

"But how will we have any privacy?" Alexa asked. "What if someone walks up when you are...?"

"Don't worry!" Nadine laughed. "We have a covenant[428] between the ladies and the gentlemen here at the camp that we've all agreed to abide by. See this tree here? This is the line of demarcation[429]," she said, pointing to an imaginary boundary line extending into the jungle. "Ladies are on this side of the line and men are on that side."

"But what about at night time?" Alexa asked. "How do you find your way through the labyrinth[430]?

"It's no different," Nadine replied. "Just take your flashlight with you."

"But what if you encroach[431] upon the gentlemen's territory in the middle of the night because you can't see where you're going?"

Nadine laughed. "Well, that would be tantamount[432] to a felony around here," she joked. "So watch where you're going! You'll learn your way around soon enough."

---

[425] **Appalling:** inspiring horror, dismay, or disgust

[426] **Neophyte:** a novice or beginner

[427] **Impervious:** not capable of being affected or disturbed

[428] **Covenant:** a usually formal, solemn, and binding agreement

[429] **Demarcation:** a boundary, separation, or distinction

[430] **Labyrinth:** a complex system of paths or tunnels in which it is easy to get lost; maze

[431] **Encroach:** to advance beyond proper or former limits

[432] **Tantamount:** equivalent in value, significance, or effect; being essentially equal to something

"But what about all of the nocturnal[433] animals in the jungle that are awake at night and waiting to pounce on any intruders in their midst?"

Nadine sighed loudly, revealing that she was beginning to feel exasperated[434] by Alexa's unending questions and inane[435] concerns. "The vast majority of the wild animals are more afraid of you than you are of them," she said. "Just use your flashlight and watch where you step. The most important thing is not to step on any snakes that might be on the path. If you don't bother them, they probably won't bother you."

Alexa rolled her eyes. She didn't believe that trite[436] saying about wild animals being more afraid of people than people being afraid of them. But sensing the impatient note in Nadine's voice, Alexa knew this was not the time to launch into a tirade[437] of complaints about the lack of a proper bathroom. If she started complaining now, Nadine would just view her as petulant[438].

So instead, Alexa vowed to view the situation with a good attitude. She knew her father expected her to integrate[439] into the camp routine without whining. If the other women at the dig found the accommodations tolerable, Alexa guessed that she could probably tolerate them, too. In fact, as time went on, Alexa grew to enjoy the solitude of these little excursions[440] into the forest.

After her first foray[441] into the jungle, Alexa headed back to camp, which was bustling with activity in the early morning twilight. The air was infused[442] with the tantalizing aroma of coffee. Alexa didn't drink coffee, but she loved the smell. It brought back memories of breakfast at home...pancakes with maple syrup, her parents lingering over the morning

---

[433] Nocturnal: most active at night

[434] Exasperate: to irritate, annoy, or make angry

[435] Inane: lacking significance, meaning, or point

[436] Trite: boring from overuse; not fresh or original; hackneyed

[437] Tirade: a long angry or violent speech

[438] Petulant: unreasonably rude or irritable

[439] Integrate: to join with something else; the process of unifying into a whole

[440] Excursion: a journey made for pleasure; an outing

[441] Foray: a venture or an initial attempt, especially outside one's usual area: *a model's foray into acting*

[442] Infuse: to fill or cause to be filled with something

paper, and then Saturday morning cartoons snuggled next to her dad on the big leather couch in their family room.

But now, of course, all of that had changed. As difficult as it was to accept, her parents were recently divorced and Alexa was painfully aware of the fact that she could never relive these old family memories. Everything had changed, Alexa acknowledged, eyeing Nadine, her father's new girlfriend, in the distance.

Alexa spotted her father eating breakfast with Nicholas and Doug and she hurried over to join them on the big slab of granite that served as a makeshift table.

"Good morning! Come have some cereal," her father beckoned.

"Sounds good," Alexa replied, grabbing a bowl and spoon. After pouring herself a bowl of cornflakes, Alexa spied the milk carton, which was in a small, square-shaped box. "Hey, this is warm," she complained when she picked up the carton.

"Oops! We forgot to bring the refrigerator," Doug joked. "Did we leave it by the palm tree at that fork in the path?"

Alexa burst out laughing. "I wasn't expecting a fancy breakfast buffet[443], but seriously though, is this milk still good? It's warm!" Alexa sniffed the carton suspiciously. It didn't have the fetid[444] odor of spoiled milk, but it didn't smell like regular milk, either.

"Don't worry," Professor McCurry assured her, "it's fit for consumption[445]. It's sterilized milk and it's stable at room temperature for months, as long as the carton is unopened. It has a bit of a funny taste, but trust me, it's better than foraging[446] for food in the jungle."

---

[443] **Buffet:** a meal at which guests serve themselves from a variety of dishes that are all set out
[444] **Fetid:** having a heavy, offensive smell
[445] **Consumption:** the act of consuming (eating, drinking, or utilizing)
[446] **Forage:** to wander in search of food or provisions

"We put in a requisition[447] for a cow, but it hasn't arrived yet," Nicholas joked.

Everyone laughed and then watched curiously as Alexa poured the milk on her cereal and tried a spoonful. They stared at her intently, waiting for her reaction. "It's fine," she said. "It tastes a little funny, but it's not so bad."

"So how are you managing without a bathroom?" Professor McCurry asked, after Alexa had taken a few spoonfuls.

"Fine," Alexa replied curtly[448] as she shot her father a disapproving look. She really didn't want to talk about bathroom issues in front of Doug and Nicholas. It was too embarrassing. Why did he have to talk about such a private matter in front of everyone? She felt so discomfited[449] by the topic of conversation that she tried to change it. "I think I saw a toucan in the forest when I was...when I was taking a walk."

"Really?" Doug asked excitedly. "What did it look like?"

"It had a bright yellow face and a huge beak. But the interesting thing about the beak was that it had several different colors, kind of like an artist's palette[450]. It was red and green and yellow..."

"Wow!" Doug exclaimed, dropping his cereal spoon into his bowl with a splash. "I bet you saw the keel-billed toucan! It's a really obscure[451] species—you are so lucky to have seen one."

"Actually, I saw two. They were flying together up near the treetops."

"A very fortuitous[452] sighting," Nicholas commented. "I've never had the opportunity to see one myself."

---

[447] **Requisition:** a formal written request for something needed

[448] **Curt:** rudely abrupt of brief

[449] **Discomfit:** to put into a state of unease, perplexity, and embarrassment

[450] **Palette:** a board, which an artist can hold while painting, that is used to mix paint

[451] **Obscure:** not readily seen or noticed; hidden

[452] **Fortuitous:** happening by fortunate accident or chance

"You must have good luck," Doug said, looking at her admiringly. "You have to come with me to look for the resplendent quetzal—you can be my good-luck charm!"

Alexa smiled, feeling a warm glow inside from Doug's compliment. But she said nothing. Out of deference[453] to José, she didn't say that she would go birding with Doug. She had never promised José that she wouldn't spend time alone with Doug, but knowing José as she did, she felt that this understanding was implicit[454].

Alexa was just finishing the last of her cereal when Nadine walked up. "Are you all ready to start working?" she asked. "Alexa and Doug, why don't you two come with me and I can show you what you'll be doing."

"This area we're excavating is one of the regions where the common folks lived," Nadine explained as they walked to the site. "The nobility and the upper echelons[455] of society tended to live closer to the center of town, where the big temples are. But here we are studying the common folks. What did they do every day? What was the quotidian[456] life of the ancient Maya? What did they eat, how did they obtain that food, and what sorts of agricultural[457] techniques did they use to farm the land? The list of questions is endless. But on this particular expedition, we're most interested in any sort of artifact that we can unearth about how these people interacted with one another to form such a successful society."

"But how could we possibly answer such a difficult question when there are no history books?" Alexa asked, as they arrived at the site. "Didn't you tell us that most of their books were burned during the conquest by the Spanish?"

---

[453] **Deference:** courteous respect or yielding to the wishes of another
[454] **Implicit:** implied or understood without direct expression: *an implicit agreement*
[455] **Echelon:** a level of responsibility or authority in a hierarchy; a rank
[456] **Quotidian:** everyday, commonplace: *a quotidian routine*
[457] **Agricultural:** relating to farming, producing crops, and raising livestock

"Yes, that's true, but as archeologists, we look for clues," Nadine said, pointing to a folding table that was covered with broken bits of pottery and other objects. "For example, take a look at this," she said, picking up a shiny black object.

"Is that an arrowhead?" Doug asked excitedly.

"No, but it is sharp. Feel this edge," Nadine urged. "This was used as a knife. But what's interesting about this particular tool is that it's made of obsidian—a volcanic rock. Obsidian makes excellent cutting knives and spear tips."

"Why is that so interesting?" Doug asked.

"Well, do you see any volcanoes around here?" Nadine asked, an amused look on her face.

Doug shook his head.

"You're right—there aren't any volcanoes in the vicinity. In fact, we've been able to do some analysis on the obsidian that we've found here, and we've figured out that it actually came from an area around Mexico City! You see, these clues help us to elucidate[458] the types of interactions that the people of Tikal had with other areas...interactions that happened over a thousand years ago."

"But how do you know it was really a thousand years ago?" Alexa asked skeptically. If you just find a piece of obsidian buried in the ground here, how do you know when it was left there?"

"Excellent question!" Nadine exclaimed. "Rest assured we don't just make a random guess—there is a way of obtaining some empirical[459] evidence. One common technique is carbon dating. When we're excavating a

---

[458] Elucidate: to make lucid (clear, understandable), especially by explanation or analysis
[459] Empirical: derived from observation or experiment: *empirical results that negated the hypothesis*

site and we come across a fireplace with pieces of charcoal in it, we can get a pretty accurate date on that charcoal by doing an analysis in the laboratory called carbon dating. Theoretically[460], the artifacts that are found at the same depth and in the same vicinity as the charcoal are from around the same time period."

"Cool," Doug commented.

"And of course, there are other clues buried in the ground as well," Nadine continued. "Certain styles of pottery and ceramics are characteristic of particular time periods. So when you find pottery or even just tiny fragments of pottery, sometimes it can help you to assign a time frame to the area that you're excavating."

"Sounds interesting," Alexa said, "kind of like solving a mystery by collecting clues."

"Exactly!" Nadine exclaimed. "I'm glad you like the idea of searching for clues, because that's what you'll be doing right here." Nadine picked up a large, rectangular-shaped frame with a screen attached to one side. "This is a sieve and it's used for sifting through the soil to recover small artifacts such as pottery shards." Nadine looked up at Alexa and Doug. "I thought it might be fun for the two of you to work together, so I have a plan."

"What's that?" Alexa asked.

"Alexa, you'll be in charge of this screen and Doug will bring you the soil that we need to sift through. Doug, you'll be using this wheelbarrow to ferry the soil from the excavation over there to Alexa and her sieve over here," Nadine pointed. "The workers at the excavation site will tell you what soil they want sifted," she said to Doug. "Alexa, I'll be showing you how to sift through the dirt for artifacts and how to catalogue[461] everything you

---

[460] **Theoretically:** based on theory
[461] **Catalogue:** to make an itemized list of

find. We keep careful records of all the artifacts and where they came from. You see, we have this whole site mapped on a grid, and each shovelful of dirt comes from a specific place with very precise coordinates."

"So I'll be sifting through dirt the whole time I'm here?" Alexa asked. As soon as the words came out of her mouth, she realized how spoiled she sounded. But she *was* disappointed. When she thought about working on a dig, she imagined actually digging in the ground with a shovel and unearthing something big and exciting. Sifting through dirt for tiny artifacts seemed like the antithesis[462] of a thrilling assignment. It looked like an insipid[463] task destined to inspire nothing but boredom.

"Yes," Nadine replied. "Don't be so disappointed," she said, looking at Alexa's downcast eyes. "You just might find something interesting." Nadine gave Alexa an encouraging smile and then walked away to confer with one of her colleagues.

As soon as Nadine was out of sight, Doug imitated her in a high-pitched, squeaky voice, "Now Alexa, don't be so disappointed—you just might find something interesting."

Alexa burst out laughing. "You sound like a parrot."

"Hey, speaking of parrots, did you know that there actually are parrots in this jungle? I'd rather be out there looking for them than here shoveling this dirt!"

"Me too," Alexa laughed. "But I think we're stuck here. We have to accede[464] to the wishes of our boss."

"Queen Nadine," Doug said mockingly. "The wicked witch of the West!"

---

[462] **Antithesis:** the exact opposite
[463] **Insipid:** lacking in interest or stimulation; dull
[464] **Accede:** to give consent, often at the insistence of another; concede

"Hey, that rhymes," Alexa laughed. He lampooned[465] Nadine so humorously that she just had to laugh along. She felt a little guilty vilifying[466] Nadine this way, but it was kind of fun to joke around with Doug. They had developed an easy rapport[467]. Doug had picked up on the uneasy feeling Alexa had about Nadine. It was hard to forget that Nadine was actually her dad's new girlfriend, usurping[468] her mother's place against Alexa's wishes. As likeable as Nadine was, sometimes Alexa wished that she didn't exist.

---

[465] **Lampoon:** a harsh satire of an individual or institution; ridicule

[466] **Vilify:** to make vicious and slanderous statements about; malign, defame

[467] **Rapport:** relationship, especially one of harmony, accord, and emotional affinity

[468] **Usurp:** to wrongfully seize someone else's place, authority, or possession

8

An Odious Operation

"**A**re you sure you want to stay here for the next couple of weeks?" Professor McCurry gave Alexa a searching look. "Because you're welcome to come back to Belize City with me if you don't feel comfortable here without me."

"I definitely want to stay," Alexa pleaded. The first few days at the dig had passed quickly, but uneventfully. Alexa had not seen José since the very first morning at the *Gran Plaza* and she desperately wanted to stay in Tikal. "Don't worry, Dad, I'll be fine," she assured him. Besides, Nadine is right here and so is Doug's father."

"Yes, and Nadine is going to watch out for you—she volunteered to be your surrogate[469] parent. So I want you to promise me that you will abide by her guidelines, OK? She's the boss when I'm not here. If you have any problems, I want you to go to her. Also, everyone here is expecting you to work hard and be conscientious and I don't want you to let them down."

---

[469] **Surrogate:** one who takes the place of another; a substitute

"OK, Dad," Alexa said, bidding her father goodbye with a heartfelt hug.

"And don't forget to take lots of pictures so I can enjoy your adventure vicariously[470] when I come back," he said, looking at her proudly. "I can't believe how much you've grown up."

"Don't get all misty-eyed, Dad," she said cheerfully. "I'll be fine." Alexa waved goodbye, watching her father walk away. She was so excited to be genuinely on her own for the first time in her life. But as soon as he was out of sight, she was surprised to feel her eyes fill with tears. All of a sudden, she felt a little homesick. She looked up at the tall trees above and felt a pang of loneliness. Instinctively, she scurried[471] back to the camp, seeking the company of other people.

After a delicious lunch of pasta with tomato sauce cooked in a big cauldron over an open fire, most of the crew took refuge from the torrid[472] midday sun under a shady tree or back in their tents for an afternoon nap. "It's siesta time," Nadine had explained when they had first arrived. "Everyone takes the early afternoon off. It's the hottest part of the day."

But Alexa never felt like taking a siesta. She simply wasn't drowsy in the afternoon like the others at the camp. Besides, she felt so lonely and she desperately wanted to find José. She was used to being in constant contact with her friends and she found the lack of e-mail at the camp to be frustrating. The communication problems were confounded[473] by the fact that their cell phones didn't work, either. They were simply too far away from civilization.

But she couldn't stop thinking about José. She was prepossessed[474] with memories of the times they had spent together. She couldn't help

---

[470] **Vicarious:** feeling the experience of someone else as if it were you: *the mother felt her daughter's pain vicariously*

[471] **Scurry:** to go with light running steps; scamper

[472] **Torrid:** scorching hot, burning

[473] **Confound:** to make something bad even worse

[474] **Prepossess:** to preoccupy the mind to the exclusion of other thoughts

but wonder what he was doing right now. He was only a couple hundred yards away, somewhere in this jungle. On the spur of the moment, Alexa made a rash[475] decision. She decided to set off into the jungle and look for José's camp by herself.

Even under the protective canopy of the jungle, the heat of the midday sun made her weary with exhaustion as she trudged[476] through the rainforest on a path that was overgrown with vines and branches. The palpable[477] humidity made it feel like a steam bath.

Alexa stopped to catch her breath. As soon as she stood still, she could hear the sound of her own heavy breathing. But she could also hear something else. A menacing noise from up ahead. It sounded like a large animal. *A jaguar?* Alexa could feel her heart pounding with fear as a rush of adrenaline coursed[478] through her veins.

Spotting a low branch on a tree, Alexa pulled herself up. Fueled by fear, she quickly ascended to a higher perch. *Can jaguars climb trees?* Alexa wondered as she watched and listened.

She couldn't hear any distinct animal noises like grunts or growls. In fact, the noise didn't really sound like footsteps of an animal at all. It was a hacking noise, as if someone was chopping away at the bushes and vines that precluded[479] access to the path. Alexa leaned forward and looked curiously.

It was José! Alexa breathed a sigh of relief that it was not a dangerous animal. Then she watched her friend curiously. José was brandishing[480] a machete, a long, sword-like knife, which he used aggressively, as if each branch before him was the dreaded enemy. With each deft[481] maneuver of his knife, he made more progress, skillfully cleaving[482] a path through the dense growth.

---

[475] **Rash:** characterized by reckless haste
[476] **Trudge:** to walk in a laborious, heavy-footed way; plod
[477] **Palpable:** capable of being touched or felt; tangible
[478] **Coursing:** to move swiftly through or over; traverse
[479] **Preclude:** to prevent or make impossible by an action taken in advance
[480] **Brandish:** to wave or flourish (typically a weapon) menacingly
[481] **Deft:** quick and skillful; adroit
[482] **Cleave:** to split or cut

High above him, Alexa looked down from her aerial[483] perch and suppressed a snicker. He didn't know that she was watching. She leaned forward and pushed the branches aside to get a better view. He never once looked up. He appeared to be completely oblivious[484] to her presence. She smiled widely as she thought about the best way to surprise him.

Before she had a chance to think of something clever, Alexa suddenly realized that she had leaned too far forward from her precarious perch. Trying to find her balance, her arms flailed desperately in an attempt to stop her fall. But much to her dismay, she couldn't regain her equilibrium[485]. She started falling, tumbling through the thin, pliable[486] branches that bent like rubber as she fell through them.

Halfway down, Alexa managed to grasp a thick vine, which she immediately clung to like a lifeline. Gripping the gnarled brown vine with all of her might, she felt a sudden sense of dread. Although the vine had slowed her fall, it was not strong enough to hold her weight. The vine was attached to a slim branch above it, which bowed portentously[487] under the strain of her weight. Alexa looked up at the branch, desperately hoping that it wouldn't give out. But the sickening sound of cracking wood presaged[488] disaster.

Still clinging to the vine as she dropped down to the ground, all Alexa could think about was how silly she looked. Why couldn't the vine work the way it did in the movies? When Tarzan grabbed a vine, it held strong and he swung through the jungle with ease and grace, like a lithe[489] trapeze artist. But when Alexa grabbed the vine, she dropped like a rock and landed with a plop, right in front of José.

---

[483] **Aerial:** high in the air; lofty

[484] **Oblivious:** lacking conscious awareness; unmindful

[485] **Equilibrium:** state of balance

[486] **Pliable:** easily bent

[487] **Portentous:** foreboding; foreshadowing something bad

[488] **Presage:** to warn of or indicate in advance; portend

[489] **Lithe:** characterized by effortless grace: *a lithe gymnast*

José dropped his machete and rushed to her side. "Alexa!" he exclaimed, his voice fraught with concern. "Are you all right?"

"I'm fine...just a few bruises, I think. I'll probably be black and blue tomorrow," she lamented as she gingerly touched the contusion[490] on her hip. "But mostly I'm just embarrassed."

"Look," he said softly, "your arm is all scraped up." José sat down on the ground beside her and carefully brushed the dirt off of her arm, where a long scratch had blood coagulating[491] on the surface. "We need to clean this up. Let's go back to my camp. I've already cut a path." José gave her a big smile. "I was making a nice path for us so that we could go back and forth between our camps."

"Good idea," she replied, mesmerized by his big brown eyes gazing into hers.

"So what the heck were you doing up there?" he asked curiously.

"Well, at first, I was just trying to come find you. But then when I heard a noise up ahead, I got scared and I climbed up that tree. Then, when I saw that it was you, I thought I might try to surprise you somehow," Alexa admitted sheepishly.

"You mean scare me, not surprise me, don't you?" he chuckled. "That wasn't nice."

Alexa shrugged. She could tell by his smile that he was just trying to tease her with a bit of good-natured criticism.

"But your little ruse[492] didn't work," he teased.

"Oh yes it did!" Alexa laughed. "You should have seen the look of surprise on your face when I came swinging down off that tree."

---

[490] **Contusion:** an injury that does not break the skin; a bruise
[491] **Coagulate:** to change from a liquid state into a solid or gel; clot
[492] **Ruse:** a deceptive maneuver designed to deceive or surprise an enemy

"OK, then, I retract[493] my words," he said. "I stand corrected. Your little ruse *did* work, because you definitely managed to catch me off guard. That's some way of saying hello."

Alexa giggled, and then all of a sudden she felt shy. It was actually the first time they'd been alone together since they arrived at Tikal, and José was still carefully brushing the dirt off of her scraped arm. Alexa looked into his limpid[494] brown eyes and felt her heart beat a little faster. It felt very intimate to be alone with him in the middle of the jungle like this, as if they were in their own little world, surrounded by the lush green leaves of the verdant[495] rainforest.

"I brought you something," José said shyly, reaching deep into the pocket of his jeans.

"Really?" Alexa asked.

"Here," he said, opening his hand to reveal a delicate bracelet made of small white seashells that had a pearly iridescence[496]. "I found the seashells myself. I thought they were really unusual. Do you like it?" he asked shyly.

"I love it," Alexa assured him genuinely. Curiously, she studied the unusual seashells. In her mind, this bracelet that she held in the palm of her hand was the perfect gift that somehow encapsulated[497] José's personality. He was unpretentious[498] and genuine, just like the seashells. But at the same time, the unusual luster of the shells reminded her of the fact that he was never dull. Whenever she was around him, it seemed that everyday events were never vapid[499] or prosaic[500]. Everything seemed exciting and alive.

"I have something else for you, too," he said.

"You do?" Alexa asked. "What is it?"

---

[493] **Retract:** to take back

[494] **Limpid:** transparent clearness: *a limpid pool*

[495] **Verdant:** green with vegetation

[496] **Iridescent:** producing a display of lustrous, rainbow-like colors

[497] **Encapsulate:** to express in a brief summary; epitomize

[498] **Unpretentious:** lacking pretension or ostentatious affectation; modest

[499] **Vapid:** lacking liveliness, animation, or interest

[500] **Prosaic:** lacking in imagination and spirit; dull

"Just a little confection[501]," he replied, handing her a gold-wrapped candy. "Something sweet for you. It's a special imported chocolate truffle. I had one yesterday and it was simply amazing—a sensual[502] delight! Go ahead, try it," he urged.

After fastening the new bracelet around her wrist, Alexa carefully opened the gold wrapper. Inside the chocolate was partially melted and was sticking to the wrapper. She took a bite of the gooey chocolate. "Mmm," she hummed. The taste was sublime[503]. "That's incredible. I've never tasted anything so heavenly before. Where did you get that?" she asked, licking the last traces of chocolate off of the wrapper.

"Rothschild has a whole case of them! He's got tons of goodies stashed away. There's a plenitude[504] of sweets at our camp, that's for sure. Enough even for a couple of gluttons[505] like Grady and Rothschild...and they eat a lot of sweets!" he laughed. "Rothschild leads a prodigal[506] life, filled with extravagances." José's tone of voice grew serious and his expression clouded with disdain as he talked about Rothschild's profligate[507] habits and lack of temperance[508]. "He simply doesn't have a clue what it's like to be poor," José said in a disparaging[509] tone of voice. Having grown up in an impoverished area, he was well aware of what it was like to be bereft[510] of the basic necessities of life. That experience made him detest pointless waste and extravagance. "But the fact that they're always overindulging...that's really not the problem..." he said, his voice trailing off.

"What are you talking about? What is going on?" Alexa asked.

"I heard Grady say something suspicious."

"What did he say?"

---

[501] **Confection:** a sweet preparation, such as candy

[502] **Sensual:** relating to gratification of the physical and especially the sexual appetites

[503] **Sublime:** inspiring awe; impressive, supreme

[504] **Plenitude:** an abundance

[505] **Glutton:** one who is prone to overindulgence or greediness in food or drink

[506] **Prodigal:** marked by wasteful extravagance

[507] **Profligate:** recklessly wasteful; wildly extravagant

[508] **Temperance:** moderation and restraint in behavior

[509] **Disparage:** to express a negative opinion of

[510] **Bereft:** deprived of something

"It was the other night, when we were staying at the hotel. I heard Grady talking to Miguel, one of the workers at the dig, outside of my door. They must have thought that I was asleep or that I couldn't hear them. But I did," he said soberly.

"What could they say that was *that* bad? Was it something profane[511]—something really vulgar that you don't want to repeat?" she asked.

"No, no, no...it was nothing like that. It was a very polite and proper conversation, but the implications make my stomach turn."

"What was it?"

"Grady said to Miguel, 'Pack this mask up with the utmost care. It's going to our most valued client.'" José scowled with disapproval, as he was forced to think about something utterly reprehensible[512].

"What was he talking about?" Alexa asked.

"I'm not one hundred percent certain," José began slowly, a pained look on his face, "but I think they were talking about a jade mask—an artifact—a real artifact from the Mayan temple that they're excavating. An hour earlier, Rothschild had shown me this incredible mask made out of jade and he told me it was a priceless artifact that they had just found."

"Maybe Grady wanted to send it somewhere for safekeeping and that's why he wanted Miguel to pack it up," Alexa said.

"Then why would he say that it was being sent to a 'valued client' as if it were being sold? These artifacts are not commodities[513]—they are not supposed to be bought and sold like modern art. That is deplorable[514]! That mask does not belong on the fireplace mantle of some rich person's mansion. The artifacts that are found here are part of the Mayan culture and they should be in a museum—a museum *here* where

---

[511] **Profane:** coarse or vulgar; characterized by profanity or cursing
[512] **Reprehensible:** deserving of blame, censure, or rebuke; blameworthy
[513] **Commodity:** an article of commerce or trade, especially goods that can be processed and resold
[514] **Deplorable:** worthy of severe condemnation: *a deplorable act of aggression*

the descendants of the Maya can see these things that their own ancestors used, things that are part of their own heritage."

"But do you really *know* that he's selling the mask? He just used the word 'client.' Maybe the 'client' is a museum," Alexa said with a nonchalant shrug of her shoulders. In her mind, Grady's statement was equivocal[515] and its interpretation was uncertain.

José shrugged. "I'm not a native speaker of English, but I am very familiar with the colloquial[516] usage of the word 'client.' I'm pretty certain it usually refers to a customer...someone who is *paying* for goods or services."

Alexa nodded. "Yes, I'd agree with that. I can see why you might surmise[517] that something sinister is going on. But it's still just conjecture[518]. You don't know for *sure* if that mask was sold to some rich client. You don't have any real, conclusive evidence to implicate[519] Grady and Rothschild in some sort of smuggling scheme, do you?"

José met her questioning gaze squarely, his eyes sparkling with intensity. "Not yet."

Alexa felt a sinking sensation in her stomach. "Uh oh," she groaned. "José, this could be dangerous. If these people really are criminals..." Alexa took a deep breath and tried to regain her composure. "Do you want me to help you?" she asked.

"Well, I didn't want to be presumptuous[520] and assume that you would help me, but of course I was hoping."

"I'll help you, you know I will," Alexa assured him. "But what do we do if we find out your suspicions are correct? What if they are selling priceless artifacts and pocketing the cash?"

"Then we expose their odious[521] operation for what it really is...a crime."

---

[515] **Equivocal:** open to two or more interpretations; ambiguous

[516] **Colloquial:** characteristic of informal spoken language or conversation

[517] **Surmise:** to infer something without sufficiently conclusive evidence

[518] **Conjecture:** a conclusion based on incomplete evidence or guesswork

[519] **Implicate:** to involve, connect intimately, or incriminate

[520] **Presumptuous:** excessively forward; going beyond what is proper

[521] **Odious:** arousing strong dislike, aversion, or intense displeasure

"But José," Alexa began, her voice wavering with emotion, "these are the very people who have awarded you a scholarship! What if they rescind[522] it? That scholarship is your one chance...your golden opportunity to go to college and escape..." Alexa stopped in mid-sentence. She didn't want to insult José by saying that he was poor.

"Poverty," he said, finishing her sentence. "Abject[523] poverty," he repeated, emphasizing his point. "I know. Believe me, I know. If they find out that we've tried to undermine[524] their operation in any way, they will likely revoke[525] my scholarship. But what can I do? If they are selling artifacts to the highest bidder and I don't report it, it would be like I approve of this type of thing. And I don't. I condemn[526] it! There's no way I could keep quiet and be complacent[527] when they are committing an egregious[528] crime right in front of us."

"Well, let's just slow down for a minute before we jump to conclusions," Alexa said, her voice shaking. The thought of José jeopardizing his scholarship really unnerved her. But at the same time, the pathos[529] evoked by his passionate speech made her want to help him. "This is your future we're talking about. I think we should defer[530] judgment until we really know what's going on." Alexa's voice gained confidence as she continued. "We have to figure out how we are going to get to the bottom of this. Then we'll decide what to do."

José flashed a triumphant smile. "I'm so happy that you're going to help me."

Alexa felt her heart surge with warmth at the sight of his captivating smile. "Was there ever any doubt in your mind?" she chuckled. "Of course I'll help you."

---

[522] **Rescind:** to take back; cancel

[523] **Abject:** of the most miserable type, wretched

[524] **Undermine:** to weaken at the foundation; to impair or hinder

[525] **Revoke:** to void or annul by recalling, withdrawing, or reversing; rescind

[526] **Condemn:** to express strong disapproval of

[527] **Complacent:** contented to a fault; satisfied and unconcerned

[528] **Egregious:** conspicuously bad or offensive

[529] **Pathos:** a quality that arouses emotions, especially pity or sorrow

[530] **Defer:** to put off; postpone

9

An Audacious Plan

"**N**ow all we have to do is to figure out how to get the evidence. But that's what you're good at," José said admiringly. "You're so smart."

Alexa could feel her face grow hot as she blushed. She wasn't used to such praise, especially from a boy she liked so much. "Uh oh," Alexa groaned, "now the pressure is on!"

José laughed at her humorous remark, but then his tone grew serious. "We need to figure out where this stuff is going," he said soberly. His face brightened as he got an idea. "Miguel is always going back and forth from the dig to the town to get supplies. Maybe we could follow him and figure out if he's carrying artifacts. We could see where he's taking them."

"I don't know..." Alexa hesitated, "I don't know if that would work so well. It might be hard to follow him without being noticed. I have a different idea. I think we need to get a hold of their notebook, the place where they record all of the artifacts they've found. If there's one thing I've learned about doing archeology, it's that you have to keep a really good written record of everything that you find. Nadine has told me so many times that the fidelity[531] of the record keeping is of paramount[532] importance."

"But how is that going to tell us if something illicit[533] is going on?" José asked. "The book would just be a list of artifacts. I highly doubt they would keep a record of an illegal sale—that would just be incriminating evidence. I don't think they would be naive enough to leave such a trail."

"Exactly!" Alexa exclaimed. "I'd bet that they wouldn't want any record of it at all. I think if they found an artifact that they wanted to sell, they probably wouldn't even write it in the book in the first place. Don't you see? That way, no one would ever know it was missing, because the fact that it was found was never written down."

"I bet you're right," José agreed. "Your theory makes so much sense. If it's true, what we need to do is to get a hold of the book and see if there's a discrepancy[534] between what was found at the dig and what was written down. If this is a legitimate[535] operation, there should be no differences between the two—no discrepancies at all."

"Right," Alexa agreed. "But if there is some type of larceny[536] going on here, there will probably be some glaring omissions in the bookkeeping."

"We could use your camera to document the evidence, right?" he suggested, eyeing the digital camera strapped to her belt.

"Uh, yeah, I guess so," Alexa said, suddenly getting the sensation that she may have gotten herself too deep in a sticky, uncertain situation.

"C'mon," he said jumping to his feet. "Let's go." José extended his hand out to help pull Alexa up to her feet. "Let's go get the notebook."

---

[531] **Fidelity:** exact correspondence with fact; accuracy
[532] **Paramount:** of highest importance or chief concern
[533] **Illicit:** contrary to accepted morality, law, or convention; unlawful
[534] **Discrepancy:** a divergence, variance, or disagreement between things; difference
[535] **Legitimate:** lawful; in accordance with the law or accepted standards
[536] **Larceny:** theft

"José, wait," Alexa pleaded. "Promise me that you'll take this one step at a time. We need to be careful. We can't just go grab the notebook in broad daylight. They'll know something is going on. We need to have a stealthy[537] plan to get our hands on that notebook without being noticed."

"Don't worry," he said with a wry smile, "I can act surreptitiously[538] when I need to. Remember how we snuck into Puerto Marino in the middle of the night and freed the baby dolphin?"

Alexa burst out laughing. "How could I ever forget that!" she exclaimed. "But I'd hardly call that surreptitious. It may have started out as a clandestine[539] operation, but it ended up on international television."

José shrugged and held his hands up in the air, as if to say, "I couldn't help it." Then he burst out laughing along with her.

Alexa felt a warm glow inside. It was so much fun to reminisce about the adventures they had shared together. But at the same time, she felt nervous about the new adventure that they were about to embark on now. Somehow it seemed so much more serious than anything they had ever done in the past. Alexa couldn't help but wish that the morass[540] of problems and suspicions would just go away and that José could accept the scholarship. Ever since she had met José and come to know him as the smart, sensitive person he was, she had dreamed a big dream for him. She wanted him to be able to go to college and to realize his potential. And secretly, she harbored another dream...that they could go to the same college—together.

As they started walking through the jungle back to José's camp, Alexa had a sinking feeling that they were about to jeopardize all of these hopes and aspirations. Deep down, she didn't want to know the answer to the questions they were seeking.

---

[537] **Stealthy:** acting with quiet, caution, and secrecy intended to avoid notice
[538] **Surreptitious:** marked by stealth; secret, clandestine
[539] **Clandestine:** conducted in secrecy
[540] **Morass:** something that traps, confuses, or impedes

But she knew her friend José very well, despite the fact that they had met just earlier that summer. If something morally questionable was going on, José was not the type of person to be apathetic[541] and sit on the sidelines doing nothing. He was a young man of integrity[542]. He possessed a strong moral compass and the certitude[543] to follow his convictions[544]. José's rectitude[545] was his defining trait—he always wanted to do the right thing. Alexa loved this about him. Even though his righteousness[546] had gotten them into trouble in the past, she loved the fact that he had a strong moral character and that he was willing to go to extreme lengths to do what he felt was right.

"Our camp is right up here," José said pointing ahead in the distance. "It's siesta time, so everyone is resting."

"Our camp also has a siesta time, but I don't want to take a nap in the middle of the day," Alexa admitted.

"Good," he said, turning to flash her a big smile. "Me neither. It's the perfect time for us to meet. I just need to finish hacking a trail between our camps."

"I can't believe how much you've done already," Alexa said admiringly as she noted all of the truncated[547] branches and vines along the path. This was a lot of work."

"Well, I couldn't let a few twigs and branches deter[548] me from seeing you," he said, smiling flirtatiously.

Alexa smiled back at him, but then she looked down at the ground, demurely[549] avoiding his gaze. She felt shy all over again.

༄ ༄

---

541 **Apathetic:** having a lack of interest or concern; indifferent

542 **Integrity:** steadfast adherence to a moral or ethical code; moral soundness

543 **Certitude:** the state of being certain; confidence

544 **Conviction:** a strong belief or position

545 **Rectitude:** moral uprightness

546 **Righteousness:** adhering to moral principles

547 **Truncate:** terminating abruptly, as if cut off

548 **Deter:** to prevent or discourage from acting, as by means of fear or doubt; dissuade, inhibit

549 **Demure:** modest and reserved in behavior; shy

"Well, well, well, what have we here?" Rothschild asked when he saw Alexa and José approaching. "Alexa, we are delighted you've come to visit our humble home away from home. How are you doing, my dear?"

"I'm fine—well, except for this scrape on my arm," she admitted.

"Oh, my gosh," he exclaimed, "did you have a run-in with a wild animal in the jungle? A feral[550] beast with sharp claws, perhaps?"

"No, no, it was nothing like that," Alexa chuckled. "It's just a scrape from a branch."

"But nevertheless, you should take care to clean the wound carefully," Rothschild cautioned. "Even a relatively benign[551] scrape can become infected here in the tropics, so I always advocate[552] the use of an antibacterial cream. José can show you where we keep our first-aid kit. Once you've dressed your wound, perhaps you would enjoy a tour of our site here?"

"Oh yes, that sounds great," Alexa said brightening up. "It looks incredible," she commented, pointing to the pyramid-shaped temple that dominated the small clearing in the jungle. Although the temple was much smaller than the huge pyramids in the *Gran Plaza,* to Alexa, it looked more intriguing. The temple itself was covered with grass, moss, and leafy plants that had only been partially cleared. It had a mysterious quality about it, as if it had just been unearthed.

"C'mon," José gently coaxed, "let's clean your wound." He took her hand and led her to a big yellow tent in the center of the clearing.

"Ouch!" Alexa exclaimed as José dabbed her wound with a wet cloth. "Be careful," she warned.

---

[550] **Feral:** wild, savage, untamed
[551] **Benign:** of a mild type that does not threaten health or life
[552] **Advocate:** to plead, argue, or speak in favor of

"I'm sorry! I would never do anything to hurt you," he said compassionately[553]. He leaned over her chair and kissed her forehead. "I just need to make sure it's really clean. I'm almost done."

Alexa felt like she was floating in the air, she was so elated. José busily dabbed antibacterial ointment on her scratch, but she didn't feel a thing. The kiss that he'd bestowed[554] on her forehead counteracted[555] the pain. It was the best form of analgesic[556] that she could imagine. She didn't even feel the stinging sensation of the ointment on her wound—all she could think about was that he had just kissed her.

"I'm almost done," he said, getting out a gauze bandage and some white first-aid tape.

"I can't wait to take a tour of this site. That was so nice of Mr. Rothschild to offer to show me around," Alexa commented.

José frowned at the mention of Rothschild's name.

"José," she whispered, "he doesn't seem like a callous[557] criminal. Mr. Rothschild is so benevolent[558] and kind. Maybe he's not the criminal you suspect he is. Maybe he's not colluding[559] with Grady."

José snorted in response. "I think you're beguiled[560] by his charm. Don't fall for that! I'll bet he's in cahoots[561] with Grady. But I still need the evidence to corroborate[562] my suspicions. So don't forget...we need to keep our eye on the ball. We have to figure out where that notebook is kept and find a way to snap some pictures of it."

"When you're working at the site here, don't you use a notebook yourself to write down your finds? Over at my excavation site, we're

---

[553] **Compassionate:** having a sympathetic concern for others' distress together with a desire to alleviate it

[554] **Bestow:** to present as a gift

[555] **Counteract:** oppose and lessen the effects of by contrary actions

[556] **Analgesic:** a medicine that reduces or eliminates pain

[557] **Callous:** emotionally hardened; unfeeling, insensitive

[558] **Benevolent:** characterized by doing good or showing kindness

[559] **Collude:** to act together secretly for illegal or deceitful purposes; conspire; plot

[560] **Beguile:** to deceive by guile (treacherous cunning and skillful deceit)

[561] **Cahoots:** a secret partnership or questionable collaboration

[562] **Corroborate:** to support with evidence; to make more certain

always writing stuff down in notebooks. We have a comprehensive[563] list of everything that's been found at the site. Don't you have that here?"

José shook his head, looking uncharacteristically sad. "No, if there is such a list here, I'm not privy[564] to it. We're going to have to figure out where it is and how to get a hold of it."

"But where are you writing down your notes about the things you find?"

"I'm not...I mean I'm not finding anything. I'm not doing any real archeology. They have me clearing the brush. That's why I'm pretty good with the machete, because that's all I'm doing here," José admitted. "Grady and Rothschild are the only archeologists at the excavation site who are actually looking for the artifacts. They've hired a bunch of local workers to help them with the manual labor—the digging and hauling and clearing the brush. I'm basically one of the worker bees, assigned to the plebeian[565] tasks." José's expression fell as he described his ignoble[566] job.

"Oh," Alexa said, feeling a stab of sympathy for him. José was the smartest boy she had ever met and she wished that he could have a job that was commensurate[567] with his considerable intellect. But instead, he was relegated to a servile[568] job. It was all so reminiscent of the first time they had met, when José was working in the kitchen of the marine biology station where Alexa was doing an internship in a DNA lab. Ever since that fateful day almost two months ago, Alexa had sensed a spark of intelligence in him that intrigued her. But beyond that, there was something else she couldn't quite put her finger on. It had something to do with the way that he made every moment of every day exciting and filled

---

[563] **Comprehensive:** covering completely or broadly; large in scope
[564] **Privy:** informed about something not generally known
[565] **Plebeian:** characteristic of commoners
[566] **Ignoble:** not of the nobility; common
[567] **Commensurate:** corresponding in size or degree; proportionate
[568] **Servile:** relating to or suitable for a slave or servant

with purpose and importance. It was intoxicating just to be around him and his indomitable[569] spirit.

But it always seemed that there was some external force that was pulling them apart. They came from such different backgrounds. He was from an isolated island off the coast of Nicaragua and she was from Ithaca, New York, where her father was a highly respected professor of molecular biology. They lived in very different worlds. It seemed like there was an enormous chasm[570] between them.

Alexa wondered how that chasm could ever be bridged if he didn't find a way to escape the isolated, insular[571] fishing village where he grew up. Alexa knew there was no way she could possibly go live on that tiny island in the Caribbean Sea, as beautiful as it was. Going to college was simply expected in her family—it was an inescapable part of her destiny. And she wanted to go. It's just that she wanted José to go, too. She didn't want him to throw away this golden opportunity to go to college in the United States. She wanted him to seize this chance to join her in her world where he could have a bright future and they could be together.

"José, maybe you could come work at our excavation," she said, hoping that he would completely forget his agenda. "I could talk to Nadine and see if you could help us with some real archeology." Alexa brightened up at the prospect of helping her friend. "I'm just sifting through dirt, but even that is better than chopping down branches."

"No, I can't do that," José said. "Not until I figure out what is going on here. C'mon, let's go."

Alexa nodded and followed him back outside. Deep down, she'd known that he wouldn't accept her offer. If she knew anything about José,

---

[569] **Indomitable:** incapable of being overcome or subdued
[570] **Chasm:** a marked division, separation, or difference
[571] **Insular:** characteristic of an isolated life, especially a narrow or provincial outlook

it was that he was a young man of great probity[572] who always tried to do the right thing, irrespective of the consequences. She just wished that the consequences didn't involve jeopardizing his future.

"Are you all patched up?" Rothschild asked, looking at Alexa's bandaged arm.

"Yes, I'm fine," she replied. "I'm so eager to see what you've found here. Is that a temple that you're excavating?"

"Yes," he replied, "although we don't yet know much about it and how it fits into the historical framework that we know about Tikal. First we need to analyze all of the artifacts we've found, but that will take years. It will take a lot of hard work to delineate[573] a sense of what happened right here over a thousand years ago."

"Where are all of the artifacts that you've found?" Alexa asked. She was desperately trying to sound casual, but she felt nervous asking such a direct question.

"They're all over there in the red tent. Grady can show you. He keeps a close tab on all of the artifacts. Why don't you go take a look? Go see what treasures the ancient Maya have bequeathed[574] to us," Rothschild suggested. "Some of them are quite stunning."

"Well, they didn't really bequeath them to *us*," José corrected him. "The artifacts are not ours to keep; it's our privilege to study them."

"Ha, ha, ha," Rothschild pretended to laugh, but his eyes narrowed and his voice had an acerbic[575] edge. "What a fine character you are, José, calling it as you see it. You're a straight shooter—no one is ever going to call you an unctuous[576] toady[577]!"

---

[572] **Probity:** complete and confirmed integrity; uprightness

[573] **Delineate:** to describe or outline

[574] **Bequeath:** to leave or give personal property by will or to hand down from one generation to the next

[575] **Acerbic:** sharp or biting, as in character or expression

[576] **Unctuous:** characterized by affected, exaggerated, or insincere earnestness (can also mean oily or slippery)

[577] **Toady:** a person who flatters or defers to others for self-serving reasons; a sycophant

"What's an unctuous toady?" Alexa asked. "It sounds like some sort of reptile."

Rothschild let out a loud guffaw. "No, my dear, an unctuous toady is not a horned toad," he laughed. "It's someone who acts in an obsequious[578] manner, flattering people, showering them with adulation[579] or acting insincerely earnest in order to get what they want. I think we can safely say that José is not a toady, nor is he unctuous!"

Alexa joined in the laughter. Rothschild's characterization of José was startlingly accurate. He would never behave like a sycophant[580], flattering his boss for self-serving reasons.

"Now José, listen up, young man. I didn't mean to imply that the artifacts are ours to keep," Rothschild replied defensively, "because of course, they are not. That would be unethical[581]. The artifacts from this excavation are all going to be studied at a university here in Guatemala. The aggregate[582] wisdom of many scholars is needed to fully analyze the artifacts that we've unearthed here. But if you're curious, why don't you go take a quick look at some of the artifacts before we have to get back to work, right, José? Siesta time is almost over." Rothschild beckoned Grady, "Why don't you show these young folks the cache[583]? I think they would enjoy seeing some of these artifacts."

Without uttering a word, Grady led them to the red tent and pulled out a key to unlock the padlock securing the zipper.

"Wow, that's a lot of security for way out here in the middle of the jungle," Alexa commented. "We don't have any locks on anything back at our camp."

---

[578] **Obsequious:** exhibiting fawning attentiveness or servile compliance
[579] **Adulation:** excessive flattery or praise
[580] **Sycophant:** a servile self-seeker who attempts to win favor by flattering influential people
[581] **Unethical:** not conforming to approved standards of social or professional behavior; dishonorable
[582] **Aggregate:** a collection of things constituting or amounting to a whole; total, collective
[583] **Cache:** a secure place of storage

"It pays to be vigilant[584]. You never know if thieves are lurking amongst you," Grady replied. "We have a lot of workers on this dig and they all appear to be trustworthy...but who knows? That just may be a pretense[585] of virtue, rather than the real thing. Sometimes criminals hide behind a mask of piety[586], so in my book, you always have to be careful."

Alexa and José exchanged wide-eyed looks while Grady busied himself unlocking the padlock. *Was Grady referring to himself?*

Grady held open the flap of the tent and Alexa and José stepped over the threshold. The sunshine streaming through the bright red nylon tent cast an otherworldly, rose-colored glow on the objects inside. The entire floor was covered with a mesmerizing array of amulets, pendants, sculptures, pottery jars, and vases. The eerie image of a man's face carved on a stone mask stared at her from across the room. "Wow!" Alexa exclaimed. "This is unbelievable." Alexa bent down to get a better look at the details of a painting on a small terra cotta vessel. In rich, earthy shades of burnt orange, sienna, and brown, a picture of an ancient Mayan man wearing an ornate[587] feathered headdress was depicted kneeling, as if in prayer.

"That was a very special cup," Grady said. "It was used for drinking the sacred, ceremonial drink of the ancient Maya—chocolate."

"They liked chocolate drinks too?" Alexa asked, amused at this commonality. She looked over at José, trying to catch his eye, but he was staring at the array of artifacts very intensely, as if he was making a mental list of everything in the tent.

"Oh yes," Grady said. "Sometimes it's surprising what we have in common with ancient civilizations."

---

[584] **Vigilant:** carefully observant and on the alert

[585] **Pretense:** the act of pretending; a false appearance intended to deceive

[586] **Piety:** the state or quality of being pious (religious devotion and reverence to God)

[587] **Ornate:** elaborately or excessively decorated

Alexa had a sudden moment of inspiration. A picture of the collection of artifacts in this tent would be invaluable. Quickly, she grabbed the camera that was dangling from her belt loop and ripped the Velcro strap open.

"No pictures!" Grady commanded. Immediately, he grabbed her arm, prohibiting her from lifting the camera up to her eyes.

"Oh!" Alexa exclaimed, shocked at the forceful way in which he grabbed her arm. "I was just trying to take a picture for my scrapbook," she said innocently.

Grady looked flustered, as if he were searching the depths of his mind for a plausible excuse as to why she shouldn't take a picture. "The flash could be damaging to the artifacts," he finally said.

"I can turn the flash off," Alexa offered.

"No pictures!" Grady repeated firmly. "Look, these artifacts are going to be professionally photographed and we don't want a bunch of amateur-quality pictures floating around out there. Shall we go?" he asked pointedly, ushering them out without waiting for an answer. "It's time to get back to work, don't you agree, José?"

"I'll be right back to work, as soon as I walk Alexa back to her camp," José replied.

José and Alexa set off on the narrow path, walking single file, with José in the lead. As soon as they were in the thick of the rainforest, far away from prying eyes and ears, José turned to face her. "Now do you believe me?" he asked. "Don't you think it was a little suspicious that Grady didn't want you to take a picture of the artifacts? There's something fishy going on and he's trying to hide it."

"I can see why you would impute[588] Grady's suspicious behavior to a criminal cover-up—it makes sense, it really does. But we still don't know for a fact that it's true," she pointed out.

José nodded silently.

"Weren't those artifacts amazing? Did you see that carved jade turtle?" she asked.

José turned to face her, a pained expression on his face. "Yes," he replied soberly, "I saw *everything*." He looked down at the ground, his forehead wrinkled with frustration as he kicked a fallen branch off the path. "You need to understand," he began, his eyes blazing with intensity, "these are not just interesting trinkets! To me they are so much more...I can't quite explain it. It's like a link to the past, my past, that is priceless...it's invaluable. It's my culture, my tradition...it's my heritage."

Alexa nodded, but she didn't try to talk. She was so touched by the strength of his sentiment that she was on the verge of tears.

"My mother is from a small village here in Guatemala, up in the highlands. I've actually never been there. We never really had the money to travel. So now, when I see these magnificent temples and artifacts from this incredible civilization that was the ancient Maya, I am deeply touched," he admitted, pointing to his heart. "And I want all of the descendants of the Maya to be able to see these things and feel what I am feeling. Don't you see?" he said, the pitch of his voice rising higher and his eyes filling with tears. "If these artifacts are sequestered[589] away in some rich person's private collection, than no one will be able to see them.

---

[588] **Impute:** to relate to a particular source; attribute the fault or responsibility to
[589] **Sequester:** to remove or set apart; segregate, isolate

When they take these artifacts from us, it's like the rich people are taking away the heart of our culture!"

"I know," Alexa said, swiping a tear off her cheek with the back of her hand. She felt like she could really understood the sentiment José was trying to communicate. When Mayan artifacts were sold and shipped off to far-off destinations, he felt like his culture was being eviscerated[590]. She couldn't help but sympathize with him. "I agree. If Grady and Rothschild are embezzling[591] from the foundation, then it's utterly despicable and it has to stop."

"It's so ironic that their foundation claims to be preserving Mayan heritage when they're actually doing the opposite. They're actively destroying our heritage by dispersing[592] artifacts to private collections all over the world, rather than keeping them in a museum here so that the Mayan people can see them. It's pure hypocrisy[593]. They profess[594] to be doing one thing when in fact, they're doing something else."

"If your suspicions are right, then I agree. These men are really duplicitous[595]. But we still don't know what's going on," she reminded him.

José's stormy expression dissipated[596] as he broke into a mischievous smile. "I think I have a plan," he said, his eyes sparkling with excitement. "Are you ready to help me?"

"That depends on what the plan is," Alexa laughed nervously. "We don't even know where Grady's notebook is. I didn't even see him with one."

"It has to be in his tent, don't you think?" he asked.

"Uh...probably. I would guess so. But we can't just walk into his tent! There are always people watching."

"Not always," José countered. "Every night Grady and Rothschild and some of the workers convene[597] around the campfire. Rothschild

---

[590] **Eviscerate:** to take away a vital or essential part of, disembowel

[591] **Embezzle:** to take property or money (entrusted to one's care) fraudulently for one's own use

[592] **Disperse:** to scatter in different directions

[593] **Hypocrisy:** professing beliefs or virtues that one does not hold; falseness

[594] **Profess:** to affirm openly; declare or claim

[595] **Duplicitous:** hiding one's true intentions with deliberately deceptive speech or behavior

[596] **Dissipate:** to attenuate to or almost to the point of vanishing: *the crowd dissipated after the music ended*

[597] **Convene:** to come together, usually for an official purpose; assemble formally

opens the brandy and starts telling stories. And then, after the liba-
tions[598] have been consumed, the chocolate comes out. Finally, after he's
satisfied his sweet tooth, he launches into song, singing these mournful
old Scottish dirges[599]. It's sad, sad music he sings, but somehow he seems
to enjoy all of that emoting[600]. I happen to think that it's pretty painful
to listen to," José laughed. "Especially when he tries to crescendo[601] up to
the high note that's a little too high for him."

Alexa laughed as her mind conjured up this amusing image. "Do
you join him?"

"No way!" he quickly exclaimed. "But Grady sometimes chimes in,
or at least he tries to. The result is pure dissonance[602] and it's not pleasant for the ears."

"At least all of that howling keeps the wild animals away."

"Actually, no! After a while, the howler monkeys start howling
along with them, joining in for the encore[603]. It turns into a raucous[604]
racket of wails and howls."

Alexa laughed uproariously. "That sounds so funny! I'd like to see
that. Actually, I think I'd like to see it, but I'm not sure I want to hear it. All
of that discordant[605] howling sounds like it would be painful to listen to."

"That's putting it mildly," José laughed. "But I'm glad you said you
want to see this campfire scene, because I think it would be the perfect
time to try to get a hold of Grady's notebook. While they're carousing[606]
by the campfire, we can be finding the proof we need."

"Do you mean that we should just brazenly[607] walk into
Grady's tent and hope he doesn't notice?" Alexa asked skeptically.
"That plan doesn't strike me as clever—it's more aptly described as pure

---

[598] **Libation:** a beverage, especially a drink containing alcohol
[599] **Dirge:** a slow, solemn, and mournful piece of music
[600] **Emote:** to express emotion, especially in an excessive or theatrical manner
[601] **Crescendo:** a steady increase in volume or intensity
[602] **Dissonance:** a harsh disagreeable combination of sounds; lack of harmony or agreement
[603] **Encore:** an additional performance at the end of a concert in response to audience demand
[604] **Raucous:** disagreeably harsh, loud, or rough sounding: *a raucous party*
[605] **Discordant:** disagreeable in sound; harsh or dissonant
[606] **Carouse:** to engage in boisterous, drunken merrymaking or excessive drinking
[607] **Brazen:** marked by flagrant boldness

effrontery[608]. Do you really just want to boldly walk into his tent and search for clues?"

"Don't worry, my plan is more cunning[609] than that," he assured her. "If you're there to help me, you could stay by the campfire with Grady and Rothschild while I sneak into Grady's tent. If Grady or Rothschild gets up, you can send me a covert[610] signal, like a whistle or something like that. Only you and I will know what the whistle means."

"I understand the plan, but I'm not sure if I have the guile[611] to pull it off," Alexa admitted. "I'm not very good at deceiving people. My mom says that I'm a terrible liar." Alexa felt a queasy sensation in her stomach. She was grasping at straws, trying to figure out a way to get José to drop this audacious[612] plan. She didn't want to be choreographing[613] a dangerous heist with José, she wanted to be talking about their future.

"I actually think this will be easier than it sounds," José replied confidently. Grady and Rothschild will be busy indulging their hedonistic[614] cravings—the chocolate, the brandy. They probably won't even notice what's going on."

"But the tent has a lock on the door. It's virtually impregnable[615]. How can you possibly get inside?" Alexa asked skeptically.

"Grady's tent doesn't have a lock, only the red tent has a lock. Everything should be fine—if you're there to help me, that is." José's wide brown eyes looked into hers. "Will you help me?"

"I will," she promised, even though her stomach churned nervously at the thought of it.

Alexa returned to work, sifting through endless piles of dirt, but her mind was preoccupied. She desperately wanted to talk to someone about

---

[608] **Effrontery:** shameless and brazen boldness

[609] **Cunning:** skillfully deceptive

[610] **Covert:** not openly carried out; secret: *covert military operations*

[611] **Guile:** treacherous cunning, skillful deceit

[612] **Audacious:** fearlessly daring, recklessly bold

[613] **Choreograph:** to arrange or direct the movement, development, or details of; orchestrate

[614] **Hedonistic:** pursuit of or devotion to pleasure

[615] **Impregnable:** impossible to enter by force or capture: *an impregnable military base*

José's suspicions. Even though she had been eager to be independent, she found herself wishing that her father hadn't left. She missed his keen interest in anything that she had to say, but even more importantly, she missed his sagacity[616]. He always had the wisdom to handle difficult situations.

Alexa wondered if she should talk to Nadine. After debating it in her mind and vacillating[617] between one course of action and another, she finally decided that she wouldn't. But when Nadine came over to ask her how she was doing, Alexa found herself confiding the problems that vexed[618] her. "Um, I'm kind of worried," she admitted to Nadine.

"About what?" she asked.

"Uh, you know my friend José, right? Well, he's got some suspicions about the people he's working with. He thinks that they may be smuggling artifacts out of the country illegally and selling them for profit. He thinks they are criminals."

Nadine gasped. "That's absurd!" she exclaimed. "I know Mr. Rothschild and his group and I can say for certain that they are people of integrity. So just drop it." Nadine's eyes flashed angrily. "Really, I mean...you can't just go around saying things of that nature. You can't just blurt out spurious[619] accusations that can harm someone else's reputation. Alexa, you need to think twice before you say something defamatory[620] about someone else. Especially when your allegations are patently[621] false. Calumny[622] is a very serious thing," she warned. "I'm sure that it's just a misconception[623] on José's part."

Alexa looked down at the ground, embarrassed at being on the receiving end of such a lecture. She simply hadn't anticipated that her

---

[616] **Sagacity:** having good judgment; wisdom

[617] **Vacillate:** to swing indecisively from one opinion to another

[618] **Vex:** to bring distress to; plague, afflict, or annoy

[619] **Spurious:** lacking authenticity or validity; false

[620] **Defamatory:** harmful and often untrue; tending to discredit or harm another person's reputation

[621] **Patently:** in a unmistakable manner; openly, plainly, or clearly

[622] **Calumny:** the utterance of maliciously false statements that harm another person's reputation

[623] **Misconception:** a mistaken thought or idea; a misunderstanding

simple confession would release such a tirade from Nadine. She wanted to explain to Nadine about the comment that José overheard and the tent full of artifacts that were not supposed to be photographed. It *was* suspicious. But she didn't want to give Nadine an excuse to pontificate[624] some more about the evils of slander. Alexa had had enough of that discourse[625]. So she decided she would keep quiet and handle the situation on her own.

[624] **Pontificate:** to talk or express opinions in a dogmatic or pompous manner
[625] **Discourse:** a formal, lengthy discussion of a subject

10

Effulgent Nuggets of Gold

"Q9, J 23-4," Doug called out as he unceremoniously dumped the contents of his wheelbarrow into Alexa's sieve.

Alexa scrambled to write down the coordinates in her notebook before sifting through the dirt that Doug had ferried over to her workstation. So far, the only things they had found were some desiccated[626] seeds from fruit that had been eaten one thousand years ago. Initially, Alexa just thought that this was just a mildly curious find. But Nadine was thrilled. "This provides yet another piece of tangible evidence to buttress[627] my theory about the varied diet of the ancient Maya," she told Alexa and Doug, after extolling[628] their keen observation skills. "This is exactly the type of thing we're looking for."

Despite her mixed feelings about Nadine, Alexa was buoyed by her praise. Every time Doug brought a new load of dirt, she felt a tingle of

---

[626] **Desiccated:** thoroughly dried out
[627] **Buttress:** something that serves to support or reinforce
[628] **Extol:** to praise highly

anticipation and she delved into her sifting with renewed avidity[629]. It was tantalizing to think that the next handful of dirt might contain something exciting...something that would give them a new insight on how the ancient Maya had lived.

"Let me help you with that," Doug offered as he watched Alexa struggle to lift the heavily laden sieve. "It will be easier if we both take a side."

"Thanks," she said gratefully.

"I was looking for you after lunch," Doug said as they lifted the sieve together. "I went on a walk in the rainforest trying to see some exotic species of birds. I'm dying to see the resplendent quetzal. I wanted to see if you wanted to join me, but I couldn't find you."

"Oh, I went over to José's camp during the siesta time," Alexa said without looking up. Her eyes were trained on the sieve as she broke apart clumps of dirt with her free hand.

"Is he your boyfriend?" Doug asked, an uncharacteristic note of vulnerability in his voice.

Alexa just shrugged. She wasn't quite sure how to answer that question.

"Is he the reason why you never showed up at the Big Squeeze for another shot of wheatgrass juice with me?"

Alexa shifted uncomfortably. His candor[630] caught her off guard. "Uh, no, I just forgot," she stammered. She could feel her face growing hotter as she hedged[631] the truth. While it was true that she had forgotten their date, she didn't want to admit openly to him that it was because she had been busy at the computer, madly exchanging e-mails with José.

"I'm going to get the next load," Doug said in a low voice. Avoiding her sympathetic gaze, he picked up the handles of the wheelbarrow and took off.

---

[629] **Avidity:** keen interest or enthusiasm

[630] **Candor:** honest, straightforward, and frank in expression

[631] **Hedge:** to avoid making a clear, direct statement; intentionally ambiguous

Alexa took a deep breath. It seemed so unbelievable at first, but now she knew in her heart that it was undeniably true. Doug *liked* her. She had certainly noticed the hints that he had been dropping, but somehow the fact of it was still surprising. In the short span of two weeks, the tables had turned. He was the popular star of the lacrosse team, and had been voted "nicest smile" and junior prom king by their classmates. She was the girl who nobody seemed to notice at school. She was the girl in his carpool with whom he had never bothered to have a conversation. But now, in this remote place so far from home, it seemed that none of the old rules applied. Doug liked her, but she already had a boyfriend.

Or did she? Alexa pondered her anticlimactic[632] reunion with José. She had expected that they would fall into each other's arms and plan their future together. But none of that was happening. He was so concerned with what he thought was a Mayan artifact scandal that they hadn't even talked about anything else. He hadn't even kissed her—just that little kiss on the forehead, but that didn't count. That didn't concretize[633] their relationship as boyfriend and girlfriend like a real kiss would.

Alexa raked her fingers through the dirt, absentmindedly working the moist soil through the sieve. Her mind was wrapped up in a jumble of thoughts and emotions when her finger touched something hard and sharp. Suddenly, she snapped out of her reverie[634] and looked at the dirt-encrusted object in her hand. Her hands trembling with excitement, she carefully brushed the soil off of its curved surface. Alexa immediately recognized the object as a shard of pottery, only two inches in diameter. But what made her heart flutter was the image of a man's face painted on the surface in earthy tones of burnt orange, copper, brown, and black. The

---

[632] **Anticlimactic:** an event that is strikingly less important than what has preceded or led up to it

[633] **Concretize:** to make something concrete, definite, or specific

[634] **Reverie:** lost in thought; daydreaming

bottom half of the image was missing, but the haunting eyes of this ancient Mayan figure gazed out at her with an intensity that thrilled her.

Alexa held the fragment up to the light and studied it. Despite the fact that this artifact had been buried under the earth for over a thousand years, the painting itself looked sharp and clear. The passage of time hadn't effaced[635] the powerful image.

Carefully, Alexa set the pottery fragment on the table. Then she began frenetically[636] sifting through the rest of the dirt, looking for more fragments. In mere minutes, she had all of the dirt through the sieve and five more shards of pottery on the table. Each piece of pottery had painting on it and she worked feverishly[637] to put the pieces of the puzzle together. Her curiosity was fired up. Every time she adjusted the orientation of the fragments, a different nuance of the image became discernable. Even though half of the pot was still missing, the broken bits, assembled on the surface of the table like a mosaic[638], allowed her to get a glimpse of something really special. It was like a window into the past.

Staring intently at the picture, all she could think about was that no one had seen this image for one thousand years. A talented artisan[639] from the distant past had poured his soul into this work of art that had not been seen by human eyes for over a millennium. After literally unearthing this treasure from the ground, she felt so privileged to be the one to first lay eyes on it. It was utterly thrilling. Alexa was so preoccupied with her exciting discovery that she didn't even notice Doug had just arrived with a new load of dirt.

"Q 9, J 23-5," Doug said mechanically as he dumped a load of mud into Alexa's sieve.

---

[635] **Efface:** to rub out or erase
[636] **Frenetic:** wildly active or excited; frantic
[637] **Feverish:** marked by intense activity or agitation
[638] **Mosaic:** a picture made up of small colored pieces (typically stone or tile) set into a surface
[639] **Artisan:** a skilled manual worker who practices a trade or handicraft; a craftsman

Alexa couldn't believe her eyes. Mud? What sort of puerile[640] prank was he trying to play? How could she possibly sift through mud? The amorphous[641] mound of wet black mud would not pass easily through the small pores of the screen. It was going to be a sticky mess. Doug turned and started walking away, avoiding her eyes. Even though his demeanor was stolid[642], Alexa could easily see through that façade. His feelings were hurt and now he was acting vindictively[643]. He wanted to give her a messy problem to deal with, so he dumped mud into her sieve.

But Alexa was too excited about her new discovery to play such petty, sophomoric[644] games. "Doug!" she called out. "Come check this out!" she beckoned.

"What's going on?" he asked cautiously, still acting aloof. Slowly, he started walking toward her.

"Come see this. There were fragments of this really cool pot in the last load. Check it out!"

His curiosity piqued, he hurried over to the table. For a moment, he was speechless with wonder. "Totally awesome," he uttered quietly. "That's the coolest thing I've ever seen. Look at this," he said, pointing to a small fragment, "doesn't that look like the paw of a jaguar? See, over here on this other fragment is the hind leg."

Huddling over the fragments next to him, Alexa studied the tantalizing hints. "I see it!" Alexa agreed triumphantly. "It does look like a jaguar...but it's missing its head."

Doug turned to her, his eyes blazing with intensity, "We have to find it!"

---

[640] **Puerile:** childish, juvenile, silly
[641] **Amorphous:** lacking definite form; shapeless
[642] **Stolid:** revealing little emotion or sensibility; impassive
[643] **Vindictive:** involving revenge; spiteful
[644] **Sophomoric:** exhibiting great immaturity and lack of judgment

"I know," she agreed enthusiastically. "We need to sift through the soil from the quadrant that was right next to the last load—the one that contained these fragments. That's where we're most likely to find the rest of the pot."

"That's what I brought you," he said sheepishly, pointing to the mound of mud in the sieve. "That's from the quadrant that's adjacent to the last one. It's Q 9, J 23-5."

"Oh..." Alexa groaned. "How are we going to search through that? That heavy mud won't pass through the sieve."

"We'll figure something out," he said confidently. "It's not an intractable[645] problem."

"I guess we could try to squeeze it through the sieve...kind of push it through with our hands." Alexa shuddered at the thought of it. "What a mess!"

"I have an idea." Doug looked at Alexa, his eyes sparkling with excitement.

"What is it?"

"Well, it's probably an unorthodox[646] solution to this problem, but I think it will work. It just might be our only viable[647] option."

"You don't want to ask Nadine, do you?" Alexa asked. As much as she wanted to share her discovery with the world, she desperately wanted to have a chance to find the missing pieces herself. She wanted to put the entire thing together without Nadine hovering over her, instructing her every move in that didactic[648] tone of voice.

"No, no," he assured her. "Let's handle this on our own. Once we've taken a stab at it, *then* we'll show them what we've found."

---

[645] **Intractable:** not easily relieved or cured

[646] **Unorthodox:** not adhering to what is commonly accepted or traditional; independent in behavior

[647] **Viable:** capable of being done; practicable: *a viable plan*

[648] **Didactic:** intended to teach or instruct

Alexa broke into a huge smile. How did he know that was exactly what she wanted to do? Somehow, he seemed to read her mind. "What's your idea?"

"Well, when I was on a walk through the jungle looking for the quetzal, I came across a stream that empties into a pool. You have to see it to believe it. It's only a couple hundred yards from here. It's kind of hard to walk through all of the plants and stuff. There's not a good path. But I was thinking that if we could carry the sieve there, we could set it in the water just part way—we wouldn't want to sink it, but if we could just let the mud dissolve into the water, all of the artifacts should be left in the sieve."

"Hmm...kind of like panning for gold."

"Yes, but instead of gold, we'll have artifacts in our sieve," he concluded.

"Let's try it!" Alexa exclaimed. "I can carry one side of the sieve."

"I'll carry it," Doug said firmly. "Just follow me." Without straining even slightly, Doug swiftly hoisted the mud-laden sieve up to his shoulder and steadied it with one arm.

Alexa looked at him in amazement. "Wow, you must be really strong—that sieve is heavy!"

"It is heavy," he admitted. "But don't worry, I can handle it. I've been lifting weights at the gym all summer long. I don't let my muscles become weak and flaccid[649] just because my coach is taking the summer off. Some of the guys on the team pass the whole summer by in indolent[650] idleness, but I've been working out every day back home." Doug turned to look her in the eye. "*And* I'm drinking wheatgrass juice." He flashed her a flirtatious smile before starting off into the rainforest. "C'mon," he urged, "follow me."

---

[649] **Flaccid:** lacking muscle tone or firmness
[650] **Indolent:** lazy, inactive; lethargic

Alexa laughed. She was relieved that he was making fun of the situation, rather than making it more awkward by acting miffed. "Are you going to keep carping[651] about the wheatgrass thing? I promise I'll try it again with you when we get back, even if it smells noxious[652] and tastes even worse."

"Good," he said. "I won't forget you said that."

Alexa could feel herself sweating profusely in the humid heat of the jungle. It was arduous[653] and time consuming to make their way through the dense growth. "Hey, I thought you said it was only a couple hundred yards?" she called out to Doug in front of her.

"It is, if you walk in a straight line. But this route has fewer branches and trees in the way, so I think it's easier, albeit[654] longer. It's a circuitous[655] route, but it will get us there faster. We're almost there. See that clearing up ahead?"

"No, I can't see anything. But I can hear the gurgling noise of water running. That sounds auspicious[656]."

"It's right here," he declared, setting the heavy sieve down on the ground with a plop. "Man, that was heavy," he said, rubbing his sore shoulder. "Wait until you see this," he said, watching her intently. "I think you're going to be impressed." Doug held aside the flexible trunk of a slim tree so that Alexa could peer through the branches.

Alexa slipped between the trees and stood next to Doug, gasping at the amazing sight before her. A pellucid[657] stream trickled over a narrow waterfall, emptying into a small reservoir[658]. The pool was placid[659], its calm waters reflecting the green foliage that surrounded it. The edges of the pool were replete[660] with colorful, delicate wildflowers that daintily

---

[651] **Carp:** to find fault in a disagreeable way; complain fretfully

[652] **Noxious:** harmful or injurious to health: *noxious pollution*

[653] **Arduous:** strenuous; demanding great effort

[654] **Albeit:** even though, although, notwithstanding

[655] **Circuitous:** a roundabout or indirect lengthy course: *they took a circuitous route to avoid the roadblock*

[656] **Auspicious:** favorable, indicative of good things

[657] **Pellucid:** clear, allowing light to pass; transparent or translucent

[658] **Reservoir:** a natural or artificial pond or lake used for the storage of water

[659] **Placid:** calm or quiet; undisturbed

[660] **Replete:** abundantly supplied or filled

decorated the perimeter. "This is breathtakingly beautiful," Alexa said, "it was worth the long walk. It's like a perfect place—a utopia[661] that you imagine in your mind but that you never actually see or experience."

"That's exactly what I thought when I saw it. That's why I wanted you to come here with me," he added softly.

Alexa heard the note of vulnerability in his voice and it tugged at her heart. Knowing Doug as well as she did, she knew he wasn't one for mawkish[662] sentimentality. He would never spout the cloyingly[663] sappy lines of a Valentine's Day card. Admitting that he wanted to come to this beautiful place with her was about as demonstrative[664] as he was likely to get.

"Almost makes you want to go for a swim, doesn't it?" he said.

"I've never seen a more beautiful place to go swimming," she agreed.

"Perfect, except for the gators."

"Gators?" she repeated.

"Yes, alligators...I saw one in the water earlier," he admitted. "So maybe a swim would not be a good idea."

Alexa couldn't decide if he was kidding or not, but she decided that she was not going to take any chances. "I think that's right," she nodded, agreeing with his judicious[665] advice. "Let's stay out of the water."

"Shall we see what's in that mud?" he asked.

"Let's do it!" she replied eagerly. Alexa picked up one side of the heavily laden sieve while Doug lifted the other side. "Do you think we can do this without getting into the water?"

"I think so," he answered. "Right down here," he pointed. "We'll just stand on the bank and lower the sieve into the water."

---

[661] **Utopia:** an imaginary and ideally perfect place

[662] **Mawkish:** excessively sentimental

[663] **Cloying:** sickeningly sweet; excessively sweet or sentimental

[664] **Demonstrative:** characterized by open expression of emotion

[665] **Judicious:** having good judgment and common sense

But as soon as they reached the edge of the water, it became obvious that this plan wouldn't work. Unless one of them got into the water, they wouldn't have enough leverage to accomplish the task.

"I'll get in," Doug offered, pulling off his heavy hiking boots and socks. "You can stay on the bank."

"I'll watch out for gators and warn you if one's about to take a nibble," Alexa offered.

"Thanks a lot!" he retorted sarcastically, making a dour face. "Just so you know...alligators are not solely aquatic[666] animals, they're terrestrial[667] as well. So just because you're standing on land doesn't mean you're safe. But don't worry, I'll warn *you* if one is about to take a nibble."

"OK," Alexa laughed.

Doug waded into the shallow water up to his knees while keeping a firm grip on the heavy sieve. As soon as they lowered the sieve into the water, the mud began to dissolve, slowly diffusing[668] into the water. The lucid[669] water of the pristine pool became sullied[670] with swirls of brown sediment. Doug held his end of the sieve with one hand while he used his free hand to stir up the mud, working it through the small pores of the screen.

"I think it's working," Alexa said. The mud is dissolving—the water is acting as a solvent[671]. This was a great idea. You deserve kudos[672] for being so clever."

Doug shrugged modestly. "Back when I was three years old, making mud pies in the puddles after it rained, I figured out that mud is soluble[673] in water. So it's not like I invented the wheel here."

Alexa laughed. It was funny to think of Doug, the quintessential[674] macho athlete, making mud pies as a toddler.

---

[666] **Aquatic:** living in water; relating to water

[667] **Terrestrial:** living on land; not aquatic

[668] **Diffuse:** to become widely dispersed or scattered; spread out

[669] **Lucid:** transparent or translucent; clear

[670] **Sully:** to mar the cleanliness of; taint, stain, or soil

[671] **Solvent:** a liquid, in which a substance can be dissolved, forming a solution

[672] **Kudos:** praise

[673] **Soluble:** something that can be dissolved to form a solution

[674] **Quintessential:** a perfect or most typical example

"OK...lift!" he commanded. In perfect harmony, they each lifted their side of the wooden frame, forcing all of the muddy water to run through the sieve. In an instant, they were able to see what they salvaged[675] from the mud. Sitting on top of the screen were six fragments of pottery, glistening in the sunshine like effulgent[676] nuggets of gold. Gingerly, they set the sieve down on the muddy bank and stared at the artifacts, too stunned to talk.

"It worked!" Alexa finally yelled out, holding her hand up in the air to give Doug a high five.

"Yahoo!" he whooped, slapping her hand triumphantly with his muddy hand. Droplets of mud went flying in all directions.

"Hey! You just spattered mud all over me," she complained, swiping the mud from her forehead.

"That's OK, it'll wash off," he said, playfully splashing her.

"Watch it," she warned, splashing him back. Alexa cringed when she saw the water hit his face. He had just splashed her a little, but she had really doused him good. Instinctively, she knew that this was going to catalyze[677] an all-out water fight. She could tell just by the look in his eye that he was going to avenge[678] her misdeed[679] with a deluge of water.

"You're in for it now!" he warned, splashing her over and over again, assailing[680] her with water.

"So are you!" Alexa said, splashing him back just as hard. Within seconds, they were both soaked, but the water fight continued unabated[681]. Water was flying everywhere and Alexa couldn't stop laughing. She had been so hot and sticky after the strenuous[682] hike through the jungle that this impromptu[683] shower felt great.

---

[675] **Salvage:** to extract something as valuable from garbage or wreckage; or to save something from destruction: *goods salvaged from the sinking ship*

[676] **Effulgent:** brilliantly shining

[677] **Catalyze:** to bring about, initiate, or increase the rate of something

[678] **Avenge:** to inflict a punishment in return for; revenge

[679] **Misdeed:** a wrong or illegal act; wrongdoing

[680] **Assail:** to attack violently; assault.

[681] **Unabated:** sustaining at the original intensity or force with no decrease

[682] **Strenuous:** requiring great exertion or effort

[683] **Impromptu:** not planned or prepared for in advance; carried out with little or no preparation

"Hey, that's enough!" she finally cried, when another torrent of water hit her face. "I think you've punished me enough for dousing you. Show a little clemency[684]! I'm already soaked," she laughed, ducking out of the way as he splashed her again. "Let's take a look at what we've found."

"OK," he laughed, slicking his wet hair back off his forehead. "I'll let you off the hook for now, but just so you know, I don't think you've fully atoned[685] for your crime. She who instigates[686] a water fight must pay the price. So when you least expect it...expect it!"

"Expect what?" Alexa asked with a mixture of curiosity and horror.

"Oh, just some mild retribution[687]...maybe a spider in your breakfast cereal or a snake in your sleeping bag," he replied. "Nothing too scary, *Dorothy!*"

"That's not funny," she moaned. "What if I apologize for splashing you? If I say I'm sorry, would that make a difference?" Alexa smiled sweetly in an attempt to convince him that she was indeed repentant[688]. He sounded like he was just teasing her in a flirtatious way, but she wanted to be absolutely certain that he was just being facetious[689]. The last thing she wanted was to be tormented with spiders and snakes.

"Hmmm," he said, pretending to look like he was carefully considering her apology. "Maybe I could consider showing a little forbearance[690] if you come birding with me later," he offered, looking at her with questioning eyes. "I want to try to see the quetzal and you can be my good-luck charm."

"Deal," she said quickly, holding out a wet hand to shake.

"Good!" he exclaimed triumphantly. "Now let's see what we got out of the mud."

---

[684] **Clemency:** demonstrating mercy in the punishment of an offender; merciful, lenient

[685] **Atone:** to make amends, as for a sin or crime

[686] **Instigate:** to stir up or provoke; incite

[687] **Retribution:** a justly deserved penalty

[688] **Repentant:** having remorse for misdeeds; penitent

[689] **Facetious:** playfully joking or kidding; humorous

[690] **Forbearance:** the act of showing patience, tolerance, or leniency when provoked

11

A Harbinger of Things to Come

Making her way through the thick growth of the rainforest and clutching the six fragments of pottery, Alexa felt elated. She couldn't wait to assemble these new fragments with the pieces that they had already found. The only damper on her mood was the soggy clothes she was wearing. As refreshing as it felt to get completely doused with water at the pond, she couldn't help but regret it as they trudged through the jungle on the way back to the camp. Her wet clothes stuck to her clammy skin and she felt anything but fresh. Even though it was hot out, the steamy humidity of the jungle prohibited the clothes from drying out thoroughly, as they would in a more arid[691] climate.

"Shhh!" Doug turned to face her. "I think I hear something up ahead," he whispered. The two of them froze in their tracks, listening intently.

---

[691] **Arid:** dry, lacking sufficient moisture, water, or rainfall

Alexa felt her heart fluttering. Was it a jaguar? Quickly, she realized that it wasn't. It was the sound of a conversation between a man and a woman. It sounded like they were discussing an artifact. Alexa tried to identify the voices without being able to see their faces. The man's voice was unmistakable—the imperious[692] tone and the pompous[693] airs gave away his identity. There was only one person who spoke with such grandiloquence[694]. It was Rothschild.

Alexa strained to hear the woman's voice. She was saying something about the remarkable quality of the jade turtle carving. Alexa felt a stab of recognition. *Nadine.* Workers at their dig had uncovered a jade carving of a turtle last week. Nadine had proudly shown her this Mayan artifact when they had first arrived. But there was also a similar jade turtle in Grady's red tent, Alexa suddenly recalled. Was it the same artifact or merely one that looked similar?

Why was Nadine meeting with Rothschild in the middle of the jungle to discuss artifacts? Was this just an innocent meeting or was Nadine involved in something more sinister? Was she warning him of José's suspicions? Alexa felt a twinge in the pit in her stomach just thinking about it. Nadine *couldn't* be a criminal, could she? It didn't make sense. She didn't seem to care about material things or money. If she had even a trace of cupidity[695] or avarice[696], she hid it well.

"It's Nadine!" Doug whispered. "Don't show her the fragments...not yet. Let's put it together first."

Alexa nodded absently. Temporarily hiding the artifacts that they found was the least of her worries now. Was Nadine involved in some sort of a devious[697] scheme to sell artifacts? It was hard not to suspect

---

[692] **Imperious:** marked by arrogant assurance; domineering

[693] **Pompous:** pretentious; characterized by exaggerated, lofty dignity and excessive self esteem

[694] **Grandiloquence:** a pompous, lofty, or bombastic style, especially in language

[695] **Cupidity:** inordinate desire for wealth; greed

[696] **Avarice:** excessive desire for wealth; greed

[697] **Devious:** departing from the accepted or correct; misleading, erring

something fishy was going on. But the thought of it made her feel sick to her stomach. Nadine was an eminent[698] scholar. And she was also her father's girlfriend.

As they resumed hiking back to the camp, Alexa was mired in thought. She realized that her already mixed feelings about Nadine had now become even more complicated. She didn't want to think of Nadine doing anything underhanded or illegal. But why had she acted so defensive about Rothschild and his reputation?

Alexa started to play through several hypothetical[699] scenarios in her mind. What if Nadine was innocent, but Rothschild was guilty and Nadine's association with him tarnished her career? Would this cause her to fall into disrepute[700]? Alexa hoped not. But something was going to happen, and soon. José was determined to blow the lid off of what he thought was a smuggling scheme, and he was also determined to get her to help him accomplish this. What would her father think of her investigating Nadine's actions? Alexa felt like she was being drawn into a very sticky situation.

That night, over a communal[701] dinner of rice and beans cooked in a big pot over the fire, Alexa and Doug showed everyone their find. The entire camp was abuzz with the new discovery. They had managed to find all of the pieces of the earthenware vessel and everyone marveled at the beauty of the painting.

Nadine was the happiest of all. After everyone finished eating, she stood up in front of the group and praised Alexa and Doug for their ingenuity and persistence. She also thanked them for finding a valuable artifact that gave credence[702] to her theory about the age of the site that they

---

[698] **Eminent:** outstanding, prominent, or distinguished in character or performance

[699] **Hypothetical:** based on hypothesis, supposed: *a hypothetical situation*

[700] **Disrepute:** damage to or loss of reputation

[701] **Communal:** shared by the people of a community

[702] **Credence:** acceptance as true or valid

were excavating. "This artifact is really important—it's yet another piece of evidence that makes my theory more tenable[703]," she said. "This find will help us confirm the timeframe during which this particular dwelling was occupied. But besides its importance from an academic standpoint, I think we can all agree that it's also quite beautiful to look at." Everyone applauded and cheered.

Alexa felt great as she basked in the warm glow of approbation[704] from all of the workers at the dig. She wished she could just forget about José's suspicions and concentrate on finding more artifacts and enjoying her time in this special place. But the problems that plagued her would not go away on their own.

"Nadine, is it OK if I go over to José's camp to visit for a little while?" Alexa asked politely.

"But it's almost dark out," she said. "Why don't you wait until tomorrow? I'm not sure your father would like you going out into the jungle after dark," she said with solicitous[705] concern.

"Don't worry, it's not dark yet and José will walk me back later. We have flashlights," Alexa pushed, sensing that Nadine might give in to her.

Nadine hesitated. "Uh, well then, I guess that would be all right," she said reluctantly. "But I want you back here by nine, OK?"

"Don't worry, I'll be back before nine. Thanks, Nadine!"

Alexa took off, setting out on the jungle trail just as the sun was setting. Her thoughts kept retuning to Nadine as she made her way through the thick rainforest. Alexa wished she could tell her father everything...José's suspicions about Rothschild and Grady, Nadine's meeting with Rothschild in the jungle...she wished she could just confess it all

---

[703] **Tenable:** rationally defensible; capable of being defended in argument: *a tenable hypothesis*

[704] **Approbation:** an expression of warm approval; praise

[705] **Solicitous:** anxious concern or care: *a solicitous mother*

to him and have him help her find the best solution to the problem. She missed her dad's keen intellect. He had such a logical way of approaching difficult circumstances. His incisive[706] mind always penetrated to the essence of the problem to come up with a solution.

But unfortunately, he wasn't here right now, and even if he was, she didn't feel right in saying anything to him about Nadine that she didn't know to be true. She didn't want to cast aspersions[707] on Nadine's integrity by alleging[708] that she did something unethical without having any proof. No, Alexa concluded, that would not be right. The best thing to do was to find the answers to all of these questions and get to the bottom of it all. They needed to uncover real evidence about where these artifacts were going. Alexa hoped that the evidence they found would exculpate[709] Nadine so that she would come out of this situation with her reputation unscathed[710].

"Alexa?" a tentative voice called out from up ahead on the trail.

"José? Is that you?" she asked.

"It's me," he said, popping into view with a big smile on his face. "I just wanted to warn you that I was coming so you didn't try to jump down on me from a treetop."

Alexa laughed heartily. They were standing in the exact same spot where she had done just that. "Am I always going to be infamous[711] for my crazy attempt to swing on a vine?"

"I think so," he laughed. "It was an inimitable[712] act of daring. I'll never forget it."

"I wouldn't ascribe[713] it to daring—it was more like an accident," Alexa admitted sheepishly. "I was falling off that branch up there and I made an effort to ameliorate[714] the situation by grabbing a vine on the way down. But it didn't work the way it was supposed to."

---

[706] **Incisive:** clear, sharp, and penetrating; acutely observant and discriminating: *incisive comments*

[707] **Aspersions:** a disparaging, damaging, or unfavorable remark; slander

[708] **Allege:** to assert to be true without proof

[709] **Exculpate:** to clear of blame or guilt

[710] **Unscathed:** not harmed, damaged, or injured

[711] **Infamous:** having an exceedingly bad reputation; notorious

[712] **Inimitable:** defying imitation; matchless

[713] **Ascribe:** to attribute to a specified cause or source

[714] **Ameliorate:** to make better; improve

José smiled, but then his expression grew serious. "Alexa, Grady and Rothschild want to have a special ceremony for me—kind of an award ceremony where they officially present me with the scholarship. It's going to be Friday evening in the *Gran Plaza*."

"Wow!" Alexa exclaimed. "That sounds spectacular—all of those magnificent temples lit by the light of the moon. I can't wait! It sounds like it's going to be so memorable. I can't imagine a more spectacular place for this. Can I come, too?" she asked hopefully. She knew he would want her there, but the note of hopefulness in her voice was because she desperately wanted him to accept this scholarship.

José squirmed uncomfortably. "Both Grady and Rothschild have been so nice to me lately. But I can't help but be suspicious of their largess[715]. So much praise—I think they are trying to blandish[716] me into silence."

"Maybe they're just trying to be nice," Alexa said.

"I don't think so," he quickly countered. "They have a profitable operation going and I'm just a problem for them. So they try to distract me with flattery and most tempting of all, a grand ceremony to present me with a scholarship."

"I don't know," Alexa said skeptically. "Rothschild seems too nice to be an obdurate[717] criminal. He kind of reminds me of the wizard in *The Wizard of Oz*. Remember how the wizard at first appeared to be so haughty and imperious, but later it turned out that he was just an old softie underneath? That's kind of how I see Rothschild—underneath all of that pretense, I think that he's a nice guy, don't you? You can't imagine a circumstance where he might be acting genuinely here?"

---

[715] **Largess:** liberal or generous in bestowing gifts, especially in a condescending manner
[716] **Blandish:** to coax by flattery or wheedling; cajole
[717] **Obdurate:** hardened in wrongdoing or wickedness

"Alexa, I'm not a misanthrope[718] who distrusts everyone. But I'm not naive either. I'm simply being realistic. I don't think that Grady and Rothschild are the paragons[719] of virtue they pretend to be."

"I know," she said softly. "But I was just hoping...hoping that we could just abort[720] this plan to expose their operation and just get on with our lives. Your future is important, too," Alexa's voice wavered with emotion. "It's *very* important to me."

José wrapped his arms around her. His warm hug felt so familiar. It evoked memories of the past that they had shared together and yet at the same time, it hinted at the future to come. But it was not a panacea[721] for their problems.

He looked down at her upturned face and wiped a tear from her cheek. "Alexa, you have to know, there's nothing in the world I would like more than to be able to go to college in the United States. I've been working toward that goal for all of my life. I've studied English *so* hard—I know English better than most Americans!" he exclaimed. José paused to catch his breath before he continued in a soft voice filled with emotion. "I want to have the best education possible, so that someday I can go back home to Nicaragua and help my compatriots[722] achieve a better life for themselves. I *need* to help them."

Alexa nodded silently. She knew that if she tried to talk now, she would end up sobbing. She had seen the poverty that afflicted his country firsthand, just a few weeks earlier. She desperately wanted José to have the opportunity to rise above his circumstances and realize the noble goals he had set for himself.

---

[718] **Misanthrope:** one who hates or mistrusts humankind
[719] **Paragon:** a model of excellence or perfection; a peerless example
[720] **Abort:** to terminate before completion
[721] **Panacea:** a cure-all; a remedy for everything
[722] **Compatriot:** a person from one's own country

"I want to go to your country and learn...with you!" José continued. "But I can't just roll over and acquiesce[723] to their plan, as tempting as it is to just say nothing. I can't just accept their money and forget about what's going on here," he said firmly. "If I accept their money without knowing the truth, it's not a trivial little thing that I could just forget about. It's not inconsequential[724]—I don't think I could live with myself if I did that."

Alexa nodded. She could tell by the determination in his voice that he was adamant[725] about finding the answers.

"Besides, I don't know if I would fit in, anyway," he admitted quietly.

"What are you talking about?" Alexa asked. "Fit in where? At college?"

"Yes," he said, looking down at the ground, his voice lacking its usual confidence. "I come from such a different place—a different background. Sometimes I wonder if I could ever really fit in the rarefied[726] atmosphere of an elite American college. I'm hardly a scion[727] of wealth—my family doesn't have money."

"So what! That's what scholarships are all about. I know you would fit in!" she quickly countered. "You're the smartest person I know."

Alexa rested her head on José's chest, listening to the sound of his heart beating. Somehow his confession of insecurity just made her want to help him all the more.

With one ear pressed to his heart and one ear listening to the multifarious[728] sounds of the jungle, she noticed that the omnipresent[729] noise of the rainforest was becoming louder and louder. Night was setting

---

[723] **Acquiesce:** to consent or agree without protest

[724] **Inconsequential:** lacking importance; trivial

[725] **Adamant:** stubbornly unyielding

[726] **Rarefied:** belonging to a small, select group

[727] **Scion:** an heir or descendant

[728] **Multifarious:** a great variety; diverse

[729] **Omnipresent:** present everywhere at all times

in and the diverse birds of the tropical jungle sang together in unrehearsed harmony. The medley[730] of songs was captivating. The lilting repetitive cadence[731] of a high-pitched songbird floated over the other voices, attracting attention like a diva soprano.

Alexa clung to José, thinking that this moment could have been the most romantic moment of her life, if only that pesky mosquito wasn't buzzing in her ear. She tried to swat it away, but the resilient[732] insect somehow managed to escape and then return to torment her again. "It's getting dark," Alexa whispered. "Did you bring a flashlight?"

"No," he whispered back, kissing the top of her head. "But I know the way back to camp by heart. Will you come with me? Will you help me?" he pleaded, his voice breaking.

Alexa nodded. How could she possibly say no? She felt so emotionally entwined[733] with him that she felt compelled to help him.

"Here," he said, holding out his hand for her to grasp, "let's get going. They're probably already sitting around the campfire, imbibing[734] and telling stories. Let's go join them—it's the perfect time for me to sneak into Grady's tent and take some pictures of the notebook. Just remember, if someone starts getting up and coming my way, you need to try to stop him or to somehow send me a signal to warn me that he's coming."

"What kind of signal? A whistle? I don't think that will work very well," she said doubtfully. "I can't just stand up and start whistling."

"You're probably right," he admitted. "It'll look too obvious if you suddenly start whistling when you're all sitting around the campfire talking."

---

[730] **Medley:** a musical arrangement made from a series of songs or melodies
[731] **Cadence:** the beat, measure, or rhythmic flow, as in music, poetry, or dance
[732] **Resilient:** marked by the ability to recover readily, as from misfortune or change
[733] **Entwined:** twisted together, interlaced, or interwoven
[734] **Imbibe:** to drink, especially alcoholic beverages

"Well then, how will I warn you if someone's coming?" she asked, handing him her digital camera.

"Just make something up. You'll think of something," he said confidently. "I know you can."

Alexa felt her stomach churn nervously. She wasn't so sure of her ability to just fabricate[735] something clever at the last minute. She felt completely out of her milieu[736]. She knew herself well enough to realize that deception and cunning were not her strong points. But she couldn't back out now. She only hoped that her ingenuous[737] nature didn't trip them up.

As they approached the camp, they heard the sound of laughter. A booming, ostentatious[738] voice presided over the laughter with an impeccable[739] British accent. Rothschild was holding court around the campfire, just as José had predicted. The glowing embers of the fire cast an orange hue on the people gathered round, who seemed so entranced[740] by Rothschild's story that they didn't even notice José and Alexa taking a seat in the campfire circle.

"There are many unanswered mysteries of the ancient Maya that we have yet to decipher," Rothschild boomed to his rapt audience. "Chief amongst them is what caused the downfall of their civilization. What caused these great cities, these architectural wonders, to be abandoned? There's no evidence of a great calamity[741]—a flood or a famine or a scourge[742] of deadly disease. And yet theses cities were abandoned. The political hegemony[743] wielded by Tikal came to an end. The written language of the ancient Maya became defunct[744] as the population spread

---

[735] **Fabricate:** to make or create, often with the intent to deceive: *a fabricated excuse*

[736] **Milieu:** an environment or setting

[737] **Ingenuous:** straightforward, lacking in cunning or guile

[738] **Ostentatious:** characterized by pretentious display that is meant to impress others; showy

[739] **Impeccable:** without fault, flaw, or error; perfect

[740] **Entrance:** to fill with delight, wonder, or enchantment

[741] **Calamity:** an event resulting in terrible loss and misfortune; catastrophe

[742] **Scourge:** a source of widespread suffering and devastation; ravage

[743] **Hegemony:** the domination of one state or group over others

[744] **Defunct:** having ceased to exist or be in use

out into the countryside. Then, their spoken language evolved into a great variety of regional dialects[745]."

The group around the campfire was quiet as they pondered Rothschild's lecture. Grady broke the silence with his hearty laughter. "Rothschild, I think you miss the lecture podium when you're out here in the wilderness. You have an inveterate[746] habit of stealing the limelight. And it looks like you've found an attentive audience for your dynamic[747] speaking skills right here around the campfire. I'm going to delegate[748] the task of entertaining the troops to you while I go do some paperwork in my tent."

"But I was just about to break out the Belgian chocolate truffles," Rothschild countered. "Do you really have the willpower to abstain[749] from indulging in these divine delicacies? There's no need to practice self-abnegation[750] out here in the jungle. You've been working hard and you deserve a little treat now and then."

Grady chuckled. "You know willpower is not my forte. It would take Herculean effort to curb my inimical[751] eating habits. But don't worry, you won't miss me. If I'm not here, you'll have center stage and I won't be here to call your bluff when you start telling mendacious[752] tales. When you tell a story that aggrandizes[753] your role in some feat of derring-do, I won't be here to say that it didn't quite happen like that."

"Mendacious tales? Self-aggrandizement?" Rothschild repeated in mock horror. "How dare you cast doubt on the veracity[754] of my stories! Every word that I say is the truth."

---

[745] **Dialect:** a regional variety of a language distinguished by features of pronunciation and grammar
[746] **Inveterate:** firmly established; ingrained, deep-rooted
[747] **Dynamic:** marked by intensity and vigor; forceful
[748] **Delegate:** to entrust to another
[749] **Abstain:** to deliberately refrain from something
[750] **Abnegation:** self-denial
[751] **Inimical:** injurious or harmful in effect; adverse
[752] **Mendacious:** lying; untruthful, or deceptive
[753] **Aggrandize:** to make appear greater; exaggerate
[754] **Veracity:** adherence or devotion to the truth; truthfulness

Everyone at the campfire burst out laughing, because they could tell by Rothschild's tone of voice that perhaps he wasn't being entirely truthful. Like an old-fashioned storyteller, Rothschild was a man who liked to spin yarns and tell tall tales that enthralled his audience, even if they hedged the truth just a bit.

"Well, I highly recommend you return promptly if you would like to partake[755] of these fine chocolates," Rothschild warned him. "I believe that the box we are about to open is the penultimate[756] box in our stash—there's only one left after this, so hurry back. Supplies are limited."

"Well, then, you had better save me at least one," Grady said. "And I don't want to miss any juicy or funny stories, either. When I come back, you can fill me in with an abridged[757] version of the story that garners the most laughter."

Alexa leaned over to José to whisper in his ear. "This isn't going to work. You can't barge into his tent if he's already in there. Let's just skip it!"

"No—he's coming right back. Let's just wait until he comes back," José whispered firmly.

"OK," she whispered reluctantly.

"José and Alexa," Rothschild boomed, "did I neglect to tell you the most important rule of the camp? No secrets at the campfire! It's most impertinent[758] of you to flout[759] the rules like that." Rothschild evinced[760] his disdain by scowling and clucking his tongue three times. "I must insist that you two reveal what you were whispering," he said with an amused twinkle in his eye. "We all want to hear the juicy secrets."

Alexa felt her face turn red. What could she possibly say? She wished she could come up with a clever witticism[761] that would make people laugh.

---

[755] **Partake:** to take or be given a part of; to participate or share

[756] **Penultimate:** next to last

[757] **Abridge:** to shorten in size, scope, or extent

[758] **Impertinent:** exceeding the limits of propriety or good manners

[759] **Flout:** to show contempt or disregard for; scorn: *flout a law*

[760] **Evince:** to show or demonstrate clearly

[761] **Witticism:** a witty remark; often clever, ironic, or funny

José didn't hesitate. Without missing a beat, he launched into a hilarious imitation of Rothschild. "We were merely commenting on the paucity[762] of chocolate truffles," José said with an affected British accent. "And Alexa came up with a rather brilliant strategy to allocate[763] the remaining chocolates in a fair and equitable fashion."

Everyone burst out laughing. José's imitation of Rothschild's bombastic[764] style of speaking was spot on. Alexa laughed too, feeling relieved that José had managed to divert attention away from their real secret.

"Ha, ha, a very clever parody[765], José," Rothschild laughed along with the group. "Miss Alexa, since you have appointed yourself as the arbiter[766] of justice here, why don't you go ahead and distribute the chocolates," he said, handing Alexa the box. "And don't try to perform any feats of legerdemain[767]—we're all watching you carefully to make sure the goods don't mysteriously disappear," he warned playfully.

"OK," she agreed, opening the top of the box. The alluring[768] aroma of chocolate wafted up toward her nose. Alexa lifted the white paper and looked at the shiny brown candies underneath. They looked absolutely irresistible. "I think the best solution is the simple one. We each take one and pass it on," she declared, taking a chocolate and popping it into her mouth. The taste was heavenly. It was a delicious amalgamation[769] of dark chocolate, cream, and cherries. The tartness of the cherry complemented[770] the sweetness of the chocolate. "Mmm, cherry," Alexa said dreamily, passing the box on to José.

"You made an excellent choice," Rothschild complimented her.

José looked at the fragrant contents of the box and then quickly passed it on without taking one.

---

[762] **Paucity:** smallness of number; an insufficiency or dearth

[763] **Allocate:** to set apart for a special purpose or distribute according to plan: *a portion of the school budget was allocated for music*

[764] **Bombastic:** pompous or ostentatiously lofty in speech or writing; grandiloquent

[765] **Parody:** an imitation done for comedy or ridicule

[766] **Arbiter:** a person who has the power to decide or judge at will

[767] **Legerdemain:** sleight of hand; an illusionary or magic trick

[768] **Alluring:** to attract or entice with something desirable

[769] **Amalgamation:** an entity resulting from the combining or uniting of elements into a unified whole

[770] **Complement:** something that completes the whole or brings to perfection

"It's just chocolate," she whispered to him.

José shook his head. As tempting as the chocolates were, he looked at the box as if it were tainted[771] with poison. He didn't want to take anything from Rothschild. Not even a single chocolate. Alexa studied the look of determination on José's face and had a sinking feeling that his seemingly simple act of declining a chocolate was merely a harbinger[772] of things to come.

---

[771] **Taint:** to affect with a tinge of something reprehensible, such as a disease or decay; contaminate

[772] **Harbinger:** an indication or foreshadowing of something to come

12

Incontrovertible Proof

Just as José had predicted, after the chocolates, out came the brandy. Soon after, Rothschild's decorous[773] behavior and polite manners started to deteriorate. He began singing loudly and urging everyone to join him. The propriety[774] that he upheld in a state of sobriety[775] completely evaporated after several rounds of drink. The haughty[776] superiority that normally colored Rothschild's language was replaced by a ribald[777] sense of humor that kept the group laughing hysterically. But Alexa was uncomfortable with the bawdy[778], off-color jokes and the scurrilous[779] language. She really wanted to leave. Discreetly, she glanced at her watch, squinting in the darkness. 9:15 P.M. Nadine had imposed a curfew of 9:00. Alexa squirmed uncomfortably. She was already late and Grady had still not returned to the campfire.

"José," she whispered tersely, "I have to get back."

---

[773] **Decorous:** proper; characterized by decorum (appropriate behavior)
[774] **Propriety:** the quality of being correct, appropriate, or proper
[775] **Sobriety:** the state of being sober, refraining from alcohol and drugs
[776] **Haughty:** arrogant superiority, scornfully proud
[777] **Ribald:** vulgar, lewd humor
[778] **Bawdy:** humorously coarse, vulgar, or lewd
[779] **Scurrilous:** vulgar or coarse language

"Just a few more minutes," he pleaded. "Grady's coming back any minute now."

Alexa nodded reluctantly. She didn't want to recant[780] her commitment to help him. Her allegiance[781] was still firm. But she desperately wanted to go back to her own camp now. She knew that if she didn't make it back on time Nadine would be sure to tell her father, and Alexa didn't relish the thought of his disapproval. Alexa thought back to the last time she had missed her curfew several months ago. Her dad didn't ground her or take away her allowance or other privileges—he wasn't much for punitive[782] measures such as those. Instead he gave her a long and stern lecture about how he was concerned for her safety. Alexa desperately wanted to avoid having Nadine censure[783] her like that, especially at the camp. There was no privacy there, and everyone would hear Nadine berating[784] her. The thought of it was mortifying.

"José, I *really* have to go," Alexa whispered again.

Before José even had a chance to respond, Grady walked up to the campfire circle and took his seat, with his back toward the cluster of tents.

José shot her a wide-eyed look. Alexa looked at his big, dark eyes that reflected the burning embers of the fire and she knew exactly what he was thinking. *Now's the time,* his expression communicated with the utmost urgency.

Looking into those eyes, Alexa didn't have the heart to say no. She gave him the tiniest nod of her head, an almost imperceptible[785] signal of affirmation[786].

José had no trouble deciphering her subtle signal. He gave her a quick smile and quietly slipped away. Alexa felt a stab of fear watching

---

[780] **Recant:** to formally retract or renounce a or previously held belief or statement

[781] **Allegiance:** loyalty

[782] **Punitive:** inflicting or involving punishment: *punitive damages*

[783] **Censure:** a strong expression of disapproval

[784] **Berate:** to scold vehemently and at length; rebuke

[785] **Imperceptible:** difficult or impossible to perceive (to become aware of via the senses)

[786] **Affirmation:** the act of supporting, confirming, or upholding the validity of

him disappear into the darkness. Now there was no turning back—she was inextricably[787] involved in this scheme. José was depending on her and she didn't want to let him down.

Alexa shifted uneasily. Behind Grady, she could see his turquoise-colored tent light up from within. A flashlight beam flitted about on the nylon surface, darting from one wall to the other. Alexa chided[788] herself for not thinking this plan through more carefully. How could they have overlooked the fact that the tent was going to light up like a firefly when José turned on his flashlight? He was in there, and his transgression[789] was in plain view to anyone who happened to look in that direction. Just like the bright lights of a railroad semaphore[790], José's flashlight sent an unmistakable signal. He had crossed the line.

"Grady, how nice of you to join us," Rothschild said, holding up the bottle of brandy. "Although some might call this warm golden liquid an indulgence, and others would consider it an elixir[791], I think that it is simply sublime—perhaps you might be persuaded to partake?"

Alexa had to snicker at Rothschild's circumlocutions[792]. His verbose[793] speech was filled with an excess of words, most of which were extraneous[794]. She only hoped his offer of brandy would distract Grady long enough for José to finish his business unnoticed.

"Actually, I think I hear the call of nature," Grady said, grabbing his flashlight and standing up. "Go ahead and pour me a drink. I'll be right back."

Alexa felt her heart leap with fear. The second Grady turned around, he would see that someone was in his tent. There was no time to stop and think. It was an exigent[795] situation and Alexa knew she had to act immediately. She regretted that she and José hadn't thought of a good

---

[787] **Inextricable:** so entangled that it is impossible to escape

[788] **Chide:** to reprimand mildly so as to correct or improve

[789] **Transgression:** the act of overstepping a boundary or violating a law

[790] **Semaphore:** a device used for visual signaling with lights, flags, or mechanically moving arms, such as is used on the railroad

[791] **Elixir:** a medicine believed to have the power to cure all ills

[792] **Circumlocution:** the use of unnecessarily wordy, roundabout, and indirect language

[793] **Verbose:** using an excessive number of words; wordy

[794] **Extraneous:** inessential or unrelated to the topic; not a vital element; irrelevant

[795] **Exigent:** requiring immediate aid, action, or remedy; urgent

signal in advance. They hadn't thoroughly planned for all of the contin-gencies[796], and now she was stuck trying to improvise something.

Leaping to her feet, Alexa shrieked, "Wait!"

Everyone immediately reacted to her piercing voice. Heads snapped around and all eyes were upon her.

Alexa felt her heart pounding. She had no idea what to say. She felt like each second was an eternity. She knew that she needed to say some-thing *now*. "Uh...*I* have to go to the bathroom! I hear nature calling too...can I go first?" she asked sheepishly.

The group around the campfire immediately broke out in a fit of raucous laughter. "There's no need to take turns," Rothschild chortled. "It's a big, big jungle out there and there's plenty of room for everyone to take care of business."

More peals of laughter erupted from the group.

Alexa felt her face turn crimson. She knew that her improvised excuse sounded fatuous[797] and it made her a target for ridicule, but it was the only thing she could think of on the spur of the moment. "Uh...um, I'd feel more comfortable if we did take turns. Mr. Grady, can I borrow your flashlight? I forgot mine. I'll be quick, I promise."

"Sure," he chuckled. "But don't forget your promise to make it fast." Grady sat back down and Rothschild handed him a drink.

Under the guise[798] of needing a bathroom break, Alexa slipped away into the darkness with Grady's flashlight. She desperately wanted to march right over to José and urge him to abandon the plan immediately. But she was reluctant to head off in the direction of the tents, lest the peo-ple at the campfire turn around to watch her go and then notice José's

---

[796] **Contingency:** an event or possibility that must be prepared for; a future emergency
[797] **Fatuous:** inanely foolish or silly
[798] **Guise:** outward appearance, semblance; sometimes indicating a false appearance or pretense

flashlight in the tent. So instead, she headed in the opposite direction, toward the trail between their two camps.

Just a few feet into the forest, Alexa turned the flashlight off and took a deep breath. She wanted to cry with frustration. In the distance, she could see the turquoise tent still lit up from within. She felt like she was being confronted with an impossibly difficult predicament in which none of the options looked good. She couldn't go warn José or else someone might see her. She couldn't go back to the campfire, because then it would be Grady's turn to go to the bathroom. She couldn't stay here too long because Grady was waiting for his flashlight. To top it off, she was late for her curfew and the minutes kept ticking by.

Alexa felt the tears well up in her eyes. She was worried about José, but at the same time, she was starting to feel mad at him. She felt aggrieved[799] by the fact that his actions had put her in this quandary[800].

Alexa stared at the turquoise tent, silently willing him to get out of that tent *now*. She was so absorbed in thought that she didn't hear the footsteps behind her.

"Alexa?" a female voice asked.

Alexa spun around, only to be accosted by the bright light of a flashlight beam right in her face. Quickly, she flicked on her own flashlight. "Nadine? Is that you?"

"Yes, it is. What are you doing out here all alone? It's nine-thirty! You were supposed to be back already," Nadine said in an annoyed tone of voice.

"I was just going to the bathroom," she said self-consciously, realizing how silly she sounded.

---

[799] **Aggrieve:** to distress; afflict
[800] **Quandary:** an unpleasant or trying situation from which extrication is difficult

"Alexa, I didn't think it was a good idea for you to come over here, but I allowed it because you said that you would be back by nine. I really don't appreciate you being so irresponsible and making me come all of the way over here to get you. You need to remember that it is a privilege to be here in Tikal and to have the opportunity to work on an archeological dig. We are a team here, and we have a lot of serious and important work to do. We don't have time to be chasing you around in the middle of the night or dealing with any such derelict[801] behavior. You need to be more considerate and realize that your actions affect everyone."

"I'm sorry," Alexa said meekly. She hoped Nadine had finished upbraiding[802] her. She wasn't sure how much more she could withstand. It had already been such a stressful evening. The last thing she needed right now was more criticism. If Nadine vituperated[803] her any more, she knew she was going to burst into tears.

"I'm sorry for being so hard on you," Nadine said, quickly making a conciliatory[804] gesture when she saw Alexa's distress. "Let's just go back. C'mon," she beckoned, putting her arm around Alexa's shoulders.

"I can't go back yet," Alexa said nervously, wondering how she was going to explain this situation to Nadine.

"Why not?" Nadine countered with mounting impatience. She was starting to get angry again.

"Uh, well...this is Mr. Grady's flashlight and I have to return it first," she said.

"Well, then, let's go give it back to him right now so that we can go. It's really getting late," Nadine said firmly.

---

[801] **Derelict:** neglectful of duties; remiss, negligent
[802] **Upbraid:** to scold severely or sharply; reproach
[803] **Vituperate:** to scold or criticize harshly or with abusive language; berate
[804] **Conciliatory:** to try to gain friendship or overcome animosity

Alexa nodded, wondering what else she could possibly do at this point. If she tried to stand up to Nadine now, a big altercation[805] was sure to develop. Nadine had just given her a glimpse of the irascible[806] side of her nature and Alexa didn't want to provoke her any further. It felt like the situation had slipped out of her control and in a way, it was a relief. It was a relief to just let go of the charade.

As they made their way back to Rothschild's campfire, all Alexa could do was hope José wouldn't get caught. But the turquoise tent was still glowing brightly like a beacon. What would Grady and Rothschild do if they caught José in the act of rifling through Grady's tent? Minimally, they would see it as a violation of trust—a perfidious[807] act. But if they truly were criminals, would the consequences be considerably worse than a slap on the wrist? Alexa shuddered to think of what might happen.

"Nadine!" Rothschild exclaimed when they walked up to the campfire circle. "What a pleasant surprise! Would you care to join our convivial[808] gathering? How about a drink? Or perhaps you would prefer some tea? You simply must stay and have something to drink with us," he insisted, ever the officious[809] host.

"No, thank you," she replied with a staid[810] expression. "I just came over to retrieve Alexa and bring her back. We really have to be going." Nadine looked at Alexa sternly, as if to prod her to hand over the flashlight to Grady immediately.

Dutifully, Alexa handed Grady his flashlight.

"Alexa, you were gone so long, we thought you had gotten lost in the forest," Rothschild teased. "I trust you found the lavatory?"

---

[805] **Altercation:** a noisy, vehement quarrel
[806] **Irascible:** hot tempered; easily angered
[807] **Perfidious:** tending to betray; treacherous
[808] **Convivial:** merry, festive, and social: *a convivial atmosphere at the birthday party*
[809] **Officious:** excessive eagerness in offering unwanted services to others
[810] **Staid:** characterized by sedate dignity and often a prim sense of propriety

Everyone broke out in laughter except for Nadine, who eyed the near-empty brandy bottle with disdain.

"We have to go now," Nadine said curtly. "C'mon, Alexa, it's late."

"But Alexa, where is that young man of yours so that you can bid him a proper farewell?" Rothschild asked.

Alexa felt her stomach tighten with dread. Nadine's eyes were darting around the campsite, scanning for José. "Uh..." Alexa stammered, desperately raking her mind for an excuse.

"I'm right here!" José exclaimed, bounding up to the campfire. His eyes were glistening with excitement. "I'll walk you back," he said, joining Alexa and Nadine.

"That won't be necessary," Nadine said curtly, grasping Alexa's arm firmly as she started marching toward the trail.

"Then just let me say goodnight to her quickly," he requested in a respectful tone of voice. "I know you're anxious to get back to camp."

Nadine hesitated for a moment. "OK," she relented, letting go of Alexa's arm. Nadine walked a few yards away to give Alexa and José a moment of privacy.

"Alexa," he whispered intensely, "I found two notebooks and you wouldn't believe what I figured out when I delved[811] into them. There is incontrovertible[812] proof that they are selling artifacts illegally. One of the notebooks was filled with all of the details about artifacts that are consigned[813] for sale. All of our suspicions are validated[814]!"

Alexa was silent. She looked behind her to make sure Nadine didn't hear José. But she was standing at the foot of the trail, safely out of earshot, eyeing Alexa and José with a suspicious glare.

---

[811] **Delve:** to make a deep and careful search for information: *delved into the files*

[812] **Incontrovertible:** impossible to deny or disprove; unquestionable

[813] **Consign:** to deliver merchandise to a dealer for sale or to be cared for

[814] **Validate:** to establish the soundness or validity of; confirm

Alexa turned back to face José. He looked exhilarated to have found what he was looking for. But all she could feel was sadness in her heart mixed with fear for the future. She had been desperately hoping that his suspicions were unfounded[815] and that they could just move on from this little episode in their lives and go to college...together. Now that dream was shattered. But equally disturbing was the fact that Nadine's world might soon be shattered, too, if she was somehow involved with these criminals. Finally Alexa spoke. "What are you going to do now?" she whispered softly.

"Alexa!" Nadine called out.

"I have to go now," Alexa whispered urgently. She could tell by Nadine's weary tone of voice that she was at the end of her rope.

"Wait a second. I saw an appointment in Grady's date book," José whispered. "There's going to be a meeting tomorrow afternoon. It's marked with a big dollar sign on his calendar—I think that this is going to be the illegal sale. Why else would there be a dollar sign after the word 'meeting'? Let's follow him and get some pictures. If he's making a sale, we could get some evidence of it. If we can document this, there's no way that anyone can deny what's going on here."

"Alexa," Nadine repeated, with mounting impatience.

"José...I don't know," Alexa wailed, her eyes filling with tears. The stress of the situation was catching up with her.

"It's OK," José whispered to Alexa, "I don't want to coerce[816] you. If you want to help me, just meet me at my camp tomorrow at siesta time. But if you don't want to, I understand." José looked down at the ground, his brow furrowed. "When I was in Grady's tent, I saw the pictures that

---

[815] **Unfounded:** not based on solid evidence or fact
[816] **Coerce:** to force or compel someone into doing something

were on your camera," he said softly. "I didn't mean to pry, but I did see the pictures that were already on there."

Alexa looked at him questioningly. "What are you talking about?" she asked. She was utterly confused, until a memory came rushing into her mind. There was the picture that Doug had taken of the two of them on top of the temple—the picture that made it look like they were girlfriend and boyfriend. Alexa groaned out loud, wondering how such a misunderstanding could have happened again. "José, it's not what you think it is," Alexa said earnestly.

José was silent for a moment before he spoke, as if he was carefully choosing his words. "Alexa," he began softly, his voice gentle and sincere, "I just want you to be happy—you're free to choose exactly what path you want to follow in life. If it doesn't include me, I understand. We're so different, you and I. We come from such different places and backgrounds, I can see why..."

Alexa felt like her heart had just been gripped in a vise. It was impossible to talk. Silently she wondered if this was what breaking up felt like. It was utterly miserable. It seemed like everything and everyone in their lives were conspiring to keep them apart. They lived in different worlds and now, with the scholarship in jeopardy, there was little hope for a future together. Alexa felt a deep sense of sadness inside. The situation seemed so hopeless and the difficulties insurmountable.

Nadine strode up to the twosome and grabbed Alexa's arm. "We are leaving now," she said adamantly, pulling Alexa away. "You two will have to finish this conversation some other time."

Alexa felt the tears spill out of her eyes. The situation seemed trag-
ically mired in adversity and confusion. She was thankful for the darkness, so that Nadine didn't see the stream of tears running down her
cheeks as they walked back to their camp. The last thing in the world she
wanted to do right now was to explain everything to Nadine.

As soon as they arrived, Nadine turned to her and started to apologize. "Alexa, I'm sorry I was so hard on you back there, but you need to
understand that I'm just trying to look out for your safety and well-being.
And I felt so responsible, because I promised your father that I would
watch out for you. I didn't want to let you go there in the first place, and
then, when you didn't come back by nine, I was so worried. I can't even
describe to you how worried I was."

"I'm sorry I was late," Alexa said contritely. She was surprised at
how nurturing[817] Nadine was acting now, given how livid[818] she had been
just a few minutes earlier. Alexa had never really thought of Nadine as
mercurial[819] before, but now she did. She had just witnessed Nadine
oscillate[820] between anger and kindness in quick succession.

"And I'm sorry for getting so angry," Nadine said. "I think I'm going
to call it a day. Are you turning in, too?"

"After I brush my teeth," Alexa said.

Nadine nodded and headed into the tent, while Alexa wandered over
to the campfire. There was no way she could possibly fall asleep right now,
especially in the crowded confines of the girls' tent. She felt too emotional
about what had just happened. She really missed the privacy of her bedroom back home—a reclusive[821] place where she could be uninhibited[822],

---

[817] **Nurturing:** to help grow and develop
[818] **Livid:** extremely angry; furious
[819] **Mercurial:** rapid and unpredictable mood changes; volatile
[820] **Oscillate:** to swing back and forth or to waver, as if between two conflicting courses of action; vacillate
[821] **Reclusive:** providing seclusion or isolation
[822] **Uninhibited:** free, open, and unrestrained

free from the prying eyes of everyone else. But right now, solitude was not an option. Someone else was spending a late night by the glowing embers of the fire. It was Doug. Alexa sat down next to him.

"Someone's in trouble, someone's in trouble," he chanted in a singsong voice. "Nadine threw a histrionic[823] fit when you didn't come back at nine. What happened? Why were you so late?"

Alexa was quiet as she stared blankly at the glowing embers of the fire. Her eyes began filling with tears again when she recalled what just happened. She certainly didn't feel like recapitulating[824] the whole story now, especially to Doug. How could she possibly talk to him about José? But it was hard to keep it all inside, too. A tear escaped her eye and ran down her cheek.

"Hey," Doug said softly. "I'm sorry—you don't have to talk. It'll be OK," he said, putting his arm around her shoulders. "Sometimes life throws you a curve ball. But that doesn't mean you can't catch it."

Alexa laughed at this remark, despite the fact that there were tears in her eyes. It just struck her as funny that Doug would give advice in the form of a sports analogy. But his pithy[825] comment was surprisingly insightful. Somehow, without even hearing the story, he could sense that something had gone awry with José. It was true—life *had* thrown her a curve ball. She had been expecting a romantic reunion with José, followed by plans for the future. Plans that involved José receiving a scholarship and coming to the United States. But none of that had happened, and now, the future looked bleak.

"Even though I don't know exactly what just happened, I do know what the remedy is," Doug said.

---

[823] **Histrionic:** excessively dramatic; characteristic of acting or actors
[824] **Recapitulate:** to summarize or repeat in concise form
[825] **Pithy:** concise and full of meaning

"What's that?" Alexa asked curiously.

"I prescribe[826] a cup of hot chocolate...it's good for people who are in hot water," he said. "I have a secret recipe," he admitted, standing up to get a carton of milk and a small pot that had been blackened by the fire. He set the pot on the hot coals and opened up a fresh carton of milk. The liquid made a sizzling sound when it hit the hot surface of the pan. Then, he rummaged around in his backpack and pulled out two chocolate kisses, wrapped in shiny red foil. "One for you and one for me," he said, unwrapping the kisses and plopping them into the pan of milk.

"That's an interesting way to make chocolate milk," Alexa laughed.

"Well, when you're out in the middle of the jungle, sometimes you have to improvise," he chuckled. "You also have to stir it a lot, or else it's a disaster," he said, grabbing a spoon.

Alexa smiled as she watched him stir the warm liquid. Doug had a way of making every situation fun, she noticed. Carefully, he poured the steaming concoction[827] into two heavy mugs and handed one to her before sitting down beside her.

"Hey, it still looks white," Alexa commented. "Isn't chocolate milk supposed to be brown?"

"Taste it," he urged.

"Let's hope it's better than that noisome[828] wheatgrass juice you made me try," she said.

"Don't crush my ego now, just try it," he pleaded.

"OK," Alexa said, lifting the cup to her lips. Gingerly, she took a sip. Immediately, she liked it. She liked it a lot. The first time she had tried the sterilized milk from the carton, she thought that it tasted weird. But

---

[826] **Prescribe:** to order the use of a medicine or remedy
[827] **Concoction:** a food or drink made by mixing different ingredients
[828] **Noisome:** offensive, disgusting, or foul: *a noisome smell*

after a few days at camp, she had grown accustomed to its unusual flavor, and in fact, had started to enjoy it. The "hot chocolate" Doug made basically tasted like warm, sterilized milk with a tiny hint of chocolate. But somehow, despite these shortcomings, it tasted delicious and comforting and just about perfect. "Well," she said, "I think it's a misnomer[829] to call this hot chocolate, but whatever it is, it's great."

Doug broke into a big smile that lit up his face. "I'm glad you like it. Hot chocolate is good for people who are in hot water," he joked. "And I think that might include you. You should have seen how mad Nadine was."

"Don't remind me," Alexa groaned.

"Don't sweat it," he advised. "Everybody gets in trouble. Even me."

"What's the most trouble that you've ever been in?" Alexa asked, her curiosity piqued.

"Oh..." Doug groaned, shaking his head. "It was bad, let's put it that way."

"What happened? What did you do?" she asked curiously.

"I'm not sure I can tell you," he said.

"Yes you can!" she exclaimed. "You have to tell me."

"Well...a long time ago, when I was eleven, I found some of my father's magazines underneath a cushion of a chair that was in our living room."

"Why did your dad keep magazines under a cushion?" Alexa asked with a puzzled expression.

Doug didn't say anything, but he gave her a look that spoke volumes.

"Ohhh," Alexa said, immediately grasping that the magazines he was talking about were prurient[830] periodicals. "Did he catch you looking

---

[829] **Misnomer: a name unsuitably applied**
[830] **Prurient: an inordinate interest in sex; lustful: *prurient thoughts***

at them?" Alexa asked, chuckling at the thought of Doug stealing a look at his father's salacious[831] magazines.

"Not right away," Doug said smugly. "He had a subscription, so every month there was a new magazine. I was able to keep abreast of the latest developments, so to speak, for two years! He didn't catch me until I was thirteen."

"What happened?" Alexa giggled, amused by his entertaining anecdote[832]. "Did he chastise[833] you? Was he mad?"

Doug rolled his eyes dramatically. "I think that's putting it mildly. Let's just say that I was subjected to quite a bit of vitriolic[834] criticism. I can laugh about now, but at the time, I was pretty embarrassed by the whole episode."

Alexa burst into laughter. "What did he say? What did he do?"

Doug just shrugged. "I can't remember exactly what he said, but I think you can summarize it by saying that he expressed his concern about my 'licentious[835] behavior.'"

"Well, he couldn't be too critical if they were his magazines," she said. "That would be hypocritical[836]. Why is it OK for him and not for you?"

"I don't know," he said. "But believe me, he delivered an invective[837]-filled speech that railed against those magazines and my behavior. He was convinced that I was sinking into the depths of depravity[838] and moral turpitude[839]. I think that as a parent, he felt he had to lay down the law and proscribe[840] pornography. But later, he must have realized he was being hypocritical, because the magazines disappeared. If he was going to

---

[831] **Salacious:** appealing to sexual desire; lascivious

[832] **Anecdote:** a short account of an incident

[833] **Chastise:** to criticize severely; rebuke

[834] **Vitriolic:** bitter, harsh, or scathing

[835] **Licentious:** lacking moral discipline, especially in sexual conduct

[836] **Hypocritical:** professing one thing while doing another; false

[837] **Invective:** abusive language; vituperation

[838] **Depravity:** moral corruption

[839] **Turpitude:** lacking moral standards; depravity, baseness

[840] **Proscribe:** to condemn as forbidden; prohibit

label me a reprobate[841] for looking at his magazines, he knew he needed to take another look at himself."

"Or maybe he just found a new hiding place," Alexa said, taking another sip of hot chocolate.

"Maybe," Doug laughed. "So what's the worst trouble you've ever been in?"

"Oh..." Alexa groaned. "It was much worse than this little episode with Nadine, that's for sure."

"What did you do?" he asked eagerly. "Tell me now, so that we can commiserate[842] together."

"I got a tattoo," she admitted quietly. "It's a dolphin tattoo, right here," she said, pointing to the back of her left hip. "I just got it a couple weeks ago—the day after I got back from Central America."

"*You?*" he exclaimed in shock. "You got a tattoo? I can't believe it!"

"Neither could my mother," Alexa admitted. "She was so angry. Somehow, in her mind, tattoos are immoral. She was convinced that I would someday regret my wanton[843] behavior. She kept telling me what poor judgment I showed by acting on such a capricious[844] whim. But I don't regret it. I love my dolphin tattoo. The whole reason that I got the tattoo was because I love dolphins. By the time I got back from Central America, I had come to the decision that I want to be a marine biologist. The dolphin tattoo was just a physical manifestation[845] of my decision. I had solemnly decided to consecrate[846] my life to the study of dolphins and so...I got a dolphin tattoo. My mom is also a marine biologist, so I thought that decision would make her very happy. Somehow, in my

---

[841] **Reprobate:** one who is morally unprincipled

[842] **Commiserate:** to feel sorrow, compassion, or pity for; sympathize with

[843] **Wanton:** being without check or limitation; undisciplined, unrestrained

[844] **Capricious:** impulsive and unpredictable

[845] **Manifestation:** a perceptible indication of the existence of something: *the first manifestation of disease occurred three days after exposure to the virus*

[846] **Consecrate:** to dedicate solemnly to a goal; devote

convoluted[847] mind, I thought she would be happy with the tattoo also, because it expressed my dedication to dolphins."

"You really thought your mother would be happy about your tattoo? What planet are you on?" Doug hooted with laughter.

"The hot water planet," Alexa laughed. "I don't think she'll ever get over it."

"That almost tops my story," he said admiringly before draining the last few drops of his hot chocolate. "Hey, so do you want to go birding with me tomorrow afternoon during siesta?

Alexa hesitated, feeling like the moment of truth had arrived. Siesta time tomorrow was precisely the time that José had proposed to go on a reconnaissance[848] mission. Now she had to decide between José and Doug. José wanted to spy on pernicious[849] criminals and gather evidence to bring down a nefarious[850] smuggling ring, while Doug wanted to go for a walk in the rainforest to look at exotic birds. One choice was safe and easy while the other was mired in danger and uncertainty. Everything about a future with José looked challenging.

"Don't forget that you promised," Doug reminded her.

"OK," Alexa relented, feeling like she had just made a fateful decision.

---

[847] **Convoluted:** complicated or intricate, as if rolled or coiled together in overlapping whorls

[848] **Reconnaissance:** an exploration or survey to gain information, especially military information about an enemy

[849] **Pernicious:** highly injurious or destructive; deadly

[850] **Nefarious:** extremely wicked

13

An Incendiary Spark

"**R**eady to go?" Doug asked. "You don't need to bring any-thing—just water to drink. I've got the book," he said holding up a tattered guide to tropical birds.

"I'm coming," Alexa said hesitantly, grabbing her water bottle from her backpack. For the first time since arriving at the camp, she actually felt like taking a siesta in the afternoon. Alexa felt her forehead, wondering if she was coming down with a virulent[851] tropical disease. But her face didn't feel inordinately hot, like it would if she had a fever. Attributing her state of lassitude[852] to the fact that she had stayed up late talking with Doug around the campfire, Alexa decided to go birding with him after all.

But after 10 minutes of hiking through the dense growth on the overgrown trail, she was exhausted. "Can we stop for a minute?" she asked. "I just need to catch my breath."

---

[851] **Virulent:** extremely infectious or poisonous; capable of causing disease
[852] **Lassitude:** a feeling of fatigue or weariness

"Sure," he responded quickly.

"No matter how many times I walk through the jungle, I still can't get over the abundance of plants and how thick it is with growth. Everywhere you look there's green."

"I know," he agreed. It's hard to believe it's not a primeval[853] forest. It's so dense and thick and filled with diversity that it's easy to assume it's always been here."

"What do you mean?" she asked.

"Well, all of this rainforest land that we're walking through now used to be used for agriculture back in the days when the Maya lived in Tikal. They practiced a form of agriculture known as slash and burn. When they needed arable[854] land to grow crops, they slashed down the forest and then burned the cuttings. The ashes from the burned vegetation helped to fertilize the soil. Then, when the soil was depleted of nutrients, instead of letting the field lie fallow[855] for a while and returning to the same land, they simply abandoned it and moved on to the next plot, where they burned down more rainforest and cultivated[856] more land."

"And then the forest grew back in the abandoned areas?" Alexa asked.

"Yes, but only after a long, long time. And then it's never quite the same. There are so many species of plants and animals, insects, fungi...the rainforest is just filled to the brim with a profusion of different species that are busy reproducing. It's a prime example of the fecundity[857] of life. Everything looks so alive and vibrant, but this environment is also surprisingly delicate. The forest can come back after it's been burned down, but in a different way. Some of the species are lost forever."

---

[853] **Primeval:** having existed since the beginning or earliest stage; original
[854] **Arable:** land fit to be cultivated
[855] **Fallow:** land left plowed but unseeded during a growing season
[856] **Cultivate:** to prepare land for raising crops
[857] **Fecundity:** the capacity for generating offspring, especially abundant offspring

"That's sad," Alexa said, disturbed by the knowledge that humans had such a deleterious[858] effect on the environment. She was sobered with the thought that extinction was so permanent and irreversible.

"I know," he agreed vehemently[859]. "Because once a species is extinct, you can't bring it back, no matter how hard you try. Back in the days of the ancient Maya, this slash-and-burn agriculture was done on such a small scale that it didn't really have a bad effect on the environment. But right now, it's still taking place and on a much larger scale, one that is in proportion with the burgeoning[860] population of the world. It's happening in the Amazon and some other places where there are amazing rainforests that can never be replaced. Some of the trees and other things may grow back at some point, but the majority of the biological diversity will be lost forever. Human beings are defacing[861] the planet without regard for the environment. We need to save these rainforests!" he exclaimed passionately.

"I agree, but how? That's such a daunting problem. If people are clearing the rainforests to grow crops, it's probably because they need the food," Alexa said. "If people need food and they're hungry, wouldn't you agree that it's hard for them to stop and think about environmental issues? I agree that the environment is really, really important, but I also can empathize with people who are struggling for food. Conservation must seem like an esoteric[862] topic for them. I think that if people have urgent needs, they are going to want to do something that is expedient[863] rather than something that is for the long-term benefit of the planet as a whole. It's important to save the rainforest, but how do you resolve that dilemma?"

---

[858] **Deleterious:** harmful or injurious
[859] **Vehement:** forcefulness of expression or extreme intensity of emotions or convictions
[860] **Burgeoning:** to grow and flourish
[861] **Deface:** to spoil or mar the appearance; disfigure
[862] **Esoteric:** confined to and understandable by a restricted number of people
[863] **Expedient:** marked by concern for self-interest rather than principle

"Of course, it's hard to reconcile[864] the needs of the people versus the environment, but I think it simply needs to be done," Doug replied. "Someone's got to do it! We need to find a new paradigm[865] that strikes a balance between environmental preservation and the needs of the people. Some radical[866] changes are necessary in the way we live if we want to save the environment. For example, some countries make a huge surplus of food. There's plenty of food to go around, it just needs to be distributed. I don't mean to belittle the problem because all of these issues are complex and difficult, but that's exactly why I want to do a dual major in environmental issues and economics in college and then go to law school. I want to be involved in environmental law and policy when I'm older. That's what I want to do."

"That sounds like a great career and a really worthy cause," Alexa said admiringly, suddenly realizing that Doug was a lot more serious about his goals in life than she initially gave him credit for. Admittedly, her opinion of him had been biased[867] by the fact that he was popular and an athlete at school. But clearly he was not the vacuous[868] jock she had thought he was.

"Look!" Doug whispered, pointing to a flowering tree.

Alexa stared at the tree blankly for a few moments before she finally saw what he was pointing to. A tiny hummingbird flitted about, poking its long beak into the pink flowers. Its wings fluttered frenetically at lightning speed, making a soft, deep buzzing noise. "Do they ever slow down?" Alexa asked. "It seems like they're always moving so fast."

"Only at night," Doug answered. "They actually go into a state called torpor[869]. It's kind of like a dormant[870], inactive state similar to

---

[864] **Reconcile:** to settle or resolve

[865] **Paradigm:** a philosophical or theoretical framework

[866] **Radical:** departing markedly from the usual or customary; extreme

[867] **Bias:** a preference or inclination, especially one that inhibits impartial judgment

[868] **Vacuous:** lacking serious purpose, intelligence, or substance

[869] **Torpor:** the dormant, inactive state of a hibernating animal

[870] **Dormant:** a condition of suspended activity; asleep or inactive

hibernation. Their metabolic rate slows down and their body temperature lowers. They use torpor to conserve energy. They need to try to save energy, because it takes a lot to fly around like that. Plus, if they have any baby birds, the mother needs to regurgitate[871] some of the food she eats to feed her young."

"Speaking of conserving energy, could we sit down for a while?" Alexa asked. "I'm really tired."

"Sure," he replied. "Actually, this is a great location to just hang out in a comfortable place and wait for the birds to come to us. See where these two trails cross right here? I've seen a lot of good stuff right here in this little clearing. I saw a really cool parrot when I was just sitting here yesterday. Sometimes it's hard to notice the birds when you're so focused on hiking. So it's good to stop every once in a while and observe quietly. Actually, if you're up for it, we can climb up this tree here and watch from up there. Sometimes, when you want to see the arboreal[872] species, the ones that live in trees, it's better to be up in a tree. Are you game? We won't go up that high. Follow me."

"OK," Alexa said, deciding not to admit that she had just fallen out of a tree a few days ago. Climbing up the tree after Doug, she focused on the task without looking down. Out of the corner of her eye, she saw a flash of scarlet wings. "Hey! Did you see that?" she asked him. "It was a scarlet-colored bird."

"Scarlet?" he repeated in an excited tone. "I wonder if it was the scarlet macaw. I wish I'd seen it, but I didn't see a thing."

"A macaw!" she exclaimed. "That's cool. I can't wait to tell everyone back home that I saw a macaw," she said enthusiastically.

---

[871] **Regurgitate:** to rush or pour back
[872] **Arboreal:** relating to trees

"Hold on a second there," he said authoritatively, turning to look down at her from his perch. "Just because you saw a flash of red doesn't mean that you saw the scarlet macaw. Color alone is not a sufficient criterion[873] to determine the species. There are several criteria that need to be met before you can positively identify which type of bird you've seen. How big was it? What did its beak look like?"

"I don't know," Alexa admitted. "It went by so fast."

"Let's stay right here and sit really quietly. Maybe it'll come back," he suggested.

Alexa nodded silently as she tried to find a comfortable way of sitting on the narrow branch. As soon as she stopped fidgeting, she succumbed[874] to the spell of the rainforest. Initially, it seemed quiet. But when they stopped moving around and talking, the subtle noises of the jungle came alive to her ears. In that tranquil moment of quiet reflection, she realized just how much she had come to love this rainforest. It was like her own personal asylum[875], a place far away from the rest of civilization where she felt at home with nature and attuned to the subtleties of her surroundings. The beautiful sight of a nascent[876] bud beginning to open, an army of ants marching single-file down the trunk of a tree, the sweet ballad[877] of a bird on a distant treetop...all of the nuances[878] and details of nature were coming alive before her eyes.

Alexa looked up at Doug and they exchanged a knowing smile. She could tell he was enjoying this quiet time as much as she was. They didn't need words to communicate how much they both enjoyed this special opportunity to commune[879] with nature. It seemed all the more special because they could share it together. Alexa felt a newfound sense of

---

[873] **Criterion:** a standard or reference point on which a judgment can be based; *plural: criteria*

[874] **Succumbed:** to yield or submit to an overpowering desire or force

[875] **Asylum:** a place of refuge or protection; a sanctuary

[876] **Nascent:** coming into existence; emerging

[877] **Ballad:** a simple song

[878] **Nuance:** a subtle distinction or variation

[879] **Commune:** to be in a state of heightened sensitivity, as with one's surroundings

respect for Doug and the fact that he wanted to save the rainforest. In her eyes, saving the rainforest was a noble goal and Doug's dedication to this worthy cause was meritorious[880].

The sound of a deep, vaguely familiar voice on the trial below shattered the tranquility. Alexa peered through the leaves and gasped out loud when she realized who was down below. It was Grady. He was standing at the intersection of the trails, talking quietly with a short man whose features were obscured. Alexa felt a chill run down her spine when she realized just what they were witnessing.

It was the meeting.

This was the illicit sale that José wanted to witness. But now, by some strange twist of fate, she and Doug were watching instead of José, unless he was also lurking somewhere in the shadows. Alexa looked up at Doug and put her finger to her lips, silently urging him to stay quiet.

"I need to take a look at the merchandise before I hand over the green," the short man said, waving a fistful of cash in Grady's face. Despite his diminutive[881] stature, his voice conveyed authority and power.

"I don't have a problem with that," Grady said confidently. "It's all right there," he said gesturing to the box at his feet. "I think you'll be impressed with the quality. Go ahead and appraise[882] it."

"I *am* impressed," the short man said, picking up a small jade carving to assess[883] its worth. He turned the object over and over again in his hands, examining all of its facets[884]. "This is great stuff. There's a dearth[885] of these authentic jade carvings on the market, and that makes for a good price. You know how the saying goes—it all boils down to supply and demand."

---

[880] **Meritorious:** deserving reward or praise; having merit
[881] **Diminutive:** very small; tiny
[882] **Appraise:** to evaluate, to estimate the quality and features of; judge
[883] **Assess:** to estimate the value of
[884] **Facet:** one of the definable aspects of an object or subject
[885] **Dearth:** a scarce supply; a lack

"And I have the supply," Grady said smugly. "That old coot Rothschild doesn't have a clue."

Alexa gasped, her hand covering her mouth to muffle the sound. Rothschild was innocent! He was not conniving[886] with Grady in the illegal trade of artifacts. He was just an eccentric old man who was unaware of the rampant[887] corruption within his own organization. It was Grady who was stealing, seemingly without compunction[888]. Rather than looking ashamed of the dark deal he was striking, he looked quite proud of himself. He was eagerly making a deal with the short man, who was evidently serving as conduit[889] for the transport and sale of the artifacts.

"No you don't!" a strong voice yelled authoritatively.

Alexa immediately recognized the voice. The fury and acrimony[890] in that voice made her tremble fearfully at the sound of it.

It was José.

But where was he? Alexa tried to peer through the branches. Down below, Grady and his cohort frantically looked in all directions, searching for the source.

They didn't have to look for long, because José was coming down toward them at lightning speed. From high on a treetop he descended, swinging precariously from a vine. Like a heavy pendulum carrying an abundance of momentum, his body was destined to impact its target with prodigious[891] force.

Alexa felt a stab of fear watching this dangerous drama unfold. José's trajectory[892] was impeccable. His outstretched legs went straight into the small of Grady's back, knocking him over as if he were a bowling pin. Grady fell into his cohort and the two men tumbled to the ground.

---

[886] **Conniving:** to cooperate secretly in an illegal or wrongful action

[887] **Rampant:** occurring unchecked and frequently or widely

[888] **Compunction:** a strong uneasiness or anxiety caused by a sense of guilt

[889] **Conduit:** a means by which something is transmitted or distributed

[890] **Acrimony:** biting sharpness and animosity in speech or disposition

[891] **Prodigious:** impressively great in size; enormous

[892] **Trajectory:** the path of a moving body through space

Like an incendiary[893] spark igniting an inferno, José's action triggered an explosive series of consequences.

"These artifacts are not yours to sell!" José yelled, his angry tone revealing the full extent of his antipathy[894] and loathing for the two men. José glared at the men lying on the ground, stunned by the turn of events. They evidently had never expected to be apprehended[895] out in the middle of a remote jungle.

Alexa felt her heart lurch. Didn't José realize that when he affronted[896] these two men, he had put himself in extreme danger? With his characteristic temerity[897], he had just charged into a treacherous situation with little regard for his own safety. Alexa desperately wanted to help him, to save him from the conflagration[898] that was sure to erupt when the two men regained their senses. She felt a compelling stab of allegiance to José and his quixotic[899] pursuits. Ever since she'd met him, he was always championing a noble cause that he pursued with vigor and firm resolve, irrespective of the practical challenges involved. He was an intransigent[900] idealist, never wavering from his righteous cause. He was simply inspiring.

But now, here he was fighting an ambitious battle all on his own. He was here by himself because she had deserted him. Alexa felt a rush of guilt and remorse. She chided herself for playing it safe and abandoning him like this. José was the one person in the world she cared about the most, but somehow, everything had gotten so screwed up. She had chosen to enjoy a simple afternoon with Doug rather than helping José in his perilous quest for justice. Now, she felt a strong and desperate desire to make up for it. She didn't care about safety, security, or simple fun anymore. She wanted to grasp life by the horns and live on the edge, just like José.

---

[893] **Incendiary:** causing fire
[894] **Antipathy:** a strong feeling of aversion or intense dislike
[895] **Apprehend:** to arrest or take into custody
[896] **Affront:** to face defiantly; confront
[897] **Temerity:** foolhardy disregard for danger; recklessness, rashness
[898] **Conflagration:** a conflict, war; can also mean a large disastrous fire
[899] **Quixotic:** foolishly impractical in the pursuit of noble deeds and idealistic goals
[900] **Intransigent:** refusing to compromise or moderate an extreme position

Alexa knew she needed to act immediately, even though she wasn't sure exactly what to do. She just had a vague, inchoate[901] idea that perhaps she could distract everyone by creating some sort of diversion[902] or somehow try to lighten the gravity of the situation.

"José!" Alexa yelled, waving wildly from her perch. She leaned forward, trying to catch everyone's attention. "José!" she yelled again, as she tried to climb down. In her haste, her foot slipped and she started descending a lot faster than she intended. She plummeted through the leaves and the palm fronds, desperately trying to grasp something firm on the way down.

"Alexa!" Doug bellowed. He nimbly ambled down the tree, trying to catch her before she landed. But he was too late.

Alexa hit the ground with a thud, landing on her back.

"Alexa! Are you OK?" Doug asked frantically.

Slowly, she opened her eyes. Both José and Doug were hovering over her with concern in their eyes. For a second, she couldn't remember where she was. But it all came flooding back to her when she glanced behind José and saw Grady getting up off the ground. "I think I just got the wind knocked out of me. I'll be OK," she said in shaky voice. "I'm all right, really."

"The two of you should go—quick!" José whispered urgently. "Pretend you know nothing."

"I'm not leaving you here alone," Alexa whispered firmly.

"You need to get her out of here safely," José appealed to Doug.

"I will," Doug said firmly, putting his arm around Alexa protectively and helping her to her feet.

"Not so fast!" Grady yelled, charging forward. He was fuming, filled with malevolent[903] rage and fury.

---

[901] **Inchoate:** imperfectly developed or formulated; vague, formless

[902] **Diversion:** something that distracts or diverts attention

[903] **Malevolent:** ill will, wishing harm to others; malicious

Alexa's mind was churning, trying to figure out a way she might be able to mollify[904] Grady's anger. She had the perspicacity[905] to realize they were in an extremely precarious position. The situation was about to turn dangerous. The truculent[906] look in Grady's eyes revealed the anger that festered within. When Alexa looked into those eyes, bubbling with rage, she knew it did not augur[907] well for a peaceful outcome to this confrontation.

Then she spied the camera. José had her digital camera strapped to his belt. Without a doubt, he had been busy chronicling[908] this illicit deal on the camera. The camera also had all of the incriminating pictures from Grady's tent. They didn't need to have this dangerous confrontation with these criminals when they already had all the evidence they needed to report the crime. All they needed to do was to find a way to get out of this contentious[909] situation unharmed and bring the camera to the authorities.

Instinctively Alexa sensed she had a much better chance of walking away from this situation with the camera in her hand than José did. Especially if she pretended that she hadn't seen anything underhanded.

Without hesitating another second, Alexa yanked the camera from José's belt before Grady reached them. The Velcro strap made a loud ripping noise as it came undone and she winced at the sound, hoping that Grady and his cohort didn't hear it and realize what she had just done.

Now, it was time for the hard part. She knew that she was going to have to summon up the best acting job of her life to pull off this feat. Alexa felt like she could do most things pretty well, but she also knew that her protean[910] talents did not include acting. Her one and only appearance on stage had been an unmitigated disaster. She thought back to the sage[911] advice of Mr. Comstock, her high school drama teacher, who

---

[904] **Mollify:** to lessen in intensity
[905] **Perspicacity:** acute mental vision, perception, or discernment; keen
[906] **Truculent:** disposed to violence; fierce
[907] **Augur:** indicate by signs; bode, foreshadow
[908] **Chronicling:** to record in the form of a historical record
[909] **Contentious:** likely to cause a dispute
[910] **Protean:** exhibiting a great variety or diversity
[911] **Sage:** marked by wisdom and good judgment

had always urged his students to breathe deeply before going on stage. Alexa took a big gulp of air.

"Hey, did you guys see that scarlet macaw? It was so cool," she enthused. "It was right over there," she pointed. "I was leaning out of the tree to see it when I fell. Did you see it?" she asked Grady sweetly, acting as if nothing had happened.

"What are you talking about?" Grady demanded brusquely[912], towering over them menacingly. His pugnacious[913] nature was underscored by his combative stance and a tone of voice that indicated he was ready to pick a fight.

Alexa felt her stomach tighten with anxiety. It was not at all clear if this plan was going to work, but at this point, she felt as if she had no choice but to play it out to the end. "I just saw a scarlet macaw! I can't believe you guys missed it. It was so beautiful," she gushed. "The only problem is that I fell out of the tree when I was trying to get a better glimpse of it and I think I hurt my ankle. I can't really stand on it." She winced, standing on one foot while she held onto Doug's arm on one side and José's on the other. "Maybe if you two both help me, I can make it back to camp," she said to Doug and José.

Alexa held her breath while she waited to see what would happen next. She knew José was aware of what she was attempting to do, but she wasn't so certain he would follow her lead and just walk away from this confrontation. She knew José very well—well enough to realize that he was a maverick[914] at heart, always thinking for himself and following his own plan. Would he follow *her* lead this time?

"We'll help you back," Doug said, sounding genuinely concerned with her faux injury. "I can carry you."

---

[912] **Brusque:** short or abrupt in manner or speech; discourteously blunt
[913] **Pugnacious:** combative and quarrelsome in nature; truculent
[914] **Maverick:** an independent individual who does not go along with a group or party; a dissenter

Alexa groaned inwardly, realizing that her acting job had been so convincing that Doug thought that she really had hurt her ankle. He had no clue about anything that was going on right now and unwittingly[915], he was about to foil[916] her plan. The goal was to get José out of this dangerous situation, which wouldn't happen if Doug carried her alone. "My left foot is still fine, so I think I can manage if you let me hold onto your arm and José's arm on the other side. C'mon, let's go," she urged them. "I need to get back to the camp and let it rest." Alexa tugged on José's arm, silently pleading him to follow her lead.

"I'll help you," José said, grasping her arm firmly. "We need to get you back to camp quickly," he added.

Alexa felt a tingling sensation as they turned to leave. José was following her lead! But were Grady and his cohort actually going to let them just walk away like this after José caught them both in an illegal act? The incriminating evidence was sitting right there in a box on the ground and Grady was clearly culpable[917]. The guilty look on his face said it all.

"Wait a minute, young man, I need to talk to you!" Grady yelled at José.

"We have nothing to talk about," José said defiantly without turning around or slowing his gait.

"Oh yes we do! Now you come over here right now," Grady demanded, like an angry parent yelling at a fractious[918] child.

"No! I'm not talking to you!" José yelled even louder, as if he was an obstreperous[919] child defying his father's orders.

"Get back here right now!" Grady yelled, his voice filled with fury and wrath[920].

---

[915] **Unwitting:** not knowing; unaware

[916] **Foil:** to prevent something from happening or being successful; thwart

[917] **Culpable:** deserving of blame or condemnation as being wrong or harmful; blameworthy

[918] **Fractious:** tending to cause trouble; unruly, irritable

[919] **Obstreperous:** stubbornly defiant and noisy

[920] **Wrath:** intense anger

José finally stopped and turned around. He looked Grady in the eyes and said in a quiet, measured tone, "There is *nothing* to talk about. I know I was really mad a minute ago, but you know that I wouldn't do or say *anything* that might jeopardize my scholarship."

Alexa winced involuntarily. To her ears, José's statement sounded highly implausible[921]. He simply had to be lying. She knew with certainty that he would not participate in a Faustian[922] bargain. He would never compromise his integrity for personal gain. If Grady thought that José was just a docile[923] person who was easily controlled, he was wrong. José was anything but malleable[924]. Instead of taking directions, he followed his own compass with strength of purpose. Ever since he had arrived at Tikal, he had taken on the role of the inquisitor[925], staunchly[926] seeking the answers to the questions that haunted his conscience.

José and Grady stared each other in the eye, as if they were silently consummating[927] a business transaction. Without spelling out the deal in precise terms, José had intimated[928] that he would keep quiet about the smuggling if they would still give him his scholarship. But would Grady accept the deal?

Alexa looked down at the ground. She didn't want to look at Grady. She was afraid her expression would reveal the panic she was feeling at this terrifying moment. Would Grady and his business partner just let them walk away? Would they actually believe that José would keep his silence in exchange for scholarship money, or would they realize that José

---

[921] **Implausible:** appearing invalid, unlikely, or unacceptable; unbelievable

[922] **Faustian:** resembling Faust, from a German legend about a man who sells his soul to the devil for power and knowledge

[923] **Docile:** willing to be led, supervised, or taught

[924] **Malleable:** easily controlled or influenced

[925] **Inquisitor:** one who inquires or makes an inquisition, especially a questioner who is excessively rigorous or hostile

[926] **Staunch:** firm and steadfast in loyalty or principle

[927] **Consummate:** to bring to completion or fruition; conclude or finish

[928] **Intimate:** to communicate delicately, subtly, and indirectly; hint

would inevitably repudiate[929] this promise? Would they fall for José's dissembled[930] greed or would they realize that he was faking it?

Without waiting for any sort of reply from Grady, José turned to leave, pulling Alexa and Doug with him.

With one arm around José and the other around Doug, Alexa kept up the pretense of having a sprained ankle. Slowly, they made it to the edge of the clearing where the trail began. Alexa felt an exhilarating thrill as she realized they were pulling it off. They were simply walking away.

"The camera!" an irate voice shouted from behind them.

Alexa glanced behind her. Grady's partner in crime was still sitting on the ground, but his finger was pointed right at her and his face was flushed an angry shade of crimson.

"The camera! Get the camera from them, you idiot," he yelled at Grady. "I can't get up. My knee is wrecked. Get them! Get the camera from the girl!"

"Run!" José yelled to Alexa and Doug, giving them a push toward the trail.

Alexa glanced at the camera that dangled from the strap around her right wrist and instinctively she grasped it tightly. Dropping the sprained-ankle routine, she burst into an all-out sprint, galloping away as fast as she could.

---

[929] **Repudiate:** to reject an obligation or to refuse to acknowledge or pay
[930] **Dissemble:** to put on a false show or appearance; feign

14

A Tortuous Trail

"**W**hat the heck is going on?" Doug yelled to Alexa as they started running down the trail.

"I'll explain later," Alexa said breathlessly. Without breaking her stride, she glanced back over her shoulder. José was not following them. Instead, he was charging straight toward Grady. Alexa immediately came to a screeching halt. "José!" she shrieked at the top of her lungs, terrified for his safety. Her strident[931] scream was so piercing that it made her own eardrums ring. Although both men were around six feet tall, Grady looked to be twice as wide as José. Juxtaposed[932] next to each other as they were, they looked terribly mismatched. Did José really think he could take on Grady? Alexa watched in horror.

José ran at top speed right toward Grady and then leapt high in the air, flying head first toward his target with his arms outstretched like Superman. At first glance, Alexa thought that he was just simply out of control, randomly flinging himself on top of Grady. But as she watched what happened next, she realized that his actions were part of a carefully

---

[931] **Strident:** sounds that are loud, grating, or shrill; discordant
[932] **Juxtaposed:** placed side by side

calibrated[933] maneuver to tackle Grady to the ground. With amazing accuracy, his full body weight hit Grady on the legs, sending him sprawling flat on his back.

Alexa gasped with surprise when she saw Grady hit the ground. She had no idea that José's manifold[934] talents included the ability to tackle like a linebacker. She was riveted to the spot, unable to run away.

José immediately scrambled to his feet, but Grady lay motionless, as if he had been anesthetized[935]. José took one look at Grady and then ran to Alexa and Doug. "Run!" he commanded them. "He's just stunned—he's going to get up in a minute!"

Alexa started running as fast as she could on the overgrown trail through the forest, with Doug and José right behind her. The protruding branches that peppered the edges of the trail scraped her bare arms as she barreled through the entanglement. Alexa tried to stay calm, but she found it hard to catch her breath. It already felt like they had been running forever.

"That was some tackle!" Doug said to José. "Are you a football player?"

"No," José said, breathless from exertion. "I've never played in my entire life."

"Well then, you've got some innate[936] ability," Doug said. "And we may need to put it to the test again—I hear someone coming. Someone's chasing us!"

"But I don't even know where we're going. I think we ran down the wrong trail," Alexa wailed. "Is this the way back to camp? This trail is tortuous[937]—there's been so many twists and turns that I don't know what direction we're heading in." Alexa stopped running and looked

---

[933] **Calibrate:** to adjust precisely for a particular function
[934] **Manifold:** many and varied
[935] **Anesthetize:** to make unconscious by use of anesthetic drugs
[936] **Innate:** inborn, possessed at birth
[937] **Tortuous:** having repeated bends, twists, or turns; winding

around her, trying to get her bearings. "I think we're lost!" Everywhere she looked there were trees and more trees. It all looked the same. There were no salient[938] features to distinguish one area of the rainforest from the next.

"I'm not exactly sure where we are either, but we have to keep going," José said. His indefatigable[939] drive was showing no signs of lagging. "I think there's a stream up there—I can hear it. If we can just get to the other side, I know a shortcut back to the camp. Let me go first," he said, skirting around them to assume the lead.

"I know the way, *I'll* go first," Doug declared, glaring at José.

"No way," José retorted, obstinately[940] refusing to budge from his position on the path.

"We don't have time to argue, guys," Alexa interjected[941], attempting to diffuse the fight that seemed destined to break out between the two boys. She had an inkling that the tension between José and Doug had something to do with her. But this was not the time to sort out complicated feelings. "I can hear someone coming," she said urgently. "Let's just get out of here."

Alexa breathed a sigh of relief when both José and Doug heeded her wishes and started heading toward the stream, rather than squabbling over who was going to go first.

"Uh oh," José groaned, coming to a dead stop.

Alexa and Doug rushed to see what was up ahead. José was standing on a precipice looking down over a bubbling stream. "This is not going to be easy to cross," Alexa said, eyeing the swift-moving water. The accretion[942] of sediment from the stream had left a muddy bank along the edge of the water several feet high, making it difficult to enter the water

---

[938] **Salient:** very conspicuous; prominent, noticeable

[939] **Indefatigable:** incapable of being exhausted or fatigued; untiring

[940] **Obstinate:** stubbornly adhering to an opinion or course of action; obdurate

[941] **Interject:** to insert in between or among other things; interpolate

[942] **Accretion:** growth by gradual addition

slowly and carefully. Alexa looked at the swirling dark water and felt a sense of dread. Although the edges of the stream looked shallow, the middle looked deep and foreboding.

"We can walk over that log," José said pointing to a fallen tree that spanned the stream. "What a boon[943] for us!" The tree trunk stretched from one bank to the other, at least five feet above the water. "Let's just get over to the other side and then we'll pull the log away so that Grady can't get over. That's how we'll bilk[944] him."

But to Alexa's eyes, the dark, smooth bark of the slim trunk looked perilously slick. "That looks so precarious," Alexa said nervously. "It's not very wide and it looks really slippery."

"I'll help you," José said.

"No, *I'll* help you!" Doug exclaimed.

"No, I'll go by myself," Alexa declared firmly, hoping that she could restore concord[945] between the two boys by refusing them both. Taking the lead, she inched along the edge of the precipice, carefully making her way down to the fallen log that spanned the water. But once she stood next to the makeshift bridge, she lost her confidence. "You guys go first, then I'll follow you," she urged them.

Doug, who was eager to take the lead, quickly whipped off his sneakers and socks and scampered over the log bridge to the other side. "Take your shoes off," he urged Alexa. "It's easy in bare feet."

José looked at Alexa, his eyes conveying his concern. "I can help you across."

"No, I'll go by myself. Just go!" she pressed.

---

[943] **Boon:** a timely blessing or benefit
[944] **Bilk:** to elude, thwart, or frustrate; can also mean to swindle
[945] **Concord:** a state of agreement or harmony

As soon as José reached the other side, Alexa knew she couldn't avoid the challenge any longer, there were no excuses left. She had simply run out of dilatory[946] tactics. Now she knew that she just had to tackle it. Alexa slipped off her sneakers and eyed the slippery log with apprehension.

"I'll come get you," Doug yelled, watching nervously from the other side.

"No, I'll do it myself," she said, mustering all of the fortitude she could. With one hand holding her sneakers and the other hand clutching her camera, Alexa climbed up onto the log and slowly started making her way across. Like a tightrope walker carefully considering each step, she kept her eyes focused on her feet, rather than looking at the mesmerizing water rushing beneath the makeshift bridge.

"You can do it! You're almost there," Doug coaxed.

Alexa glanced up to give José and Doug an encouraging smile, just a little signal to let them know that she was doing OK. But when she looked up at them, she realized that something was terribly wrong. Neither one of them was focused on her. Instead they were looking over at the other side of the stream with an alarmed expression. It could only mean one thing. Grady had caught up with them.

Alexa's head snapped around to look behind her. Sure enough, there he was, standing on the bank, a mere 10 feet away. Alexa felt a stab of fear when she saw his ominous[947] glare directed right at her. His penetrating focus was like a laser that cut right through her. The look in his eyes was so frightening that she inadvertently screamed.

Alexa quickly looked away and whipped her head around to face forward. Instantly, she was fighting to regain her balance. The simple act

---

[946] **Dilatory:** causing delay
[947] **Ominous:** menacing, threatening, or alarming; foreshadowing evil or disaster

of turning her head had set her off kilter. In hindsight, she wished she could have just stayed focused on her goal of reaching the other side, but regrettably, she had succumbed to the temptation of looking behind her and now she couldn't take back that foolish mistake. Her hips gyrated forward and then backward as her arms flailed wildly. In that moment of desperation, Alexa completely lost her grip on the items she was holding in both of her hands. The frantic thrashing of her arms sent her sneakers flying into the air, while the camera, which she had been clutching diligently, dangled precariously from the slim Velcro strap around her right wrist.

Alexa heard the horrifying sound of her two sneakers splashing down into the rushing brook and hoped she was not about to suffer a similar fate. But she still had not regained her balance. Her arms were pumping the air in big backward circles, desperately trying to offset her unstable stance. As her right arm flailed around and around, the camera, still dangling from the loop around her wrist, was concomitantly[948] making its own revolutions around her arm, gaining speed and momentum like a slingshot.

Alexa felt the horrifying sensation of the strap slipping right off her wrist. The camera, propelled by the rapid rotations, shot off her arm like a ballistic missile and flew high into the air. After making one last desperate lunge for the camera, Alexa knew that her fate was sealed. There was no way she could regain her balance now. Feeling a sense of inexorable[949] doom, she knew she was going down. Instinctively, she tried to grab the log as she fell so that she wouldn't end up careening all of the way down into the water.

Her hands grasped the slippery log, but the rest of her body kept falling. She ended up dangling from the log, clinging to it with all of her

---

[948] **Concomitant:** occurring, existing, or happening at the same time
[949] **Inexorable:** not to be persuaded or appeased by entreaty (requests or pleas); relentless

might, while her bare feet splashed down into the surface of the water below.

Before she had a chance to collect her wits, the camera came hurling down from sky and landed in the water right next to her, making a sickening plop as it splashed down and descended into the dark depths. When Alexa saw the camera land in the water, she felt like it was an ominous sign that portended[950] her own fate. Her hands slipped right off the smooth tree trunk and she slid right into the water.

Her vertical body sliced through the water and her bare feet painfully hit the rocky bottom of the stream before her head went under. "Ahh!" Alexa shrieked.

"Alexa! Are you OK?" José yelled out.

"Alexa!" Doug exclaimed.

Both boys jumped into the water at the same moment to perform the chivalrous[951] rescue. But Doug got there first. Sweeping her up into his arms, he whisked her to the bank of the river and set her down.

José lingered in the water and dove down under, resurfacing with the waterlogged camera in hand. Standing in the shallow water at the edge of the stream, he gingerly opened up the camera to access the memory card. They all watched, transfixed by the sight of water pouring out from inside the camera. It was ruined.

Alexa felt a deep sense of guilt and remorse. The camera itself had been retrieved, but the evidence might just as well have vaporized[952] into thin air. It was simply gone.

"Ha, ha, ha!" Grady laughed fiendishly[953], while witnessing the demise[954] of the camera. "Serves you meddling kids right," he said smugly,

---

[950] **Portend:** to serve as an omen or a warning of; presage, forecast

[951] **Chivalrous:** characterized by consideration, gallantry, and courtesy, especially toward women

[952] **Vaporize:** to convert into a vapor (gaseous state); to vanish as if vaporized

[953] **Fiendish:** extremely wicked

[954] **Demise:** the end of existence or activity; death; termination

the corners of his mouth curled upward in a diabolical[955] smile. He looked as if he was savoring the moment. "As for you," Grady glared at José, "I've never seen such insolent[956] and ungrateful behavior in my life."

"Save the rhetoric[957]," José said. "We both know exactly what's going on here."

"All I know is that an incorrigible[958] young man assaulted me and my friend, resulting in multiple injuries. If we decide to press charges, I think you'll be looking at a pretty stiff penalty," Grady warned. "If you so much as say a single word, I will litigate[959], and believe me, I will prevail[960]. You'll be ordered by the courts to pay restitution[961] to your assault victims, and I'm willing to bet there would be jail time as well." Grady smiled superciliously[962] and folded his arms across his chest, assuming a cocky, self-satisfied stance. He knew he had just made a trenchant[963] argument for José to comply with his demands. He was confident that he had just defeated his opponent.

Alexa cringed with horror at the thought of José ending up in a jail cell. But the thought of him entering into a covenant of silence with Grady was equally horrifying.

José seethed with anger, his lips pressed tightly together. Finally, he spoke. "I'm not saying anything," he said quietly. "I suggest you go help your friend—it looked like he was going to need some help walking out of here." José calmly turned his back on Grady and began making his way downstream to retrieve Alexa's sneakers.

Grady paused, staring straight at Alexa and Doug, as if he was wondering what to do about them. Then, without uttering a word, he turned and walked away.

---

[955] **Diabolical:** characteristic of the devil; devilish
[956] **Insolent:** audaciously rude, disrespectful, or insulting; impertinent
[957] **Rhetoric:** language that is pretentious, insincere, or intellectually vacuous
[958] **Incorrigible:** difficult to control, manage, or reform
[959] **Litigate:** to engage in legal proceedings
[960] **Prevail:** to prove superior; to triumph
[961] **Restitution:** the act of compensating for loss, damage, or injury
[962] **Supercilious:** arrogant superiority, haughty disdain
[963] **Trenchant:** forceful, penetrating, and effective

"Whoa!" Doug exclaimed when Grady was out of earshot. "What was that all about?"

"Smuggling," Alexa replied. "José figured out that Grady was illegally selling some of the artifacts that they unearthed at the dig and he wanted to stop them."

"Why doesn't he just tell someone instead of acting like a vigilante[964]?" Doug asked. "It's dangerous to take the law into your own hands. If they're criminals, they could be violent—what's the point of reeling them in on your own when that's the job of the police?"

"It's more complicated than that," Alexa countered. "He wanted to have some evidence before he accused these people of a crime."

"But I still don't see what the big deal is. Why is it worth all of the danger?" Doug asked.

José, who had just heard the tail end of their conversation, walked up to Doug and threw Alexa's soaked sneakers at his feet. "I'll tell you why," José said defensively. "These artifacts are not just pretty trinkets for some rich person's collection. They are priceless artifacts from a lost civilization. To sell them like they are trinkets is to desecrate[965] their sacred value for the Mayan people. These artifacts are part of our heritage and we deserve to have this link to our own past. Nobody has the right to take them away from us!" José's eyes flashed with emotion and his face was flushed with anger.

Doug had a skeptical look on his face as he listened to José's emotional explanation. Doug simply didn't understand José's maudlin[966] concern for the fate of a box full of artifacts.

---

[964] **Vigilante:** one who takes law enforcement into his or her own hands
[965] **Desecrate:** to violate the sacredness of; profane
[966] **Maudlin:** effusively sentimental; mushy

But Alexa understood very well. She knew José well enough to realize that this was not sanctimonious[967] preaching. It was genuine, heartfelt emotion for this tangible link to the history of his people.

"I'm going to put an end to it," José declared decisively.

"But you heard what Grady said—he's going to sue you for assaulting him if you say anything," Alexa pointed out.

"No, he won't," José replied confidently. "He's operating on the premise[968] that the evidence was destroyed." José said, holding up the waterlogged camera.

"But it was, wasn't it?" Alexa asked skeptically.

"No," he replied, his eyes sparkling with a hint of mischief.

---

[967] **Sanctimonious:** feigning piety or righteousness

[968] **Premise:** something assumed to be true and upon which an argument is based or conclusion drawn

15

The Day of Reckoning

"**B**ut the pictures were ruined," Alexa countered. "That was not meant to be an underwater camera. That memory card was decimated[969] by the water—I'm sure of it."

"But I have a copy," José replied.

"You do?" she asked incredulously.

"Yes, of some of them, at least. Remember when I borrowed your camera and went into Grady's tent to look for evidence?"

"Yeah, I remember that very well," Alexa said. "How could I forget," she added with a trace of sarcasm, remembering the agonizing wait for José to emerge.

"When I was in his tent, I took pictures of his notebook and records, and then I downloaded the memory card from the camera onto Grady's hard drive. That's why it took me so long."

---

[969] **Decimate:** to destroy a large part of

"Wait a minute," Doug interjected. "You snuck into his tent, took pictures of the evidence, and then downloaded the pictures onto *his* computer?"

"Yes, I did," José admitted. "I just made a new folder with a funky name and hid it on his hard drive. If he did a search for it, he would find it—it's right there. But if he's not looking for it, he'll never find it."

"That takes guts, man!" Doug said, with a note of admiration in his voice.

"What did you name the file?" Alexa asked curiously.

"Y-T-I-R-G-E-T-N-I," he said, spelling out each letter. "That's 'integrity' spelled backwards. It just looks like one of those nonsensical files on your computer and you have no idea what they're doing there or how they got there." José chuckled at his own ingenuity.

"But wait a minute," Alexa interjected, "you can't have pictures of what just happened here in the jungle—you just took the pictures and then the camera landed in the water."

"I know," he admitted. "But we have three eyewitnesses of that. The only pictures that are downloaded on his computer are the ones that I took that night in his tent. Oh, and there were a few other pictures already on the memory card that you took."

Alexa quickly looked down at the ground. She knew exactly what pictures he was talking about. There was the picture of Alexa and Doug in front of the airport terminal, the picture of Doug in the ramshackle van that brought them to Tikal, and the picture of herself and Doug together on top of Temple IV, among others. Alexa looked into José's eyes and she knew that he had been acting reserved with her for a reason. He had seen the pictures that she had taken of Doug and he had seen the pictures of them together. He had drawn the conclusion that Doug was her boyfriend.

Somehow, their signals had gotten crossed yet again and Alexa had a sinking feeling that this time, it was irrevocable. She wondered if those pictures were a self-fulfilling prophecy[970]. Maybe Doug *was* destined to be her boyfriend. For a fleeting moment, Alexa felt as if she got a glimpse of the future and she wasn't sure if she was ready to go there. She wanted to linger in the past, dawdling on a serene beach in the Caribbean with José.

"Anyway," José continued, "I think I have enough evidence, but I need to copy those files from his computer. I need to copy those pictures onto a memory stick or a disk or a CD or something like that so I don't have to take his computer with me when I go."

"Go where?" Alexa asked.

"To the authorities," he said succinctly. "I'm going to hike back to the center of Tikal. I need to make it to the hotel so that I can make a phone call. But first, I need to get those files off of Grady's computer."

"You can't possibly do that now—not after what just happened with Grady," Alexa pointed out. "I doubt they'll let you set foot on that campsite ever again."

"I'm sure you're right about that," José agreed. "As soon as Grady makes it back to camp, he's going to tell everyone to keep me away. But the way I see it, we have a window of opportunity here. If we can get to the camp before Grady does, I will go into his tent, copy the files, and then high-tail it out of there and head straight for the authorities."

"Let's go!" Doug said, "We'll help you."

---

[970] **Prophecy:** a prediction of something to come in the future

"No, I don't want the two of you to get involved any more than you already are. I feel like I've already put you in a dangerous situation and I don't want to do it again."

"I'm going with you," Alexa said decisively. "And I'm doing it of my own volition[971]. I don't want you to go there alone." Alexa hurriedly put on her soggy sneakers.

"And I'm coming too," Doug added.

"Well then, let's go," he said solemnly. "This way," he beckoned. "We don't have much time."

José led the way through the dense underbrush, while Alexa, following in his footsteps, dwelled on the uncertain future. If José was able to get a hold of the files on Grady's computer and give them to the authorities, the whole situation was destined to blow up. Would Nadine be caught in the fray? Was she as guilty as Grady or was she innocent like Rothschild? Whenever Alexa thought about Nadine, her mind kept returning to her father. Would he view her actions as an attack on Nadine and his relationship with her? Alexa felt as if everything in her life, everything she held dear to her heart, was resting in the balance.

As they approached the camp, José turned to Alexa and Doug and raised his finger to his lips, urging them to be as quiet as possible. "It's still siesta time," he said. "It looks quiet. I think I'm just going to walk right into Grady's tent and get what I need. You guys should stay here."

Alexa surveyed the quiet camp. It was an opportune moment to sneak around unnoticed, but she worried, nevertheless. "You're just going to walk right into his tent and pray that no one sees you?"

---

[971] **Volition:** the act of choosing or determining

"Yes and no," he replied. "Yes, I'm just going to walk in there. What do I have to lose at this point? The 'no' part is for the praying. I'm not going to do that. I'm agnostic[972]."

"You don't believe in God?" Doug asked him incredulously.

"I didn't say that I'm an atheist, I said that I'm an agnostic, meaning that I don't know if there is a God or not," José explained. "I don't think that it's knowable."

"How can you say that?" Doug asked, looking at José with a worried expression.

"I'm not trying to demean[973] anyone else's beliefs—I'm a very tolerant person. I think that people should be allowed to believe or not believe anything they want to. But for myself as an individual, I simply don't espouse[974] religion."

Doug looked shocked at José's bold statement, but Alexa wasn't surprised at all. Earlier in the summer, during long, lazy afternoons on the beach, they had had many deep discussions. At this point, she knew José well enough that his nonconformist[975] opinions didn't surprise her. He abhorred following the crowd and he disliked authority, especially when it reigned over him. Like an anarchist[976] who deems government as oppressive and undesirable, José wanted to forge through life rebelling against the establishment in all of its forms.

There was something about José's fierce independence that inspired Alexa. It made her feel so alive and empowered[977] with the ability to change the world. It made her think that she didn't have to meekly follow the path that was laid out before her. She felt emboldened[978] to branch out

---

[972] **Agnostic:** one who believes that it is impossible to know if God exists
[973] **Demean:** reduce in dignity, worth, or character
[974] **Espouse:** to give one's loyalty or support to
[975] **Nonconformist:** one who refuses to be bound by accepted beliefs, customs, or practices
[976] **Anarchist:** one who rebels against any authority, established order, or coercive control
[977] **Empower:** to give an ability or quality to; enable
[978] **Embolden:** to instill boldness or courage in

and do the unexpected. It was liberating and exciting to be around him. But at the same time, José's reckless abandon scared her. It made her worry about the danger that was around the corner, just as she was worrying right now.

"Here I go," he said deliberately, giving Alexa a final, probing look.

"Be careful," Alexa admonished, her voice breaking. Something about the raw emotion in his dark eyes made her wince. He looked at her with sadness and resolve. It was as if their special friendship was collapsing right at that very moment. It was the nadir[979] of their relationship.

Alexa had never felt so conflicted in her life. Part of her wanted to jump off the edge with him and live life precariously. The other part was terrified at the thought of it and wanted to cower in safety here in the bushes with Doug, who was always so predictable, reliable, and secure.

José walked away, boldly marching through the stillness of the sleeping campsite. With a forceful flick of his wrist, he yanked at the zipper on Grady's tent. The harsh, grating noise of the zipper reverberated throughout the clearing. Alexa felt as if her heart stopped beating while she waited to see if anyone heard the noise. But all was quiet, and José ducked under the open flap.

"Man, he's got guts," Doug said, in awe of José's bold actions.

Alexa nodded absently, her unswerving[980] gaze trained on Grady's tent. "What's taking him so long?" Alexa asked anxiously after a couple minutes passed.

"He's probably trying to copy the files," Doug reminded her. "But he'd better hurry, because Grady's going to be back any second now. Even

---

[979] **Nadir:** the lowest point
[980] **Unswerving:** constant; steady and unfaltering

if Grady's carrying his friend all of the way back here, it's not going to take him much longer!"

Alexa sighed and slumped to the ground, feeling enervated[981] after the tumultuous events of the afternoon. "I can't watch, he's going to get caught," she moaned.

"No, here he comes!" Doug exclaimed. "Oh my gosh, is he taking the whole computer with him? I thought he was just going to copy some files!"

Alexa jumped to her feet and peered through the bushes. José was running toward them with Grady's laptop tucked under his arm.

"Let's go!" José said breathlessly. "I've got to get out of here and fast. If I can just make it back to the hotel before they catch me, I can make a phone call to the authorities. This way," he beckoned, walking hurriedly toward the trail to Alexa's camp. "I'm going to take the trail that starts at your camp— that's the fastest way to the hotel." After a few paces, he broke into a run.

"That's at least an hour away by foot," Alexa said, as she and Doug started running behind him.

"But there's no other way to get there," he countered, glancing back at her over his shoulder. "And I have to take this computer because I couldn't find a disk to transfer the files to."

"You've got a head start and you're a lot faster than Grady," Doug said. "The trail to the hotel is just on the other side of our camp. You're going to make it," he said firmly. "They can't catch up. Nothing's going to stop you now."

As soon as Doug uttered those fateful words, José stopped dead in his tracks.

---

[981] **Enervate:** lacking strength or vigor; debilitated

"What's going on?" Alexa asked, peering over his shoulder on the narrow trail. Alexa gasped with shock when she saw who stood before them. Doug was wrong. Someone could stop José.

It was Nadine.

Standing like a sentinel[982] in the middle of the trail, Nadine had her arms folded across her chest as she glared at José reproachfully[983]. "Whose computer is that and what are you doing with it?" she demanded.

Alexa felt a stab of alarm penetrate her body. The day of reckoning[984] had arrived and questions raced through her mind. Was Nadine complicit[985] in the smuggling scheme? Whose side was she on? For a moment Alexa considered saying that the computer was broken and José was bringing it to town to be fixed. But then she reconsidered. Nadine was sure to see through such a tenuous[986] excuse. Finally, Alexa blurted out the truth. "Mr. Grady is selling artifacts illegally and José has the evidence on this computer. He's taking it to the authorities." Alexa took a deep breath to steady her nerves as she watched Nadine carefully, wondering if she was going to stop them.

Nadine's eyebrows furrowed as she looked at José questioningly. "Are you sure about this? These are very serious allegations."

"I'm sure," José said.

"We all saw him doing it," Alexa said defensively. "There's a preponderance[987] of evidence. But we have to go quickly," she said urgently. "Before he catches up to us." Alexa knew that Nadine was shrewd enough to see exactly what was going on. If she let José go, the smuggling ring was destined to go down in flames. But if she stalled them there until Grady caught up to them, he would surely seize the evidence. If she was guilty,

---

[982] **Sentinel:** a guard

[983] **Reproach:** to express disapproval or criticism of; admonish

[984] **Reckoning:** a settling of accounts

[985] **Complicit:** association with or participation in a wrongful act

[986] **Tenuous:** lacking strength or substance; flimsy

[987] **Preponderance:** a superiority in weight, importance, or strength

she would try to stop them, Alexa reasoned. Did Nadine expect to be implicated in a crime or completely absolved[988] of any wrongdoing? Alexa fervently hoped it was the latter.

Nadine hesitated for a moment, her stoic[989] expression revealing nothing about her inner thoughts. Finally, she spoke. "Well then, you had better hurry," she said to José.

Alexa let out a big sigh of relief. Nadine certainly wasn't acting guilty. She was letting José walk away with the evidence.

"Thanks," José said quietly, walking right past Nadine.

"Wait a minute!" Nadine put her hand up to stop Alexa and Doug from following him. "I don't want the two of you going anywhere. I'm responsible for your safety and I'm not letting you out of my sight. We're heading right back to camp, and Alexa, I'm going to call your father so that he's apprised[990] of the situation here."

"Can't we just go with José to the trailhead to say goodbye?" Alexa begged.

Nadine sighed, "OK, but I'm coming with you. I meant what I said about not letting you out of my sight."

By the time they reached the trailhead, Alexa felt her eyes welling with tears.

"José, why don't you take my backpack?" Doug offered. "You can put the laptop in there. It will be easier to carry and it won't look so conspicuous."

"Really?" he said, surprised by Doug's gesture.

"Yes," Doug said, slipping the straps off his shoulders.

---

[988] **Absolve:** to pronounce clear of guilt or liability
[989] **Stoic:** seemingly indifferent to pleasure, pain, or grief
[990] **Apprise:** to give notice to; inform

José slipped the computer into the backpack. It was a perfect fit. But before he put it on, he looked at Doug. "I don't know when I can return it," he said somberly.

Alexa choked on a sob welling up in her throat. The grim reality was imminent. José was leaving and she knew he wouldn't be coming back to Tikal. But even sadder yet was the thought that she might not ever see him again.

"That's OK. You can keep it. Good luck," Doug said, walking a few paces away to stand with Nadine and give Alexa some privacy to say goodbye.

"I've got to go," José said quietly.

"I know," she whispered.

Alexa looked into his eyes, hoping for some sign or signal that their special friendship was still intact.

"Don't forget me," he said quietly.

"I won't," she promised. "I can't."

José turned and walked away, silently disappearing into the depths of the jungle.

Alexa stood motionless, as if rooted to the spot. Too stunned to talk and still reeling from life's vicissitudes[991], she didn't want to process what had just happened. She didn't want to move on and return home to her mundane existence, without the hope of having José in her life in a meaningful way.

"Look!" Doug whispered urgently.

Alexa spun around to see Doug pointing to the treetops above them. There, in mid-flight, was the most spectacular bird Alexa had ever

---

[991] **Vicissitude:** one of the sudden or unexpected changes or hardships encountered in one's life, activities, or surroundings

seen. Its long serpentine tail feathers were a brilliant shade of emerald green and its breast a vibrant shade of crimson. It was the resplendent quetzal, the most prized and sacred of all birds for the ancient Maya.

Alexa gasped at the sight of this magnificent bird, mesmerized by the luster of the long green feathers. She could easily see why the ancient Maya revered this exceptional bird. But what she couldn't fathom is why this rare creature had revealed itself to her at this poignant[992] moment in her life. It felt like a message bubbling up from the distant past or a signal pointing to her future, but she couldn't quite decipher it. The elusive, majestic bird quickly disappeared into the rainforest canopy, but the questions it evoked[993] lingered in her mind.

Alexa slowly lifted her eyes from the treetops and looked at Doug standing next to her, a euphoric glow lighting up his face. "You're my good-luck charm," he said softly, staring into her eyes.

---

[992] **Poignant:** profoundly moving; touching
[993] **Evoke:** to call forth or summon

16

Hackneyed Advice

Alexa walked into the Big Squeeze and immediately her eyes locked with Laurie's. The two friends ran to hug each other.

"I'm so glad you're back!" Laurie exclaimed. "I can't wait to hear *everything*," she said, looking searchingly into Alexa's eyes. "I can't believe you went to a place that doesn't have e-mail—I've been dying to hear what's going on. How is that boyfriend of yours? Did you see José there?"

Alexa looked down at the ground. Just hearing his name spoken out loud gave her a stabbing pain in her heart. She felt so acutely disconnected from him. When she and José had said their quick goodbyes and he had walked down that jungle path with Grady's laptop, Alexa had the sensation he was literally walking right out of her life. Where was he now? Did he even realize that his brave actions successfully brought down a large smuggling ring, or did he return to the insular world of his small Caribbean island without hearing about any of the drama that unfolded after the authorities examined Grady's laptop? Did he know that Rothschild and Nadine had been shown to be completely innocent and had both sung his praises for uncovering the insidious smuggling ring at great personal expense? Alexa had spent a lot of time pondering these questions, but mostly, she filled the lonely hours of her existence wondering if José missed her the same way she missed him.

"Yeah, he was there," she finally answered, her eyes downcast. Fittingly, the radio was playing a melancholy song about the demise of a romance. For the first time in her life, Alexa felt like she really understood it—the mournful melody and lamenting lyrics all made sense. She felt it resonating in the core of her being.

"What happened?" Laurie asked sympathetically. "I can tell something went wrong. Did you break up?"

Alexa hesitated to answer. Her heart was feeling heavier than ever. She felt like she was going to burst into tears if she tried to talk about it. "I don't know," she said still staring at the floor. "I don't even know what happened or why. It's just that everything got screwed up somehow."

"What happened?" Laurie asked again, her voice brimming with concern and curiosity.

When Alexa finally looked up from the floor to face her friend, she saw someone approaching them. It was Doug.

"Hey Alexa, ready for some wheatgrass juice?" Doug asked, his face lighting up with a mischievous grin.

Alexa managed a weak smile and a nod in return.

"Good, I'll go get us one. You'll like it better this time, I promise. Do you want one too, Laurie?"

"No, thanks," Laurie replied, turning to look at Alexa with wide-eyed surprise. As soon as Doug walked away, Laurie peppered her with questions. "What's going on? Are you guys an item?" she asked in a hushed tone that couldn't mask her excitement.

Alexa shrugged. "I don't know," she said nonchalantly.

"*I* think that you are," she said, "I can just tell." Laurie grinned and spontaneously gave her friend another hug. "Alexa, this is going to catapult your popularity into the stratosphere! We all know that Doug's going to be homecoming king...and that means you'll be queen. Your coronation[994] is just around the corner—I can feel it!"

Alexa snickered at Laurie's prediction, but she didn't really believe it, given the fickle[995] nature of popularity contests. "Half the people don't even bother to vote in those stupid contests, so the winner is just arbitrary[996]. Besides, you know I don't care about stuff like that," she said.

"Yeah, right! Whether you care or not, I think it's going to happen," Laurie said in a singsong, teasing voice. "And," she added pointedly, "it's not true that people don't bother voting for homecoming king and queen. The voting takes place right during fifth period when everyone is at school. The entire student body is enfranchised[997]—everyone has a vote and a voice. So when you're sitting on that throne, don't forget all of the little people who helped you get there," she teased. "Or better yet, can you have Doug introduce me to some of his friends on the lacrosse team?" she asked hopefully.

"I'll see what I can do," Alexa laughed, watching Doug walk up to them carrying two small paper cups.

"Here you go," he said, flashing his famous smile.

---

[994] **Coronation:** the act of crowning a new sovereign
[995] **Fickle:** erratic changeableness in affections or attachments
[996] **Arbitrary:** determined by chance rather than necessity or reason
[997] **Enfranchised:** to endow with the privileges of citizenship, especially the right to vote

Alexa felt the slimy green liquid on her tongue. It was true...it did taste better than the first time. It tasted bittersweet, a mixed blessing, part good and part bad, just the way she was feeling about her life at that very moment. Yes, it was true that the most popular boy at Ithaca High School had fallen for her, but she couldn't help but wonder about what might have been.

Her mind kept returning to Tikal, searching for the reasons why things turned out so differently than she had hoped. She wondered what would have happened if she had been brave during the moments when she'd acted so cautiously. What would have happened if she had told José that she stood behind him 100 percent and supported his decision to refuse the tainted scholarship? What if she had offered to help him find a new scholarship instead of resigning herself to the fact that he was not going to come to the United States? In retrospect, things began to look crystal clear. Alexa knew that she had given up on José and the whole hope of being together when it became evident that he was going to lose his scholarship. Even though the two of them hadn't expressly discussed breaking up, he had sensed her lack of commitment to him and they had ended up going their separate ways. Finally, she felt like she was beginning to understand what had happened.

Alexa had the distinct sensation that she was letting life happen *to* her rather than grasping it by the horns, the way that José did. He always thought about his goal and then he committed himself to it. Alexa wondered if perhaps the reason why she liked José so much was because she wanted to be more like him. It was intoxicating to be around him because he had so much strength of purpose. When they were together, *his* all-consuming goals effectively masked the fact that she hadn't set her own.

Alexa fingered the delicate white seashell bracelet on her wrist and decided that it was time to stop thinking wistfully[998] about the past. Senior year was starting imminently and it was time to think about the future. She downed the last sip of wheatgrass juice in one decisive swig and gave Doug a smile. He was a good friend, but that was all. Because deep down, when she thought about what she really wanted from life, it wasn't the safe and easy path. Her true goal in life didn't consist of winning a popularity contest or being someone else's good-luck charm. In fact, her real dream wasn't anywhere to be found in Ithaca, New York.

The persistent dream that was growing within her involved becoming a marine biologist and seeing the world, especially the oceans. She wanted to know more about the mysterious sea creatures that lived below the surface. She wanted to go scuba diving in exotic locations and study dolphins in their natural habitat. She wanted to learn more about the ecology of the ocean and find a way to make a positive contribution to the preservation of the marine environment.

Alexa heard her mother's voice echoing in her mind, telling her to study for the SATs and prepare for her future. Alexa had gotten so tired of hearing this hackneyed[999] advice that she had completely discounted its merit. But now, she was beginning to change her mind. Studying wasn't about dutifully obeying her parents' wishes, she realized. It was all about making your own goals a reality.

Alexa crushed the little paper cup in her hand and threw it into the garbage can several feet away. The wadded wet cup landed squarely in the middle of the open receptacle.

"Hey, great shot!" Doug said admiringly, wadding up his own empty cup and aiming to toss it into the trash with hers. But his shot fell

---

[998] **Wistful:** full of wishful yearning or desire, often tinged with melancholy
[999] **Hackneyed:** excessively familiar through overuse; trite, banal

short and the cup bounced off the rim of the receptacle. "Oh..." he groaned loudly, his face turning red. He looked at Alexa sheepishly. "A couple of us guys are going to the lake today for a swim," he said. "Do you two want to come?"

"No thanks," Alexa said. "I have to go—I'm spending the day studying for the SATs. I'll see you guys later," she said turning to leave.

Laurie came running after her. "Are you crazy?" she asked irately as soon as they were out the door. "You *must* be crazy, because you just snubbed him, not to mention the fact that you just ruined a perfect opportunity to introduce me to his friends." Laurie let out an exasperated sigh. "He's not going to ask you out again after that little scene. I can't believe that you gave him such a lame excuse! Who studies during summer break?"

"I do," Alexa said confidently, striding purposefully down the sidewalk. "I'm going to study all morning, and then in the afternoon I'm going to write an e-mail to José and spend some time scouring the Internet for scholarships that he can apply for. He lost his scholarship and I want to help him find a new one."

"But what about Doug?" she asked incredulously. "He likes you!"

Alexa shrugged. "I know, but that doesn't mean I'm automatically going to feel the same way about him, despite the fact that he is popular and all that. The truth is that I still like José, and I'm not ready to let go of the dream that someday we could be together at the same college. But if I'm going to make that happen, I'm going to have to help find him a new scholarship, and I have to study for the SATs. I'm never going to get into a marine biology program if I don't improve my score, so it's really important that I study and give it my best shot."

"Well, I hope your lofty ambitions come true, because the reality of the situation now is that you've just abdicated[1000] the throne—the throne reserved for the homecoming queen," Laurie joked.

Alexa laughed at her friend's wisecrack and then quickened her pace on the sidewalk, heading for home. With every determined step, she felt her dreams coming closer to fruition.

[1000] **Abdicate:** to formally give up a high office or responsibility, especially that of a monarch

Exercises

The exercises presented here are designed to reinforce the vocabulary presented in *The Mayan Mission* and allow you to test your retention. The first section, *Tricky Twosomes*, presents troublesome pairs such as *inimical* and *inimitable*—vocabulary words that look similar at first glance but have vastly different meanings. The *Tricky Twosome* section will walk you through these challenging vocabulary words by providing the definition as well as an example of how they are used in context. Test your retention with the fill-in-the-blank questions that follow each pair of words.

The *Hot Topics for SAT Vocabulary* reviews some of the more challenging vocabulary words by topic. Rather than looking at mind-numbing lists and endless definitions, *Hot Topics* provides a more meaningful way for you to review these words and improve your retention. Each subject review is followed by questions to test your burgeoning vocabulary.

The *Chapter Review* section has 100 questions that are organized by chapter and correspond to the vocabulary presented in *The Mayan Mission*. If you like to test your vocabulary retention while you are reading the novel, this section will allow you to take a short test at the end of each chapter. Alternatively, this section may be tackled after reading the entire novel. If you have trouble with the questions in a particular chapter, you may want to think about rereading a given chapter or consulting the Vocabulary List to review the definitions.

Tricky Twosomes

These pairs of challenging SAT words look deceptively similar, but their meanings are distinct. Each Tricky Twosome that follows is incorporated into a sentence. When reading the sentences (*in italics*), practice gleaning the meaning of the vocabulary words from the context. Then, check yourself with the definitions provided, and finally, test your retention by filling in the blank with one of the Tricky Twosomes. To see how you did, turn to the Answers section.

Ascetic   Aesthetic

*The **ascetic** monks were devoted to spiritual enlightenment. They were not concerned with the **aesthetics** of the monastery and spent little effort on its beautification.*

An **ascetic** is one who renounces material comforts and practices self-denial, usually in the context of enhancing his or her spiritualism. The word **aesthetic** concerns beauty and the appreciation of beauty and good taste.

Question 1: When the architect accepted the job of designing a new art museum, he knew that the _____ qualities of the building would be of paramount importance.

Adverse   Avarice

*After performing in her first starring role on stage, Clarissa was crushed by the **adverse** reviews in the paper the next day. She didn't care about the fat paycheck in her pocket—she didn't have a trace of **avarice**—she just wanted people to like her.*

Adverse is something that is unfavorable, difficult, or contrary to one's interests. **Avarice** is an excessive desire for wealth; greediness.

Question 2: Although it was challenging to preach about the evils of _____ to a congregation comprised primarily of wealthy businessmen, Father McDougal managed to capture their attention with a poignant story about a greedy merchant.

Blandish   Brandish

*The weary samurai was initially quite reluctant to go into battle again, but the emperor **blandished** him so relentlessly that he ceded the emperor's wishes. He charged into battle and the enemy cowered in fear when the samurai **brandished** his sword.*

To **blandish** is to cajole or coax someone by flattery or wheedling. To **brandish** is to wave or flourish something menacingly, usually a weapon of some sort.

Question 3: _____ by Seth's charms, Gwen agreed to go to the movies with him.

Commensurate   Commiserate

*In the sentencing phase of the trial, the judge felt compelled to dole out a punishment that was **commensurate** with the crime. But the tragic circumstances of the perpetrator's upbringing made the judge want to **commiserate** with him.*

Commensurate is a way of describing things that are the same size as each other or are proportionate in extent or degree. When you **commiserate**, you express sorrow or pity for someone; you sympathize with that person.

Question 4: On the day that Sarah lost her dog to a tragic car accident, a group of her friends stopped by to _____ with her.

Compliment   Complement

*Jason showered the chef with **compliments** about the creative feast she had prepared. He particularly liked the way that the tartness of the lemon vinaigrette **complemented** the asparagus salad.*

A **compliment** is an expression of praise or admiration. When something **complements** another, it completes it, makes it whole, or brings it to perfection.

Question 5: Judy sold copious quantities of anti-virus software packages by telling her clients that the product would _____ their existing software.

Compliant   Complicit

*The students at the boarding school were generally **compliant** with the behavioral guidelines set by the principal. But a glaring exception was discovered when several students were found to be **complicit** in a drug ring that operated on campus.*

Compliant means disposed or willing to comply—to act in accordance with someone else's rules or direction. When somebody participates in or is associated with a crime or questionable act, they are **complicit**.

Question 6: The prisoner-abuse scandal at the Abu Ghraib Prison led many to question if the administration was _____ with torture in Iraq.

Congenial   Congenital

*The **congenial** doctor immediately set her young patient at ease with her warm smile and gentle mannerisms. After chatting with her patient for a few minutes, she finally listened to his errant heartbeat, a **congenital** abnormality that had plagued him since the day he was born.*

Congenial describes a disposition that is friendly and sociable. **Congenital** refers to a condition that is present at birth.

Question 7: The _____ host of the party set all of her guests at ease with her friendly banter.

Consummate   Consecrate

After completing a pilgrimage that **consummated** *a lifelong spiritual quest, the weary but euphoric man* **consecrated** *his life to the service of the Lord.*

To **consummate** is to complete, conclude, or bring to fruition. To **consecrate** is to set something apart as sacred (*consecrate a church*) or to solemnly dedicate oneself to a goal.

Question 8: The two businessmen shook hands, silently _____ the transaction that had taken months to negotiate.

Indigent   Indigenous

Fresh produce was an unheard-of luxury for the destitute and **indigent** *inhabitants of the refugee camps.*

Given the prevalence of tomato sauce in Italian cuisine, many people are surprised to find out that the tomato plant is actually **indigenous** *to South America and wasn't brought to Italy until the sixteenth century.*

An **indigent** person is someone who is needy, poor, or destitute. An **indigenous** person is one who originates from and lives in a particular area. An **indigenous** plant occurs naturally in a particular area.

Question 9: The _____ inhabitants of the Americas succumbed to many diseases when the European settlers arrived.

Ingenious   Ingenuous

After being accused of embezzling from the firm, the stockbroker was unable to invent an **ingenious** *explanation for the missing funds. Instead, he* **ingenuously** *admitted succumbing to greed.*

An **ingenious** person or idea is inventive, clever, or cunning. An **ingenuous** person has difficulty hiding his or her feelings; he or she has a lack of guile, deviousness, or deceptiveness.

Question 10: The _____ money-laundering scheme was the most complex and effective deception that the officers had ever seen.

Inimical   Inimitable

*The workers at the chemical factory always put on a protective suit before entering the **inimical** environment of the production facility.*

*Griffin's **inimitable** sense of humor was truly unique.*

Inimical describes something that is injurious or harmful in effect. **Inimitable** describes something that defies imitation or copying; it's matchless.

Question 11: During her six-week stay at the drug rehabilitation center, Jenna was taught the tools to curb her _____ habits.

Obstreperous   Obsequious

*The **obstreperous** child kicked and screamed, stubbornly defying his mother's attempts to strap him into his car seat.*

*When the famous movie star stepped into the humble restaurant, the **obsequious** waiter fawned over him incessantly, never leaving him alone for a minute.*

Obstreperous describes behavior that is noisily and stubbornly defiant. **Obsequious** behavior is characterized by fawning attentiveness or servile compliance.

Question 12: Throughout the shooting of the film, the director was always flanked by his _____ assistant, who was ready to fetch a cup of coffee at a moment's notice.

Palette   Palate

*The artist set down his paintbrush and **palette** to take a lunch break, but when he took a look at the buffet, nothing appealed to his **palate**.*

A **palette** refers to the flat board that artists sometimes hold while painting and use to mix paint colors. The **palate** is the sense of taste. When something is appealing to eat, it is **palatable**.

Question 13: It was George's insatiable appetite and discriminating _____ that attracted him to the position of restaurant critic for the Chicago newspaper.

Perfidious   Penurious

*After signing the treaty to great fanfare, the rogue government deliberately violated its tenets, committing a **perfidious** act that alienated the people.*

*After fulfilling a lifelong dream of moving to Los Angeles to pursue an acting career, the penniless man embraced the **penurious** lifestyle of the struggling artist when he finally arrived in California.*

A **perfidious** act or person deliberately violates trust and is characterized by betrayal and treachery. **Penurious** is poverty-stricken or destitute. It can also describe someone who is stingy and reluctant to spend money.

Question 14: Oftentimes teenage runaways end up on the streets, living in appalling, _____ circumstances that they didn't foresee.

Perspicacity   Pernicious

*Even though Ebola outbreaks are exceedingly rare, the young doctor had the **perspicacity** to diagnose the early symptoms of this **pernicious** viral infection.*

Perspicacity is keen perception, acute discernment, and the capacity to assess situations shrewdly. Something that is exceedingly harmful, injurious, or deadly is **pernicious**.

Question 15: The shrewd businessman knew that negotiating a deal with his biggest competitor was going to require both _____ and perseverance.

Proscribe   Prescribe

*Although the use of drugs in school was specifically **proscribed**, exceptions were made for students who had a particular medication **prescribed** by their doctor.*

Proscribe is to denounce, condemn, or prohibit. **Prescribe** is to order the use of a particular medication or treatment.

Question 16: In order to foster a nurturing environment in their home, Dan's parents _____ all movies and television shows that contained violence.

Prodigious   Prodigal

*The **prodigious** mansion was so grand in scale that it awed even the most jaded real estate agents. Its twenty-three bedrooms, three swimming pools, and lavish décor throughout were perfectly suited to a wealthy buyer who wanted to live a **prodigal** lifestyle.*

Prodigious is something that is impressively great in size or extent. **Prodigal** is excessively or wastefully extravagant.

Question 17: The movie star's _____ lifestyle ultimately led him to accumulate a massive debt that he could never repay.

Prurient   Puritan

*Henry's **prurient** thoughts gave him great cause for guilt and shame. The **puritan** values of his small-town upbringing were deeply ingrained within him.*

Prurient is characterized by lust or an inordinate interest in sex. The **Puritans** were a group of English Protestants living in the sixteenth and seventeenth centuries who advocated strict religious discipline. As an adjective, **puritan** means morally strict and opposed to sensual pleasures.

Question 18: The concerned parents installed a parental lock software package on their computer in order to prohibit their young children from accessing the _____ websites on the Internet.

Sophomoric   Soporific

*After discovering the pine cone on his chair, the professor scowled at his students for pulling such a **sophomoric** prank.*

*Even though Jenny was having trouble sleeping at night, she was reluctant to take any type of **soporific** agent.*

Sophomoric means to show great immaturity or lack of judgment. **Soporific** describes something that induces sleep.

Question 19: When the group of young mothers assembled to discuss the best way to encourage their infants to go to sleep at night, the _____ effect of warm milk was touted by several of them.

Tenuous   Tenable   Trenchant

*Sara was reluctant to face her parents after she missed her curfew, because she knew that her **tenuous** excuse—she forgot to look at her watch—wouldn't get her off the hook. She wished that she had a **tenable** excuse—something that was reasonable and defensible, like a flat tire. After carefully considering what she was going to say, Sara presented a **trenchant** argument that convinced her parents to forgive her transgression and relax the stringent curfew they had imposed last year.*

Tenuous describes something that is flimsy or thin. **Tenable** describes something that is rationally defensible and capable of being maintained in an argument. **Trenchant** describes something that is forceful, vigorous, and effective.

Question 20: The prosecuting attorney was eager to cross-examine the witness. He knew that the witness' explanation of the events was not _____ and would fall apart when challenged.

Tortuous   Torturous

*The bus driver went as fast as he dared on the **tortuous** highway that wound its way up the mountainside. Fred, who always succumbed to motion sickness, found the constant turning to be **torturous** on his delicate stomach.*

Tortuous describes something that is winding, twisting, or has repeated turns. **Torturous** describes something that is extremely painful or related to torture.

Question 21: The _____ trail through the forest caused many of the hikers to become confused about their orientation.

Vindicate   Vindictive

*When the "not guilty" verdict was announced, Bart was thankful that he was finally **vindicated**. He felt like lashing out at his accusers in order to seek revenge, but he managed to suppress his **vindictive** urges.*

To **vindicate** is to clear of all suspicion, blame, or doubt with supporting proof. A **vindictive** person or act is concerned with seeking revenge.

Question 22: When he was fired from his job as a computer programmer, David couldn't resist his _____ desires and he unleashed a computer virus in the company's network.

Hot Topics for SAT Vocabulary

There are certain topics that are chock-full of challenging SAT vocabulary words. Below, these words are grouped by subject matter and cursory definitions are provided in the Hot Topic summaries (for complete definitions, see the Vocabulary List section). You've seen these vocabulary words in the text of *The Mayan Mission*, but they're reviewed again here in a different context as an additional learning aid. Read the "Hot Topics" to refresh your memory of these vocabulary words and then test your retention with the sentence completion questions below. To see how you did, turn to the Answers section.

Law

Litigation is a legal proceeding in a court of law. A **litigant** is a party who is engaged in a lawsuit. When a lawsuit is filed, one party **alleges** that the other party has done something unlawful—they make an **allegation**, which is an assertion that is not proven. During the course of the trial, the prosecution will try to prove that the **allegations** are true by providing supporting evidence. They will try to prove that the defendant (the person defending himself from the allegations) is **culpable**, meaning that he is deserving of blame.

The defendant's attorney will try to **refute** the allegations and provide **exculpatory** evidence—evidence that will clear the defendant from blame. The defense attorney will try to **rebut** the prosecution's argument by providing an opposing argument. If the defendant is ultimately cleared of blame, you could say that he has been **absolved** of guilt or that he has been **vindicated, exonerated,** or **exculpated.**

Each side tries to amass a **preponderance** of evidence that proves their stance, so that they will **prevail** (to be greater in strength or effectiveness). They will try to present convincing, conclusive evidence, as opposed to **conjecture** or **speculation,** both of which describe a conclusion or opinion based on guesswork or inconclusive evidence.

If the defendant is proven guilty, the law may stipulate **punitive** measures—something that punishes. The law defines the appropriate **retribution** for particular crimes. For example, the offender may be sent to jail or required to pay **restitution** to his victims. But if the judge shows **clemency,** this means that the judge is merciful or lenient in doling out the punishment and he may shorten the jail sentence.

If the offender feels remorse for his misdeeds, he may try to **atone** for his crime in some way. For example, he might make a heartfelt speech saying that he is sorry for his actions. To **atone** is to make amends for.

1. Jerry adamantly proclaimed his innocence when his mother accused him of taking the whole pan of brownies. But it wasn't until the family dog appeared, his furry face smeared with chocolate, that Jerry was finally _____.

   A. atoned

   B. culpable

   C. litigated

   D. negated

   E. vindicated

2. When the suspect revealed that he had an airtight alibi for the night of the robbery, the police officer knew that this man couldn't possibly be _____ .

   A. vindicated
   B. absolved
   C. exculpated
   D. exonerated
   E. culpable

3. The solid DNA evidence presented at the trial was _____ and consequently, the accused was exonerated of the crime.

   A. exculpatory
   B. punitive
   C. culpable
   D. conjecture
   E. restitution

4. The _____ murderer watched the jury file into the court-room and nervously waited to hear if they would pronounce him guilty or innocent of the heinous crime.

   A. vindicated
   B. exonerated
   C. alleged
   D. culpable
   E. prevailing

Fighting Words

What do you do when you are really mad at someone and you want to express it? If you're just a little bit angry and you want to scold the person mildly, you might **chide** him, **admonish** him, or give him a **reproving** glance. If harsh criticism is in order, you might **censure** him. **Censure** is also an appropriate way of expressing strong disapproval in an official capacity or formal setting, such as in government.

If you feel like scolding someone severely, you could **vituperate**, **berate**, or **upbraid** the person. These are all ways of **rebuking** someone when you feel that he or she has done you wrong.

If your anger is extreme—you're really **livid** and you feel like using some harsh language to express your anger—you might give the person some **vitriolic** criticism. You might feel like delivering an **invective** that **rails** against his behavior and **castigates** him for his misdeeds.

If you feel like you want to start a fight, you might describe it as feeling **antagonistic** or **truculent**. If you always feel like you want to fight and you're **belligerent** and combative in nature, you might describe yourself as **pugnacious**. If you're easily angered and prone to outbursts of temper, you are **irascible**. If you're quarrelsome in nature, you are **contentious**.

But be careful—you might start an **altercation** (a noisy quarrel) that escalates into a full-fledged **conflagration**. A **conflagration** is a disastrous fire or other event, such as a conflict or war.

5. Kathy didn't want to be too critical of her son's first attempt to write a story, but she did want to gently _____ him for revealing several embarrassing family secrets.
   A. vituperate
   B. admonish
   C. antagonize
   D. congratulate
   E. praise

6. In the history of the United States, several presidents, including Polk, Jackson, and Clinton, have been _____ by Congress for their various misdeeds.
   A. censured
   B. extolled
   C. lauded
   D. lavished
   E. venerated

7. What started out as a small forest fire quickly grew into a large and destructive _____.
   A. altercation
   B. aesthetic
   C. complement
   D. conflagration
   E. invective

Demeanor and Styles of Speaking

There are many ways of describing how someone speaks. An **inarticulate** person has trouble speaking clearly or even speaking at all. **Laconic** speech is terse, concise, and uses very few words. Conversely, **verbose** speech is wordy and uses an excessive number of words. A **loquacious** person is very talkative. A roundabout expression that is unnecessarily wordy is described as a **circumlocution**.

A **cordial** person is friendly. A **convivial** person likes to party and socialize. A **nonchalant** person acts indifferent or coolly unconcerned. An **aloof** person acts reserved or remote.

A long, angry, or violent speech is a **tirade**.

An **eloquent** speaker expresses himself clearly and effectively. But a **grandiloquent** speaker is **pompous** or **bombastic**, which means ostentatiously lofty or pretentious in style. **Haughty** describes arrogant superiority, looking down on other people or views with disdain. **Imperious** is arrogant assurance, a domineering, dictatorial style. Someone who jokes a lot is **jocular**.

A **trite** or **hackneyed** saying has become too familiar through overuse and has lost the power to evoke interest.

A person who is insincerely earnest is **unctuous**. An **obsequious** person is attentive or fawning in an ingratiating manner. A person who flatters influential people in order to get what he wants from them can be described as a **sycophant** or a **toady**.

8. The congressional candidate gave a(n)_____ speech that alienated the voters, most of whom detested such bombastic rhetoric.

A. laconic

B. cordial

C. convivial

D. grandiloquent

E. eloquent

9. Jerry tried to act _____ when he asked Belinda to go to the prom, but he couldn't hide his trepidation.

A. trite

B. nonchalant

C. hackneyed

D. inarticulate

E. verbose

10. The glamorous movie star knew that her dress was terribly unflattering, despite the fact that everyone in her entourage kept telling her it looked marvelous. She realized that she was surrounded by _____ who would take every opportunity to flatter her.

A. sycophants

B. circumlocutions

C. pompous people

D. laconic people

E. nonchalant people

11. The egotistical rock star swaggered into the club and headed straight to the V.I.P. section on the upper level, where he looked down at the regular folks with an air of _____disdain.

A. toady

B. loquacious

C. haughty

D. eloquent

E. trite

Money

There are several ways of describing someone who is poor and needy. An **impecunious** person is penniless and doesn't have the money for necessities. If a person is experiencing extreme poverty and destitution, he is living in **penury, privation,** or **indigence. Penurious** can mean impoverished, or it can also be used to describe someone who is stingy and unwilling to spend money.

A **frugal** person is very thrifty and careful to avoid waste. A **parsimonious** person is **frugal** to the point of stinginess.

Someone who likes to plan and save for the future is **provident.** Someone who is recklessly extravagant is **prodigal.**

People who are greedy and have an inordinate desire for wealth have **cupidity** or **avarice.**

12. Jeff's insatiable _____ was not lessened in the slightest by the fortune he had already amassed.
    A. penury
    B. privation
    C. indigence
    D. provident
    E. cupidity

13. Living in _____ for much of her childhood gave Alisha a profound appreciation for the simple pleasures in life, such as a warm meal and a clean bed.
    A. privation
    B. cupidity
    C. avarice
    D. wealth
    E. luxury

14. The _____ habits of the Indian tribe were evidenced by the ample supply of food that was stored away for winter.
    A. impecunious
    B. penurious
    C. prodigal
    D. provident
    E. complicit

The Future

Sometimes people describe the future as **nebulous**, meaning that it's vague or unformed. But quite a few SAT vocabulary words describe predicting the future in some fashion. For example, a **prescient** prediction or a **prescient** person has knowledge of events before they occur. A **clairvoyant** has the ability to see objects and events that can't be perceived by the senses.

When there is a sign that indicates or warns about the future, it **presages** or **portends** something that is going to occur. For example, a **harbinger** is something that foreshadows what is to come. Sometimes, these signs about the future are **auspicious** or **propitious**, both of which indicate favorable circumstances or good luck. A favorable sign **augurs** well for the future. Conversely, an **inauspicious** sign is unfavorable, like a bad omen.

Prophecy is a prediction of the future that is viewed as a revelation of divine will. It is generally used in the context of an inspired vision of the future, such as when the **prophets** of biblical times were reportedly inspired by God to predict the future. The book of Revelation, last book of the Bible, is full of colorful and dreamlike **prophesies** concerning the end of the world. If someone in modern times utters a prediction of the future in a manner that suggests divine inspiration, you could say that the person's words are **prophetic**.

15. When John predicted that a devastating tornado was going to touch down in their small community, no one believed him. When his prediction came true, the townspeople were sorry they hadn't listened to his _____ words.

    A. nebulous
    B. prophetic
    C. auspicious
    D. propitious
    E. inconclusive

16. When Jason found a penny on the sidewalk, he interpreted it as a(n) _____ of good things to come.

    A. harbinger
    B. clairvoyant
    C. nebulous
    D. inauspicious sign
    E. ominous sign

17. The wildly inflated stock prices _____ a disastrous market crash.

    A. portended
    B. nonplused
    C. oscillated
    D. pontificated
    E. proselytized

Friendly and Unfriendly

There are subtle shades of meaning among these adjectives (see the Vocabulary List for more complete definitions), but basically all of the following words describe someone who is acting friendly and warm: **amicable, amiable, affable, congenial, genial**, and **cordial**.

Someone who is **convivial** enjoys a good party—the person is sociable and fond of feasting, drinking, and merrymaking.

But it is hard to be friendly when you are feeling **animosity, acrimony,** or **enmity**—all expressions of bitter hatred. **Aversion** and **antipathy** describe a feeling of repugnance—a strong feeling of dislike and/or desire to avoid something unpleasant.

18. The deep-seated _____ between the two tribes was destined to culminate in a ferocious battle.
    A. geniality
    B. congeniality
    C. cupidity
    D. avarice
    E. enmity

19. After experiencing food poisoning from eating linguine with clam sauce, Lisa developed a strong _____ shellfish, and she hasn't eaten any since.
    A. affinity for
    B. aversion to
    C. reverence for
    D. ardor for
    E. partiality for

20. The leaders of the two warring tribes were able to set aside their mutual _____ long enough to sit down at the negotiation table and strike a deal for peace.
    A. respect
    B. affinity
    C. antipathy
    D. rapport
    E. repose

Religion

The belief in a **divine** power, a God or Gods, is called **theism**. Conversely, the lack of a belief in God(s) is called **atheism**. An **agnostic** thinks that it is impossible to know whether there is a God or not.

Someone who has a religious devotion and reverence to God is **pious**. A person who tries to induce others to join his religious faith is **proselytizing** his religion. A **missionary proselytizes** his faith typically by traveling to a foreign country to convert others to his faith and/or to do charitable work.

The **clergy** are people who have been ordained for religious service. For example, a priest or a minister is a member of the **clergy**.

To **consecrate** is to set apart as sacred, or to solemnly dedicate one-self to a particular goal. To **desecrate** is to violate the sacredness of some-thing: *The townspeople gathered to **consecrate** the new church. The prison guards **desecrated** the inmate's Bible when they threw it in the toilet.* Something that is set apart as holy or sacred is **hallowed**: *the hallowed ground of the ancient burial site.* The act of setting something apart as sacred is to **sanctify**.

When a person feels remorse for his sins or misdeeds, he is **repentant**. A related word is **penitence**, which also describes the condition of being **penitent**—feeling regret for wrongdoing. Another synonym is **contrition**, which again describes a feeling of regret for one's sins or misdeeds. **Compunction** is a strong feeling of uneasiness caused by a sense of guilt.

21. The Native American tribe was horrified to see their sacred burial ground _____ by the building of a new mall right on top of it.
    A. consecrated
    B. hallowed
    C. sanctified
    D. desecrated
    E. divined

22. The famous movie star was so excited about her controversial religion that she seized every public forum as an opportunity to _____.

    A. desecrate
    B. consecrate
    C. proselytize
    D. sanctify
    E. repent

23. The convicted burglar showed such _____ for his misdeeds that he managed to engender the sympathy of everyone in the courtroom.

    A. desecration
    B. contrition
    C. agnosticism
    D. theism
    E. plaudits

Medicine

When a person falls down and gets cuts and bruises, you could describe the injuries as **lacerations** (cuts) and **contusions** (bruises). Lacerations break the surface of the skin and typically involve bleeding. When the blood clots, it **coagulates,** meaning that it transforms from a liquid into a solid.

A **congenital** condition is present at birth, as opposed to something that develops later in life. A **virulent** disease is extremely infectious. A doctor might **prescribe** a medication to combat the disease. If pain is involved, a doctor might recommend an **analgesic** to counteract the pain. If poison is involved, the doctor might prescribe an **antidote** to counteract it. An **elixir** is a substance with the power to cure all ills. An **elixir** can also describe the sweet syrup that is used as a vehicle for medicine, hiding its unpleasant flavor.

Lassitude is a condition of weariness or listlessness.

24. When her sister came down with a _____ strain of the flu, Alyssa rushed her to the doctor's office.

    A. congenital

    B. virulent

    C. analgesic

    D. coagulating

    E. benevolent

25. When Fred fell out of the tree and suffered multiple lacerations and contusions, his doctor recommended an over-the-counter _____ to counteract the pain.

    A. antidote

    B. analgesic

    C. elixir

    D. coagulation

    E. congenital

26. On her 30th birthday, Velma felt lonely, sick, depressed, and miserable. She wished that there existed a(n) _____ that she could take to cure all of her ills.

    A. elixir

    B. analgesic

    C. coagulation

    D. laceration

    E. contusion

Politics and Government

A **monarchy** is a government that is ruled by a **monarch**, such as a king or queen, who typically inherits the position and keeps it for life. The act or ceremony of crowning a new **monarch** is called a **coronation**. **Nobility** refers to a privileged class in some societies that hold hereditary titles, such as dukes, duchesses, etc. **Ignoble** describes something that is characteristic of commoners, not of the **nobility**.

A **despot** is a ruler who has absolute power and wields that power oppressively. A **demagogue** is a leader who gains power or stirs up the people by appealing to the passions and prejudices of his audience.

Hegemony is the influence or domination of one state over another.

A **lobby** is a group of people who have organized to try to influence legislators in favor of a particular cause: *The agricultural lobby has been very powerful in convincing Congress to maintain price supports for dairy products.*

A **pacifist** believes that disputes should be resolved peacefully, without resorting to violence or war. A **utopia** is an ideally perfect place (often imaginary), particularly with respect to its social and political aspects. **Utopia** often refers to an idealistic, impractical ideal for society.

To **enfranchise** is to endow with the rights of citizenship. It is most commonly used in the context of the right to vote. To be **enfranchised** is to have the right to vote, while conversely, to be **disenfranchised** is to be deprived of the right to vote: *The suffragettes worked tirelessly to enfranchise American women.*

27. A consummate _____, the leader of the rogue government rapidly rose to power following a series of speeches that appealed to the people's deep-seated desire for a religious state and played on their fear of foreign influences on their society.

    A. pacifist

    B. demagogue

    C. monarch

    D. lobbyist

    E. elixir

28. The widespread influence of Hellenistic culture in the Mediterranean came to an end with the rise of Roman _____.

    A. pacifists

    B. utopia

    C. hegemony

    D. lobbyists

    E. coagulates

29. After suffering through two years of unemployment, Harriet was ready to take any job, even jobs she had in the past considered to be _____.
   A. enfranchised
   B. disenfranchised
   C. despot
   D. ignoble
   E. noble

Indulgence

Both **prodigal** and **profligate** describes someone who is recklessly extravagant. The person spends money or uses resources in a wild, wasteful manner. A **glutton** is prone to overindulgence or greediness in the consumption of food or drink. By contrast, an **abstemious** person eats and drinks in moderation. **Temperance** is moderation in behavior and avoidance of excess. **Temperance** can also be used to describe restraint or **abstinence** from alcoholic beverages. When someone **abstains** from something, the person is refraining from it by choice.

Abnegation is self-denial—limiting or restraining one's own desires. An **ascetic** is someone who renounces material comforts and practices self-denial, usually in the context of enhancing his or her spiritualism.

30. When Mrs. Lee opened the credit card bill, she immediately called her _____ daughter at her dorm room and threatened to cancel her card if the extravagant expenditures didn't stop immediately.
   A. profligate
   B. abstemious
   C. ascetic
   D. abnegating
   E. frugal

31. Upon opening the refrigerator and finding that an entire birthday cake and a six-pack of beer had disappeared in the middle of the night, Jack concluded that his new roommate lacked _____.

   A. gluttony
   B. indulgence
   C. profligate tendencies
   D. prodigal habits
   E. temperance

32. Jim's _____ eating habits kept his weight down to a healthy level.

   A. profligate
   B. prodigal
   C. abstemious
   D. extravagant
   E. capricious

Walking

There are a handful of SAT vocabulary words that describe different ways of walking. To **scurry** and to **scamper** both mean to go with light running steps. To **traipse** is to walk or tramp about. To **trudge** or to **plod** both mean to walk in a laborious, heavy-footed way. To **swagger** is to walk or conduct oneself with a proud, arrogant air.

33. When he was announced as most valuable player, Seth _____ up to the stage like a proud peacock to accept his prize.

   A. trudged
   B. plodded
   C. swaggered
   D. dissolved
   E. diffused

34. The frightened squirrel _____ up the tree trunk when it saw us coming.
    A. swaggered
    B. strutted
    C. plodded
    D. trudged
    E. scurried

Chemistry

Sugar is **soluble** in water. This means that it can be dissolved to form a solution. When you add a teaspoon of sugar to a glass of water and stir it until it dissolves, it will form a solution of sweet water. In this example, the water is acting as the **solvent**, the liquid in which a substance is dissolved, and the sugar is the **solute**.

When you first add the sugar to the water, it begins to **diffuse** throughout the water. To **diffuse** means to become widely dispersed. If you add a lot of sugar to the glass of water and heat it up to help it dissolve, you may find that the sugar **precipitates** out of solution when you allow the water to cool down again. To **precipitate** is to cause a solid substance to be separated from a solution. In a more general sense, the word **precipitate** means to cause something to happen: *The mass hysteria on Wall Street **precipitated** an enormous stock market crash.*

To **catalyze** is to speed the rate of a chemical reaction by catalysis. But in a more general sense, the word **catalyze** means to bring about or initiate: *The highly publicized student protest **catalyzed** a substantive change in the university's policies.*

To **desiccate** is to dry out thoroughly.

35. Belinda knew that the paint stain on the rug wouldn't come out with water, so she hunted through the cabinet looking for a chemical _____ that could dissolve the paint.

   A. diffuser

   B. desiccator

   C. solvent

   D. precipitate

   E. coagulate

36. The newspaper article hinting at corruption within the administration _____ an investigation by the authorities.

   A. desiccated

   B. precipitated

   C. solubilized

   D. coagulated

   E. commiserated

Chapter Reviews

Selected vocabulary words from each chapter of *The Mayan Mission* are reviewed in the following sentence completion questions. For the questions below, read the entire sentence and pick the vocabulary word that best fits the sentence as a whole. To see how you did, turn to the Answers section.

Chapter 1

1. After Hank lost the family savings in a scam, his wife encouraged him to be more _____ about investing.
   A. savory
   B. flabbergasted
   C. circumspect
   D. apocryphal
   E. congenial

2. When the teacher handed out the _____assignment, all of the students groaned, because they knew that it would take them all weekend to complete it.

   A. amicable

   B. palatable

   C. disparate

   D. irreverent

   E. onerous

3. The two _____ styles, shabby and sophisticated, were awkwardly melded together in the designer's new collection.

   A. disparate

   B. pejorative

   C. prescient

   D. erudite

   E. ravenous

4. The smell of cow manure was so _____ that Daniella felt compelled to flee from the barn for a breath of fresh air.

   A. exalting

   B. banal

   C. enthralling

   D. repugnant

   E. insatiable

5. Mike made a(n) _____ prediction about the effectiveness of a new drug that was later substantiated by dozens of clinical trials.

   A. pejorative

   B. prescient

   C. despondent

   D. penchant

   E. antiquated

6. Harry's _____ for the high life has left him with a massive debt.
   - A. ambivalence
   - B. indifference
   - C. predilection
   - D. nonchalance
   - E. repugnance

7. A(n) _____ scholar of entomology, Belinda had read every book about bugs that was published in the last decade.
   - A. erudite
   - B. philanthropist
   - C. waning
   - D. pungent
   - E. amicable

8. In order to _____ her guilty feelings, Jenny wrote a long letter of apology.
   - A. stupefy
   - B. procure
   - C. relish
   - D. assuage
   - E. enthrall

Chapter 2

9. The spacious master bedroom has a(n) _____ bathroom with three sinks, an oversize hot tub, and plenty of floor space to move about.
   - A. rational
   - B. commodious
   - C. epistolary
   - D. fastidious
   - E. utilitarian

10. The documentary focuses on Darren, a(n) _____ orphan who struggles to escape the suffocating veil of poverty.

    A. euphoric

    B. wealthy

    C. elated

    D. exorbitant

    E. impecunious

11. When Jerry was in jail, he maintained a(n) _____ relationship with his girlfriend and wrote her a long letter every single day.

    A. epistolary

    B. cosmopolitan

    C. commodious

    D. archaic

    E. vindicated

12. Patrick showed a profound disrespect for authority by _____ the direct orders of his supervisor and consequently, he was expelled from the military school.

    A. accommodating

    B. coveting

    C. contravening

    D. aspiring

    E. satiating

13. Howard was _____ about personal hygiene; he scrupulously washed his hands at least 20 times a day.

    A. commodious

    B. frugal

    C. provident

    D. impecunious

    E. fastidious

Chapter 3

14. The _____ story kept Jane engrossed in the novel.
    A. scintillating
    B. interminable
    C. punctilious
    D. implacable
    E. abstruse

15. After being convicted of a(n) _____ crime, the man hid his head in shame and tried to avoid the prying eyes of the assembled crowd.
    A. literal
    B. serendipitous
    C. cordial
    D. lethargic
    E. ignominious

16. Harold kept his car scrupulously clean; he vacuumed it _____ after every family outing.
    A. irrevocably
    B. supinely
    C. enigmatically
    D. meticulously
    E. adversely

17. Overcoming _____ odds, Frieda managed to win the state lottery twice.
    A. eloquent
    B. tacit
    C. insuperable
    D. scathing
    E. parsimonious

18. Jared was so _____ that he refused to spend a mere 50 cents on parking and instead, he would walk the three miles to the theater.

   A. ubiquitous

   B. grandiose

   C. nostalgic

   D. parsimonious

   E. animated

19. The _____ talents of the dance company were on full display during the sold-out show. They superbly performed every style from classical ballet to hip-hop.

   A. myriad

   B. dubious

   C. impudent

   D. elusive

   E. imperative

20. _____, Sam bought the videos for his kids, but his wife suspected otherwise when she saw how much Sam enjoyed watching the videos himself.

   A. Grievously

   B. Lethargically

   C. Ostensibly

   D. Eloquently

   E. Impudently

21. Brenda tried everything from acupuncture to hypnotism in her tireless search for a way to _____ her chronic pain.

   A. palliate

   B. speculate

   C. proselytize

   D. simulate

   E. capitulate

22. Bill's _____ remarks about his ex-wife's new husband caused a violent brawl to break out between the two men.

    A. cordial

    B. impassive

    C. enlightened

    D. caustic

    E. genial

23. After fighting with her parents for hours, Hailey finally gave up and _____ their demands.

    A. goaded

    B. capitulated to

    C. effervesced

    D. permeated

    E. proselytized

24. Gwen and her best friend were complete opposites; Gwen was animated and excited about everything, while her best friend always appeared _____.

    A. impassive

    B. zealous

    C. gregarious

    D. effervescent

    E. convivial

Chapter 4

25. The warm _____ among the students at the boarding school kept Sarah from feeling lonely.

    A. quagmire

    B. privation

    C. conundrum

    D. camaraderie

    E. hierarchy

26. When walking home alone at night, Brian was always cautious and _____ of danger.
    A. hapless
    B. wary
    C. nebulous
    D. propitious
    E. dissuaded

27. Taking a _____ from the intense stress of her job, Susan relaxed at the beach for a week.
    A. duress
    B. pittance
    C. interlocutor
    D. conundrum
    E. reprieve

28. The politician's speech was so trite and full of meaningless _____ that the audience quickly lost interest.
    A. platitudes
    B. prowess
    C. plaudits
    D. conundrums
    E. innovations

29. When Carrie's father reprimanded her, he made it clear that he didn't _____ her irresponsible behavior.
    A. discern
    B. abhor
    C. elegate
    D. condone
    E. dispatch

Chapter 5

30. When a huge traffic jam materialized at rush hour, the impatient commuters expressed their frustrations in a(n) _____ of blaring car horns.

   A. atrophy

   B. cacophony

   C. laceration

   D. commendation

   E. inequity

31. Even in the face of great hardship, Ashley was _____; she always looked at the bright side of any situation.

   A. antiseptic

   B. quiescent

   C. unnerved

   D. sanguine

   E. bashful

32. After playing on the professional tennis circuit for 10 years, George still loved to work out daily; he couldn't stand the thought of slowing down and living a _____ lifestyle.

   A. amorous

   B. swarthy

   C. cognizant

   D. luminous

   E. sedentary

33. The cartoon show depicted endless variations on the theme of a menacing cat chasing a _____ little mouse who cowered in fear.

   A. colossal

   B. timorous

   C. diaphanous

   D. evanescent

   E. enamored

34. Jared's mother tried to counsel him to respond to situations rationally and after careful thought, rather than emotionally and _____, as he was known to do.

    A. atrophied
    B. wizened
    C. impetuously
    D. scrupulously
    E. incessantly

35. Harry's gregarious behavior at the party was a big departure from his typically _____ demeanor.

    A. convivial
    B. congenial
    C. vociferous
    D. taciturn
    E. evanescent

36. Wendy felt much better after Harold apologized profusely; his sincere apology was like a _____ for her wounds.

    A. antecedent
    B. despot
    C. salve
    D. consortium
    E. cacophony

37. Trying not to say anything contentious, the talk-show host restricted her commentary to _____ generalities.

    A. innocuous
    B. forlorn
    C. indignant
    D. deprecating
    E. acute

38. When Kathy became a pacifist, she declared that she was going to adamantly _____ violence in favor of negotiation as a strategy to resolve disputes.

A. flourish

B. divine

C. elicit

D. eschew

E. dither

Chapter 6

39. The beautiful supermodel achieved spectacular international success; she was widely regarded as a woman of great _____.

A. innuendo

B. pulchritude

C. aberrations

D. macabre

E. penury

40. The school principal warned the student body that the dedication ceremony was to be a solemn, respectful event and that _____ and laughter would be inappropriate.

A. corpulence

B. aesthetics

C. mitigation

D. reconciliation

E. levity

41. Although the politician didn't expressly state anything derogatory about his opponent, the _____ was clear.

A. swagger

B. innuendo

C. fodder

D. corpulence

E. pulchritude

42. The jury was not likely to be lenient after hearing the _____ crime described in horrifying detail.

   A. aesthetic

   B. ascetic

   C. pacifist

   D. execrable

   E. jocular

Chapter 7

43. The show was so boring and repetitious that the audience was lulled into a(n) _____ state.

   A. somnolent

   B. sophomoric

   C. petulant

   D. obscure

   E. empirical

44. John shifted uneasily in his chair, _____ by the embarrassing revelation.

   A. integrated

   B. catalogued

   C. discomfited

   D. delighted

   E. foraged

45. _____ the rain, Joshua played happily in the midst of a downpour.

   A. Nocturnal in

   B. Impervious to

   C. Implicit in

   D. Insipid in

   E. Petulant in

46. After practicing basketball all day long, Harry was _____ the fact that he still was unable to make a single basket.

   A. obscured by
   B. exuberant about
   C. integrated with
   D. exasperated by
   E. clamoring for

47. Mike was so sick of the _____ chicken that was served on every flight that he decided to bring his own meal on the airplane.

   A. petulant
   B. covenant
   C. insipid
   D. theoretical
   E. vilified

Chapter 8

48. The teacher explained things in such a dull and unimaginative fashion that he managed to make even the most interesting topics seem _____.

   A. sensual
   B. sublime
   C. palpable
   D. iridescent
   E. prosaic

49. The politician's remarks were _____ and no one in the room could figure out what side of the issue he stood on.

   A. presumptuous
   B. equivocal
   C. sublime
   D. condemning
   E. palpable

50. The conditions in the nursing home were so _____ that the health inspector shut down the home.
    A. iridescent
    B. unpretentious
    C. deplorable
    D. complacent
    E. sublime

51. The short magazine article successfully managed to _____ the complexities of the difficult issue.
    A. bereft
    B. brandish
    C. coagulate
    D. encapsulate
    E. trudge

52. The _____ dark clouds in the sky presaged an ominous storm.
    A. portentous
    B. pliable
    C. profligate
    D. presumptuous
    E. lithe

53. Regretting the contentious things that she said, but unable to _____ her words, Katrina apologized profusely.
    A. encapsulate
    B. retract
    C. coagulate
    D. presage
    E. prepossess

Chapter 9

54. The _____ party was so loud and unruly that one of the neighbors called the police.

    A. analgesic

    B. apathetic

    C. compassionate

    D. raucous

    E. servile

55. The investigators _____ the cause of the fire to a faulty wire.

    A. bequeathed

    B. truncated

    C. deterred

    D. emoted

    E. imputed

56. The _____ article about the movie star was filled with derogatory statements and lies.

    A. benevolent

    B. defamatory

    C. demure

    D. compassionate

    E. ignoble

57. Thomas knew that the accusations were _____ false, so he stood up to tell everyone in the room the real truth.

    A. benevolently

    B. covertly

    C. hedonistically

    D. patently

    E. vigilantly

58. The young man led a double life; he managed to ingratiate himself into high society while hiding his _____ roots.

    A. plebeian
    B. benign
    C. ornate
    D. sagacious
    E. benevolent

59. Greg climbed the corporate ladder by constantly flattering his boss and acting like a _____.

    A. morass
    B. analgesic
    C. toady
    D. libation
    E. dirge

60. Jake's mother tried everything to get her son interested in his schoolwork and excited about learning. But despite her efforts, Jake continued to be _____ about his studies.

    A. cunning
    B. compassionate
    C. vigilant
    D. beguiled
    E. apathetic

61. Amanda was _____; she told her boss that she was content with her job, but in reality, she was busy searching for a new job.

    A. comprehensive
    B. duplicitous
    C. ignoble
    D. indomitable
    E. legitimate

62. Garry kept up a _____ of virtue, but soon everyone began to realize that this was a façade.

    A. chasm
    B. dissonance
    C. dirge
    D. pretense
    E. privy

63. When a person makes a statement that is maliciously intended to damage the reputation of another person, it is called _____.

    A. discourse
    B. probity
    C. calumny
    D. effrontery
    E. sagacity

Chapter 10

64. Without rehearsing or even using a script, the kids staged a(n) _____ show.

    A. impromptu
    B. desiccated
    C. artisan
    D. catalyzed
    E. hedged

65. Grace preferred learning on the job rather than a(n) _____ approach to learning, consisting of endless textbooks and lectures.

    A. desiccated
    B. didactic
    C. salvaged
    D. facetious
    E. effaced

66. Brenda didn't want to eat another bite of the birthday cake. She found the thick, sweet icing to be _____.
    A. aquatic
    B. lucid
    C. pellucid
    D. cloying
    E. demonstrative

67. Rather than wearing the same type of outfits that everyone else wore to school, Gwen decided to break with convention and wear something _____.
    A. intractable
    B. indolent
    C. circuitous
    D. unabated
    E. unorthodox

68. After winning a fierce battle, the victors showed _____ in sparing the enemy commanders and allowing the defeated army to retreat.
    A. avidity
    B. reverie
    C. clemency
    D. kudos
    E. candor

69. The _____ commercial was so excessively sentimental that everyone in the room groaned when it came on.
    A. mawkish
    B. flaccid
    C. quintessential
    D. avenged
    E. concretized

Chapter 11

70. A(n) _____ of fashion, the magazine editor personally picked out the clothes for every cover shoot.
    A. misanthrope
    B. scourge
    C. abnegation
    D. paucity
    E. arbiter

71. The reporter thought that his newspaper article was _____, so he was quite surprised when the article sparked such an important series of events.
    A. multifarious
    B. unscathed
    C. inconsequential
    D. resilient
    E. communal

72. When a scathing article was published about the mayor, he immediately made a statement railing against the newspaper for printing a(n) _____ article filled with lies.
    A. mendacious
    B. alluring
    C. solicitous
    D. panacea
    E. omnipresent

73. The _____ of grizzly bears in the region prompted the local legislators to propose a bill that would put the grizzly bear on the endangered species list.
    A. panacea
    B. paucity
    C. credence
    D. parody
    E. abnegation

74. The _____ of the defendant's story was challenged by the prosecuting attorney, an astute and experienced lawyer who deftly pointed out the inconsistencies in the defendant's version of events.
    A. approbation
    B. largess
    C. harbinger
    D. veracity
    E. allocation

75. Kara did not believe a word of Jerry's excuse. After many years and many fabricated excuses, she knew that Jerry was a(n) _____ liar.
    A. defunct
    B. inveterate
    C. compatriot
    D. penultimate
    E. communal

76. George decided to _____ convention and do something completely unorthodox.
    A. ascribe
    B. aggrandize
    C. allure
    D. entwine
    E. flout

77. The _____ of the poem was really catchy and the students enjoyed reciting the rhythmic rhymes.
    A. avarice
    B. credence
    C. cadence
    D. scion
    E. largess

Chapter 12

78. The legislator proposed setting aside some of the budget to be reserved for _____circumstances, so that when an urgent matter arises that requires immediate action, the money would already be allocated.

    A. exigent

    B. fatuous

    C. irascible

    D. recapitulated

    E. hypocritical

79. Larry was in a _____; none of his options looked good.

    A. misnomer

    B. circumlocution

    C. elixir

    D. semaphore

    E. quandary

80. Justin knew that he was destined to go to jail. The evidence against him was _____.

    A. convoluted

    B. wanton

    C. conciliatory

    D. incontrovertible

    E. fatuous

81. A base or depraved act is a(n) _____.

    A. invective

    B. quandary

    C. turpitude

    D. misnomer

    E. affirmation

82. When the story of the politician's affair with the intern broke, it sparked a deluge of _____ news articles that focused on the details of the affair.
    A. convivial
    B. salacious
    C. imperceptible
    D. staid
    E. nurturing

83. Greg was given to _____ decisions and whims of fancy; he was simply unpredictable and impulsive.
    A. meticulous
    B. staid
    C. validated
    D. logical
    E. capricious

84. Henry was a(n) _____ man; he loved a good party.
    A. censured
    B. staid
    C. convivial
    D. unfounded
    E. perfidious

85. When Ruth discovered that the company's treasury had been raided, she knew that it had to be one of the employees who committed the _____ act.
    A. perfidious
    B. reclusive
    C. decorous
    D. haughty
    E. officious

Chapter 13

86. Greta decided to quit smoking because she knew that it was _____ to her health.

    A. vacuous

    B. dormant

    C. arable

    D. deleterious

    E. intransigent

87. The _____ spark that ignited the conflagration was ultimately attributed to a frayed electrical wire.

    A. Faustian

    B. rampant

    C. incendiary

    D. esoteric

    E. docile

88. George's _____ talents were on full display in the one-man show, during which he did amazing impersonations of a wide variety of people, from political figures to famous actors.

    A. diminutive

    B. protean

    C. truculent

    D. culpable

    E. vacuous

89. Jared cheated without _____; he didn't feel a trace of uneasiness or guilt when he looked on his neighbor's answer sheet during the exam.

    A. compunction

    B. bias

    C. torpor

    D. fecundity

    E. expediency

90. The causes championed by the lobby group were _____;
    they were not of interest to the majority of the population.
    A. appraised
    B. protean
    C. esoteric
    D. meritorious
    E. primeval

91. Rob's plan for the future was _____ and unformed. He knew
    that he needed more time to formulate something more concrete.
    A. arboreal
    B. dissembled
    C. culpable
    D. sage
    E. inchoate

92. The veterinarian had a great deal of difficulty with the _____
    animal; it refused to stay on the examination table and was stub-
    bornly resistant to any form of control.
    A. fractious
    B. vacuous
    C. arable
    D. fallow
    E. compliant

93. The _____ beast was always growling and looking for a
    fight.
    A. expedient
    B. torpid
    C. intimate
    D. pugnacious
    E. mollified

Chapter 14

94. The _____ toddler never obeyed his mother or responded to her reprimands.
    A. congenial
    B. salient
    C. incorrigible
    D. chivalrous
    E. maudlin

95. Jim took the time to carefully _____ his thermometer before he did the experiment so that it would accurately read the temperature of the solution.
    A. anesthetize
    B. juxtapose
    C. calibrate
    D. bilk
    E. desecrate

96. After seeing the gruesome crime scene, the policeman said that only a _____ criminal could commit such a heinous crime.
    A. maudlin
    B. diabolical
    C. dilatory
    D. chivalrous
    E. genial

97. The haughty professor had such a _____ air about him that he made his students feel inferior and unworthy.
    A. fiendish
    B. chivalrous
    C. strident
    D. supercilious
    E. vigilante

Chapter 15

98. Grace did not get fired. She left the job of her own _____.
   A. prophecy
   B. nadir
   C. volition
   D. decimation
   E. sentinel

99. The _____ walked the perimeter of the compound all night long, vigilantly guarding against any intruders.
   A. agnostics
   B. anarchists
   C. sentinels
   D. nonconformists
   E. merrymakers

Chapter 16

100. Many people in the kingdom wondered if the young royal would _____ the throne, because he seemed more interested in fishing than in ruling.
   A. enfranchise
   B. coronate
   C. reckon
   D. privy
   E. abdicate

Answers

Tricky Twosomes

1. aesthetic
2. avarice
3. blandished
4. commiserate
5. complement
6. complicit
7. congenial
8. consummating
9. indigenous
10. ingenious
11. inimical
12. obsequious
13. palate
14. penurious
15. perspicacity
16. proscribed
17. prodigal
18. prurient
19. soporific
20. tenable
21. tortuous
22. vindictive

Hot Topics for SAT Vocabulary

1. E
2. E
3. A
4. C
5. B
6. A
7. D
8. D
9. B
10. A
11. C
12. E
13. A
14. D
15. B
16. A
17. A
18. E

19. B	28. C
20. C	29. D
21. D	30. A
22. C	31. E
23. B	32. C
24. B	33. C
25. B	34. E
26. A	35. C
27. B	36. B

Chapter Reviews

1. C	23. B
2. E	24. A
3. A	25. D
4. D	26. B
5. B	27. E
6. C	28. A
7. A	29. D
8. D	30. B
9. B	31. D
10. E	32. E
11. A	33. B
12. C	34. C
13. E	35. D
14. A	36. C
15. E	37. A
16. D	38. D
17. C	39. B
18. D	40. E
19. A	41. B
20. C	42. D
21. A	43. A
22. D	44. C

45.	B	73.	B
46.	D	74.	D
47.	C	75.	B
48.	E	76.	E
49.	B	77.	C
50.	C	78.	A
51.	D	79.	E
52.	A	80.	D
53.	B	81.	C
54.	D	82.	B
55.	E	83.	E
56.	B	84.	C
57.	D	85.	A
58.	A	86.	D
59.	C	87.	C
60.	E	88.	B
61.	B	89.	A
62.	D	90.	C
63.	C	91.	E
64.	A	92.	A
65.	B	93.	D
66.	D	94.	C
67.	E	95.	C
68.	C	96.	B
69.	A	97.	D
70.	E	98.	C
71.	C	99.	C
72.	A	100.	E

Vocabulary List

The Vocabulary List and the footnotes in *The Mayan Mission* provide simplified definitions that explain the meaning of the vocabulary words as they are used in the context of the story. Some vocabulary words may have multiple definitions that are not included here. For complete definitions, consult a dictionary.

Abate   to reduce; lessen

Abdicate   to formally give up a high office or responsibility, especially that of a monarch

Aberration   a departure from the normal or typical

Abhor   to regard with loathing or horror; detest

Abide   to conform to; comply with

Abject   of the most miserable type, wretched

Abjure   to give up or abstain from

Abnegation   self-denial

Abort   to terminate before completion

Abridge   to shorten in size, scope, or extent

Absolve   to pronounce clear of guilt or liability

Abstain   to deliberately refrain from something

Abstemious   marked by restraint and moderation, especially as applied to eating and drinking

Abstruse   hard to understand; incomprehensible

Accede   to give consent, often at the insistence of another; concede

Acclaim   to praise enthusiastically and often publicly; applaud

Accolade   an expression of approval; praise

Accommodate   to adapt oneself, become adjusted

Accost   to approach and speak to boldly or aggressively, as with a demand or request

Accretion   growth by gradual addition

Acerbic   sharp or biting, as in character or expression

Acquiesce   to consent or agree without protest

Acrid   unpleasantly sharp or bitter to the taste or smell

Acrimony   biting sharpness and animosity in speech or disposition

Acute   reacting readily to stimuli or impressions; keenly perceptive; sensitive

Adamant   stubbornly unyielding

Adept   very skilled

Adhere   to carry out without deviation

Admonish   to gently express warning or disapproval

Adorn   to lend beauty to, enhance or decorate

Adroit   quick, skillful, or adept in action or thought; dexterous

Adulation   excessive flattery or praise

Adumbrate   to give a sketchy outline of

Adverse   contrary or against one's interests; difficult or unfavorable: *adverse criticism*

Advocate   to plead, argue, or speak in favor of

Aerial   high in the air; lofty

Aesthetic   relating to beauty and the appreciation of beauty and good taste

Affable   pleasant and easy to talk to

Affirmation   the act of supporting, confirming, or upholding the validity of

Affront   to face defiantly; confront

Aggrandize   to make appear greater; exaggerate

Aggregate   a collection of things constituting or amounting to a whole; total, collective

Aggrieve   to distress; afflict

Agile   characterized by quickness, lightness, and ease of movement; nimble

Agnostic   one who believes that it is impossible to know if God exists

Agricultural   relating to farming, producing crops, and raising livestock

Alacrity   promptness in response; cheerful readiness

Albeit   even though, although, notwithstanding

Allay   reduce in intensity or severity; alleviate, relieve

Allege   to assert to be true without proof

Allegiance   loyalty

Alleviate   to relieve or make more bearable: *aspirin alleviated the pain*

Allocate   to set apart for a special purpose or distribute according to plan: *a portion of the school budget was allocated for music*

Alluring   to attract or entice with something desirable

Aloof   emotionally distant, reserved, or remote

Altercation   a noisy, vehement quarrel

Amalgamation   an entity resulting from the combining or uniting of elements into a unified whole

Ambivalent   having a mixture of opposite feelings

Ameliorate   to make better; improve

Amenable   readily brought to yield or cooperate; willing

Amenities   something that confers material or physical comfort

Amiable   friendly, sociable

Amicable   friendly

Amorous   indicative of love or sexual desire

Amorphous   lacking definite form; shapeless

Analgesic   a medicine that reduces or eliminates pain

Analogy   a comparison based on similarities between things that are otherwise dissimilar

Anarchist   one who rebels against any authority, established order, or coercive control

Anathema   someone or something intensely loathed or shunned

Anecdote   a short account of an incident

Anesthetize   to make unconscious by use of anesthetic drugs

Animated   lively, spirited, or zestful

Anomaly   deviation from the common rule; irregularity

Anonymous   name unknown

Antecedents   one's ancestors or something that goes before or precedes

Antediluvian   extremely old and antiquated

Anticlimactic   an event that is strikingly less important than what has preceded or led up to it

Antipathy   a strong feeling of aversion or intense dislike

Antiquated   too old to be useful or fashionable; outdated

Antiseptic   a substance that inhibits the growth and reproduction of disease-causing microorganisms

Antithesis   the exact opposite

Apathetic   having a lack of interest or concern; indifferent

Apocryphal   of doubtful authenticity

Appalling   inspiring horror, dismay, or disgust

Appease   to bring peace or quiet to; soothe

Appraise   to evaluate, to estimate the quality and features of; judge

Apprehend   to arrest or take into custody

Apprise   to give notice to; inform

Approbation   an expression of warm approval; praise

Aquatic   living in water; relating to water

Arable   land fit to be cultivated

Arbiter   a person who has the power to decide or judge at will

Arbitrary   determined by chance rather than necessity or reason

Arboreal   relating to trees

Arcane   known or understood by only a few: *arcane economic theories*

Archaic   characteristic of an earlier or more primitive time; antiquated

Archetypal   an ideal example of a type

Ardent   characterized by strong enthusiasm or devotion; fervent

Arduous   strenuous; demanding great effort

Arid   dry, lacking sufficient moisture, water, or rainfall

Artisan   a skilled manual worker who practices a trade or handicraft; a craftsman

Ascertain   to find out or learn with certainty; discover

Ascetic   one who renounces material comforts and practices self-denial as a measure of personal and especially spiritual discipline.

Ascribe   to attribute to a specified cause or source

Aspersions   a disparaging, damaging, or unfavorable remark; slander

Aspiration   a strong desire or ambition to achieve

Assail   to attack violently; assault.

Assert   to state positively; affirm

Assess   to estimate the value of

Assuage   to put an end to by satisfying; quench, appease

Astute   having shrewdness and discernment

Asylum   a place of refuge or protection; a sanctuary

Atone   to make amends, as for a sin or crime

Atrophy   decrease in size or wasting away of a body part or tissue

Attune   to make aware or responsive

Atypical   not conforming to type; unusual or irregular

Audacious   fearlessly daring, recklessly bold

Audible   that is heard or is able to be heard

Augur   indicate by signs; bode, foreshadow

Auspicious   favorable, indicative of good things

Austere   severely simple or stark

Avarice   excessive desire for wealth; greed

Avenge   to inflict a punishment in return for; revenge

Avidity   keen interest or enthusiasm

Balk   to stop short and refuse to proceed

Ballad   a simple song

Banal   lacking originality, freshness, or novelty

Bashful   shy, self-conscious, and awkward

Bawdy   humorously coarse, vulgar, or lewd

Beguile   to deceive by guile (treacherous cunning and skillful deceit)

Behemoth   something of enormous size or power

Benefactor   one who gives aid, especially financial aid

Benevolent   characterized by doing good or showing kindness

Benign   of a mild type that does not threaten health or life

Bequeath   to leave or give personal property by will or to hand down from one generation to the next

Berate   to scold vehemently and at length; rebuke

Bereft   deprived of something

Beseech   to beg for urgently; implore

Bestow   to present as a gift

Bias   a preference or inclination, especially one that inhibits impartial judgment

Bilk   to elude, thwart, or frustrate; can also mean to swindle

Blandish   to coax by flattery or wheedling; cajole

Boisterous   loud and lacking in restraint; rowdy

Bombastic   pompous or ostentatiously lofty in speech or writing; grandiloquent

Boon   a timely blessing or benefit

Brandish   to wave or flourish (typically a weapon) menacingly

Brazen   marked by flagrant boldness

Brusque   short or abrupt in manner or speech; discourteously blunt

Buffet   a meal at which guests serve themselves from a variety of dishes that are all set out

Buffoonery   ridiculous, joking, or clowning behavior

Burgeoning   to grow and flourish

Buttress   something that serves to support or reinforce

Cache   a secure place of storage

Cacophony   jarring, discordant sound; dissonance

Cadence   the beat, measure, or rhythmic flow, as in music, poetry, or dance

Cahoots   a secret partnership or questionable collaboration

Cajole   to repeatedly urge with gentle appeals, teasing, or flattery; wheedle

Calamity   an event resulting in terrible loss and misfortune; catastrophe

Calibrate   to adjust precisely for a particular function

Callous   emotionally hardened; unfeeling, insensitive

Calumny   the utterance of maliciously false statements that harm another person's reputation

Camaraderie   lighthearted rapport and goodwill between friends

Candor   honest, straightforward, and frank in expression

Canvas   a piece of such fabric on which a painting is executed

Capacious   capable of containing a large quantity; spacious, roomy

Capitulate   to cease resisting; acquiesce

Capricious   impulsive and unpredictable

Captivate   to attract and hold by beauty, charm or excellence

Carouse   to engage in boisterous, drunken merrymaking or excessive drinking

Carp   to find fault in a disagreeable way; complain fretfully

Catalogue   to make an itemized list of

Catalyze   to bring about, initiate, or increase the rate of something

Caustic   marked by incisive sarcasm; cutting

Cavort   to bound or prance about in a playful, boisterous, or sprightly manner

Censure   a strong expression of disapproval

Certitude   the state of being certain; confidence

Chaos   a condition of great disorder or confusion

Chasm   a marked division, separation, or difference

Chastise   to criticize severely; rebuke

Chide   to reprimand mildly so as to correct or improve

Chivalrous   characterized by consideration, gallantry, and courtesy, especially toward women

Choreograph   to arrange or direct the movement, development, or details of; orchestrate

Chronicling   to record in the form of a historical record

Chronological   arranged in order of time of occurrence

Circuitous   a roundabout or indirect lengthy course: *they took a circuitous route to avoid the roadblock*

Circumlocution   the use of unnecessarily wordy, roundabout, and indirect language

Circumscribe   to draw a line around or surround by a boundary

Circumspect   careful to consider all possible consequences; prudent, cautious

Circumvent   to manage to avoid or get around; bypass

Clamor   to make loud, insistent demands or complaints

Clandestine   conducted in secrecy

Cleave   to split or cut

Clemency   demonstrating mercy in the punishment of an offender; merciful, lenient

Cloying   sickeningly sweet; excessively sweet or sentimental

Coagulate   to change from a liquid state into a solid or gel; clot

Coerce   to force or compel someone into doing something

Cogent   appealing to the intellect or powers of reasoning; valid and persuasive: *a cogent analysis*

Cognizant   fully informed; conscious, aware

Coherent   marked by an orderly and logical relation of parts: *a coherent argument*

Colloquial   characteristic of informal spoken language or conversation

Collude   to act together secretly for illegal or deceitful purposes; conspire; plot

Colossal   of a size, extent, or bulk that elicits astonishment; immense

Colossus   a huge statue (for example, the Statue of Liberty)

Commendation   something, especially an official award, that commends (expresses approval or praise)

Commensurate   corresponding in size or degree; proportionate

Commiserate   to feel sorrow, compassion, or pity for; sympathize with

Commodious   roomy, spacious

Commodity   an article of commerce or trade, especially goods that can be processed and resold

Communal   shared by the people of a community

Commune   to be in a state of heightened sensitivity, as with one's surroundings

Compassionate   having a sympathetic concern for others' distress together with a desire to alleviate it

Compatriot   a person from one's own country

Compensate   to make satisfactory payment or reparation to

Complacent   contented to a fault; satisfied and unconcerned

Complement   something that completes the whole or brings to perfection

Compliant   willing to carry out the orders or wishes of another

Complicit   association with or participation in an wrongful act

Comprehensive   covering completely or broadly; large in scope

Compunction   a strong uneasiness or anxiety caused by a sense of guilt

Concede   to make a concession; yield

Conciliatory   to try to gain friendship or overcome animosity

Concoction   a food or drink made by mixing different ingredients

Concomitant   occurring, existing, or happening at the same time

Concord   a state of agreement or harmony

Concretize   to make something concrete, definite, or specific

Condemn   to express strong disapproval of

Condone   to forgive, excuse, or overlook

Conduit   a means by which something is transmitted or distributed

Confection   a sweet preparation, such as candy

Conflagration   a conflict, war; can also mean a large disastrous fire

Confluence   the coming or flowing together at one place

Confound   to make something bad even worse

Congenial   friendly and sociable; having a pleasant disposition

Congregate   to come together in a group or crowd

Conjecture   a conclusion based on incomplete evidence or guesswork

Conniving   to cooperate secretly in an illegal or wrongful action

Consecrate   to dedicate solemnly to a goal; devote

Consensus   an opinion reached by a group as a whole

Consign   to deliver merchandise to a dealer for sale or to be cared for

Consortium   a cooperative arrangement among groups or institutions

Constrain   to secure, confine, or keep within close bounds

Construe   to explain the meaning of; interpret

Consummate   to bring to completion or fruition; conclude or finish

Consumption   the act of consuming (eating, drinking, or utilizing)

Contemporaneously   occurring during the same time period

Contempt   the act of despising, hating

Contentious   likely to cause a dispute

Contingency   an event or possibility that must be prepared for; a future emergency

Contravene   to act or be counter to; violate

Contrite   feeling regret and sorrow for one's sins or offenses; penitent

Contusion   an injury that does not break the skin; a bruise

Conundrum a difficult or insoluble problem; a dilemma

Convene to come together, usually for an official purpose; assemble formally

Conviction a strong belief or position

Convivial merry, festive, and social: *a convivial atmosphere at the birthday party*

Convoluted complicated or intricate, as if rolled or coiled together in overlapping whorls

Copious large in quantity; abundant

Cordial warm and sincere; friendly

Coronation the act of crowning a new sovereign

Corpulence the condition of being excessively fat; obesity

Corroborate to support with evidence; to make more certain

Cosmopolitan having wide international sophistication

Counteract oppose and lessen the effects of by contrary actions

Coup a brilliant, sudden, and usually highly successful stroke or act; a triumph

Coursing to move swiftly through or over; traverse

Covenant a usually formal, solemn, and binding agreement

Covert not openly carried out; secret: *covert military operations*

Covet to wish for longingly

Cower to cringe in fear

Credence acceptance as true or valid

Credulity willingness to believe, especially on slight or uncertain evidence

Crescendo a steady increase in volume or intensity

Criterion   a standard or reference point on which a judgment can be based; *plural: criteria*

Culpable   deserving of blame or condemnation as being wrong or harmful; blameworthy

Cultivate   to prepare land for raising crops

Cunning   skillfully deceptive

Cupidity   inordinate desire for wealth; greed

Cursory   performed hastily and without attention to detail

Curt   rudely abrupt of brief

Curtail   to cut short; reduce

Daunting   having the effect of lessening courage or discouraging through fear

Dearth   a scarce supply; a lack

Decimate   to destroy a large part of

Decorous   proper; characterized by decorum (appropriate behavior)

Deface   to spoil or mar the appearance; disfigure

Defamatory   harmful and often untrue; tending to discredit or harm another person's reputation

Defer   to put off; postpone

Deference   courteous respect or yielding to the wishes of another

Defile   to corrupt the purity or perfection of; sully, dishonor: *defiling the flag*

Deft   quick and skillful; adroit

Defunct   having ceased to exist or be in use

Delegate   to entrust to another

Deleterious   harmful or injurious

Delineate   to describe or outline

Delve   to make a deep and careful search for information: *delved into the files*

Demarcation   a boundary, separation, or distinction

Demean   reduce in dignity, worth, or character

Demise   the end of existence or activity; death; termination

Demonstrative   characterized by open expression of emotion

Demure   modest and reserved in behavior; shy

Denigrate   to belittle, disparage, or minimize

Denounce   to condemn openly as evil or reprehensible

Deplorable   worthy of severe condemnation: *a deplorable act of aggression*

Depravity   moral corruption

Deprecate   to belittle, depreciate

Derelict   neglectful of duties; remiss, negligent

Desecrate   to violate the sacredness of; profane

Desiccated   thoroughly dried out

Desolate   devoid of inhabitants; deserted

Despondent   extreme discouragement, dejection, or depression

Despot   a person who wields power oppressively; a tyrant

Deter   to prevent or discourage from acting, as by means of fear or doubt; dissuade, inhibit

Devious   departing from the accepted or correct; misleading, erring

Diabolical   characteristic of the devil; devilish

Dialect   a regional variety of a language distinguished by features of pronunciation and grammar

Diaphanous   of such fine texture as to be transparent or translucent

Didactic   intended to teach or instruct

Diffuse   to become widely dispersed or scattered; spread out

Dilatory   causing delay

Diligent   characterized by steady and earnest effort

Diminutive   very small; tiny

Dirge   a slow, solemn, and mournful piece of music

Disaffected   resentful and rebellious, especially against authority

Discern   to perceive with the eyes or intellect; detect

Disclose   to make known something that was previously secret; divulge

Discomfit   to put into a state of unease, perplexity, and embarrassment

Discordant   disagreeable in sound; harsh or dissonant

Discourse   a formal, lengthy discussion of a subject

Discrepancy   a divergence, variance, or disagreement between things; difference

Disdain   a feeling or show of contempt and aloofness; scorn

Disgruntle   to make ill-humored or discontented

Disheartened   to cause to lose spirit or morale

Disparage   to express a negative opinion of

Disparate   fundamentally different or dissimilar

Dispatch   the act of sending off, as to a specific destination

Disperse   to scatter in different directions

Disrepute   damage to or loss of reputation

Dissemble   to put on a false show or appearance; feign

Dissipate   to attenuate to or almost to the point of vanishing: *the crowd dissipated after the music ended*

Dissonance   a harsh disagreeable combination of sounds; lack of harmony or agreement

Dissuade   to deter someone from a course of action by persuasion

Dither   to act nervously indecisive

Diversion   something that distracts or diverts attention

Divine   God-like, having the nature of a deity; superhuman

Divulge   to make known or public something that was previously secret; reveal

Docile   willing to be led, supervised, or taught

Dogmatic   characterized by an authoritative, arrogant assertion of unproved principles

Dormant   a condition of suspended activity; asleep or inactive

Dour   silently ill-humored or gloomy

Dubious   unsettled in opinion; doubtful

Duplicitous   hiding one's true intentions with deliberately deceptive speech or behavior

Duress   constraint by threat; coercion: *confessed under duress*

Dynamic   marked by intensity and vigor; forceful

Ebullient   zestfully enthusiastic

Echelon   a level of responsibility or authority in a hierarchy; a rank

Eclectic   made up of a variety of different elements or sources: *eclectic taste in fashion*

Ecstatic   a state of intense joy or delight

Edict   an order or decree issued by an authority

Edify   to instruct, inform, or enlighten

Efface   to rub out or erase

Effervesce   exhibiting liveliness, high spirits, or exhilaration

Efficacious   having the power to produce a desired effect

Effrontery   shameless and brazen boldness

Effulgent   brilliantly shining

Egregious   conspicuously bad or offensive

Elaborate   to express at greater length or in greater detail

Elate   to fill with joy or pride

Elicit   to bring or draw out

Elixir   a medicine believed to have the power to cure all ills

Eloquent   marked by persuasive, fluent speech: *an eloquent speaker*

Elucidate   to make lucid (clear, understandable), especially by explanation or analysis

Elusive   tending to evade grasp or pursuit

Emaciate   to become extremely thin, especially as a result of starvation

Embezzle   to take property or money (entrusted to one's care) fraudulently for one's own use

Embolden   to instill boldness or courage in

Eminent   outstanding, prominent, or distinguished in character or performance

Emote   to express emotion, especially in an excessive or theatrical manner

Empathy   direct identification with and understanding of another person's situation or feelings

Emphatic   expressed with emphasis; forceful and definite

Empirical   derived from observation or experiment: *empirical results that negated the hypothesis*

Empower   to give an ability or quality to; enable

Enamor   to inspire with love; captivate

Encapsulate   to express in a brief summary; epitomize

Encompass   to constitute or include

Encore   an additional performance at the end of a concert in response to audience demand

Encroach   to advance beyond proper or former limits

Encumber   to put a heavy load on; burden

Endeavor   an activity directed toward a specific goal

Enervate   lacking strength or vigor; debilitated

Enfranchised   to endow with the privileges of citizenship, especially the right to vote

Enigmatic   resembling an enigma (something puzzling, ambiguous, or inexplicable); mysterious

Enlighten   to give information or knowledge to; illuminate, inform, or instruct

Enmity   mutual hatred or ill will

Entail   to have, impose, or require as a necessary accompaniment or consequence

Enthrall   to hold spellbound; captivate

Entrance   to fill with delight, wonder, or enchantment

Entwined   twisted together, interlaced, or interwoven

Ephemeral   lasting a very short time

Epistolary   carried on by or composed of letters

Epitome   a standard, typical, or representative example of a class or type

Equanimity   evenness of mind especially under stress; composure

Equilibrium   state of balance

Equivocal   open to two or more interpretations; ambiguous

Erudite   having or displaying deep, extensive knowledge

Eschew   avoid, shun

Esoteric   confined to and understandable by a restricted number of people

Espouse   to give one's loyalty or support to

Esteem   to regard with respect

Ethereal   not of this world; heavenly

Euphoric   exaggerated feeling of great happiness, elation, or well-being

Evanescent   tending to vanish like vapor; fleeting

Evince   to show or demonstrate clearly

Eviscerate   to take away a vital or essential part of, disembowel

Evoke   to call forth or summon

Exacerbate   to increase the severity of; aggravate

Exalt   to raise in rank, power; elevate

Exasperate   to irritate, annoy, or make angry

Excavation   the act of exposing or uncovering by digging

Exclusive   tending to exclude most from entry, membership, or participation: *an exclusive nightclub*

Exculpate   to clear of blame or guilt

Excursion   a journey made for pleasure; an outing

Execrable   detestable, very bad: *execrable crimes*

Exemplary   deserving imitation because of excellence

Exhort   to urge strongly by argument, advice, or appeal

Exigent   requiring immediate aid, action, or remedy; urgent

Exonerate   to free from blame

Exorbitant   exceeding all bounds of what is customary or fair: *exorbitant prices*

Expedient   marked by concern for self-interest rather than principle

Expunge   to strike out, obliterate, erase, or destroy

Extant   still in existence; not destroyed, lost, or extinct

Extenuating   partially excusing or justifying

Extol   to praise highly

Extraneous   inessential or unrelated to the topic; not a vital element; irrelevant

Extricate   to release from entanglement or difficulty

Fabricate   to make or create, often with the intent to deceive: *a fabricated excuse*

Façade   a showy misrepresentation intended to conceal something unpleasant

Facet   one of the definable aspects of an object or subject

Facetious   playfully joking or kidding; humorous

Fallow   land left plowed but unseeded during a growing season

Fastidious   displaying careful, meticulous attention to detail

Fathom   to understand the meaning or nature of; comprehend

Fatuous   inanely foolish or silly

Faustian   resembling Faust, from a German legend about a man who sells his soul to the devil for power and knowledge

Fecundity   the capacity for generating offspring, especially abundant offspring

Felicitous   marked by good fortune or happiness

Feral   wild, savage, untamed

Fervent   having great emotion or zeal

Fetid   having a heavy, offensive smell

Feverish   marked by intense activity or agitation

Fickle   erratic changeableness in affections or attachments

Fidelity   exact correspondence with fact; accuracy

Fiendish   extremely wicked

Flabbergast   to overwhelm with shock or astonishment; dumbfound

Flaccid   lacking muscle tone or firmness

Flourish   to grow well, thrive

Flout   to show contempt or disregard for; scorn: *flout a law*

Fodder   a consumable, such as feed for livestock, that is used to supply a heavy demand

Foil   to prevent something from happening or being successful; thwart

Forage   to wander in search of food or provisions

Foray   a venture or an initial attempt, especially outside one's usual area: *a model's foray into acting*

Forbearance   the act of showing patience, tolerance, or leniency when provoked

Forestall   to delay or prevent by taking precautionary measures beforehand

Forlorn   appearing sad or lonely

Formidable   difficult to undertake or surmount

Forsake   to give up

Fortitude   strength of mind that allows one to endure adversity with courage

Fortuitous   happening by fortunate accident or chance

Foster   to promote the growth and development of; nurture, cultivate

Fractious   tending to cause trouble; unruly, irritable

Fraught   filled with a specified element; charged: *a situation fraught with danger*

Frenetic   wildly active or excited; frantic

Frugal   marked by economy in spending; thrifty, sparing

Furtive   characterized by stealth or secrecy; surreptitious

Garish   excessively vivid or flashy; gaudy: *garish eye makeup*

Genial   having a pleasant or friendly disposition or manner

Glutton   one who is prone to overindulgence or greediness in food or drink

Goad   to urge or prod, as if with a pointed stick

Grandiloquence   a pompous, lofty, or bombastic style, especially in language

Grandiose   uncommonly large and impressive in scope or intent; grand

Gregarious   marked by seeking and enjoying the company of others; sociable

Grievous   characterized by severe pain, suffering, or sorrow: *a grievous loss*

Guile   treacherous cunning, skillful deceit

Guise   outward appearance, semblance; sometimes indicating a false appearance or pretense

Hackneyed   excessively familiar through overuse; trite, banal

Hallowed   holy or sacred: *a hallowed cemetery*

Hapless   having no luck; unfortunate

Harbinger   an indication or foreshadowing of something to come

Hardy   capable of withstanding unfavorable conditions; sturdy, robust, and healthy

Harrowing   extremely distressing; agonizing

Haughty   arrogant superiority, scornfully proud

Hedge   to avoid making a clear, direct statement; intentionally ambiguous

Hedonistic   pursuit of or devotion to pleasure

Hegemony   the domination of one state or group over others

Hiatus   a gap or interruption; a break

Hierarchy   a group of people categorized according to rank, ability, or status

Histrionic   excessively dramatic; characteristic of acting or actors

Hyperbole   extravagant exaggeration; as in *I ate a ton of food*

Hypocrisy   professing beliefs or virtues that one does not hold; falseness

Hypocritical   professing one thing while doing another; false

Hypothetical   based on hypothesis, supposed: *a hypothetical situation*

Idolatrous   given to blind or excessive devotion to something

Ignoble   not of the nobility; common

Ignominious   deserving of shame or infamy; despicable

Illicit   contrary to accepted morality, law, or convention; unlawful

Imbibe   to drink, especially alcoholic beverages

Imbroglio   a very embarrassing misunderstanding

Impassive   devoid of emotion; expressionless

Impeccable   without fault, flaw, or error; perfect

Impecunious   lacking money; penniless

Imperative   not to be avoided or evaded; necessary: *an imperative duty*

Imperceptible   difficult or impossible to perceive (to become aware of via the senses)

Imperious   marked by arrogant assurance; domineering

Impertinent   exceeding the limits of propriety or good manners

Impervious   not capable of being affected or disturbed

Impetuous   characterized by haste and lack of thought; impulsive and passionate

Implacable   impossible to placate or appease

Implausible   appearing invalid, unlikely, or unacceptable; unbelievable

Implicate   to involve, connect intimately, or incriminate

Implicit   implied or understood without direct expression: *an implicit agreement*

Impregnable   impossible to enter by force or capture: *an impregnable military base*

Impromptu   not planned or prepared for in advance; carried out with little or no preparation

Impudent   marked by offensive or cocky boldness; impertinent

Impute   to relate to a particular source; attribute the fault or responsibility to

Inane   lacking significance, meaning, or point

Inarticulate   unable to speak clearly

Incendiary   causing fire

Incessant   continuing without interruption; unceasing

Inchoate   imperfectly developed or formulated; vague, formless

Incisive   clear, sharp, and penetrating; acutely observant and discriminating: *incisive comments*

Inclined   to be disposed to a certain preference or course of action

Inconsequential   lacking importance; trivial

Incontrovertible   impossible to deny or disprove; unquestionable

Incorrigible   difficult to control, manage, or reform

Increment   the process of increasing in number, size, or value

Incumbent   imposed as an obligation or duty; obligatory

Indefatigable   incapable of being exhausted or fatigued; untiring

Indifferent   having no marked feeling, interest, or concern

Indigenous   having originated in a particular area or environment; native

Indigent   experiencing want or need; poor, impoverished

Indignation   a feeling of righteous anger aroused from something mean or unjust

Indolent   lazy, inactive; lethargic

Indomitable   incapable of being overcome or subdued

Ineffable   incapable of being expressed; indescribable

Inequity   injustice; unfairness

Inexorable   not to be persuaded or appeased by entreaty (requests or pleas); relentless

Inextricable   so entangled that it is impossible to escape

Infamous   having an exceedingly bad reputation; notorious

Infuse   to fill or cause to be filled with something

Ingenious   marked by inventive skill, imagination, or cunning; clever

Ingenuous   straightforward, lacking in cunning or guile

Inimical   injurious or harmful in effect; adverse

Inimitable   defying imitation; matchless

Iniquity   a wicked act or thing; a sin or gross injustice

Innate   inborn, possessed at birth

Innocuous   having no adverse effect; harmless

Innovative   marked by the act of introducing something new, such as a creation or invention

Innuendo   an indirect or subtle implication (usually derogatory) in expression; an insinuation

Inquisitor   one who inquires or makes an inquisition, especially a questioner who is excessively rigorous or hostile

Insatiable   incapable of being satisfied

Insipid   lacking in interest or stimulation; dull

Insolent   audaciously rude, disrespectful, or insulting; impertinent

Instigate   to stir up or provoke; incite

Insular   characteristic of an isolated life, especially a narrow or provincial outlook

Insuperable   impossible to overcome; insurmountable

Integrate   to join with something else; the process of unifying into a whole

Integrity   steadfast adherence to a moral or ethical code; moral soundness

Interject   to insert in between or among other things; interpolate

Interlocutor   one who takes part in dialogue or conversation, often in an official capacity

Interminable   seeming to never end; endless

Intimate   to communicate delicately, subtly, and indirectly; hint

Intractable   not easily relieved or cured

Intransigent   refusing to compromise or moderate an extreme position

Intrepid   characterized by resolute fearlessness, courage, and endurance: *an intrepid explorer*

Inundate   to overwhelm, as if with a flood of water: *the museum was inundated with visitors*

Inure   to habituate to something undesirable, especially by prolonged exposure; accustom

Invective   abusive language; vituperation

Inveterate   firmly established; ingrained, deep-rooted

Irascible   hot tempered; easily angered

Iridescent   producing a display of lustrous, rainbow-like colors

Irreverent   critical of what is generally accepted or respected; satirical: *irreverent humor*

Irrevocable   impossible to retract or revoke

Jocular   characterized by joking behavior and good humor

Judicious   having good judgment and common sense

Juxtaposed   placed side by side

Kudos   praise

Labyrinth   a complex system of paths or tunnels in which it is easy to get lost; maze

Laceration   a jagged cut or wound

Laconic   using few words; terse or concise

Laggard   one who lags or lingers

Lampoon   a harsh satire of an individual or institution; ridicule

Languid   sluggish; lacking energy

Larceny   theft

Largess   liberal or generous in bestowing gifts, especially in a condescending manner

Lassitude   a feeling of fatigue or weariness

Laud   to praise, extol

Lavish   to give in abundance; very generous

Legerdemain   sleight of hand; an illusionary or magic trick

Legitimate   lawful; in accordance with the law or accepted standards

Lethargic   lacking alertness or activity; sluggish

Levity   lightness of manner or speech, especially when inappropriate; excessive frivolity

Liability   something that holds one back or acts as a disadvantage; drawback

Libation   a beverage, especially a drink containing alcohol

Licentious   lacking moral discipline, especially in sexual conduct

Limpid   transparent clearness: *a limpid pool*

Literally   in a literal or strict sense

Lithe   characterized by effortless grace: *a lithe gymnast*

Litigate   to engage in legal proceedings

Livid   extremely angry; furious

Lobby   a group of persons engaged in trying to influence legislators in favor of a specific cause

Lucid   transparent or translucent; clear

Luminous   emitting or reflecting light

Macabre   suggesting the horror of death; gruesome

Magnanimous   courageously noble and generous in spirit

Malevolent   ill will, wishing harm to others; malicious

Malleable   easily controlled or influenced

Mandate   an authoritative command or instruction

Manifestation   a perceptible indication of the existence of something: *the first manifestation of disease occurred three days after exposure to the virus*

Manifold   many and varied

Mar   to impair or spoil

Maudlin   effusively sentimental; mushy

Maverick   an independent individual who does not go along with a group or party; a dissenter

Mawkish   excessively sentimental

Meager   deficient in quantity or amount; scanty

Medley   a musical arrangement made from a series of songs or melodies

Mendacious   lying; untruthful, or deceptive

Mercenary   one who serves merely for wages, especially a soldier hired into a foreign service

Mercurial   rapid and unpredictable mood changes; volatile

Meritorious   deserving reward or praise; having merit

Metamorphose   to change into a wholly different form or appearance; transform

Meticulous   extremely concerned with details

Milieu   an environment or setting

Mirth   gladness and great merriment, especially as expressed by laughter

Misanthrope   one who hates or mistrusts humankind

Misconception   a mistaken thought or idea; a misunderstanding

Misdeed   a wrong or illegal act; wrongdoing

Misnomer   a name unsuitably applied

Missionary   one who is sent on a mission, particularly to do religious work in a foreign country

Missive   a written message; a letter

Mitigate   to make less severe; alleviate

Moderation   being within reasonable limits; not excessive or extreme

Mollify   to lessen in intensity

Monarch   one who reigns over a state or territory, usually for life and by hereditary right

Morass   something that traps, confuses, or impedes

Mores   moral attitudes

Morose   sullenly melancholy; gloomy

Mosaic   a picture made up of small colored pieces (typically stone or tile) set into a surface

Multifarious   a great variety; diverse

Munificence   showing great generosity

Myriad   a large, indefinite number; innumerable: *myriad fish in the sea*

Nadir   the lowest point

Nascent   coming into existence; emerging

Nebulous   indistinct, vague

Nefarious   extremely wicked

Neophyte   a novice or beginner

Nobility   a privileged class holding hereditary titles such as dukes, duchesses, earls, countesses, etc.

Nocturnal   most active at night

Noisome   offensive, disgusting, or foul: *a noisome smell*

Nominal   insignificantly small; trifling

Nonchalant   seeming to be coolly indifferent or unconcerned

Nonconformist   one who refuses to be bound by accepted beliefs, customs, or practices

Nonplus   to put at a loss as to what to say or do; bewilder

Nostalgic   a bittersweet longing for things of the past

Notoriety   the state of being generally known and talked of, especially in an unfavorable way; ill fame

Noxious   harmful or injurious to health: *noxious pollution*

Nuance   a subtle distinction or variation

Nurturing   to help grow and develop

Obdurate   hardened in wrongdoing or wickedness

Obfuscate   to render indistinct, obscure, or difficult to see; to hide by covering

Oblivious   lacking conscious awareness; unmindful

Obscure   not readily seen or noticed; hidden

Obsequious   exhibiting fawning attentiveness or servile compliance

Obstinate   stubbornly adhering to an opinion or course of action; obdurate

Obstreperous   stubbornly defiant and noisy

Odious   arousing strong dislike, aversion, or intense displeasure

Officious   excessive eagerness in offering unwanted services to others

Ominous   menacing, threatening, or alarming; foreshadowing evil or disaster

Omnipresent   present everywhere at all times

Onerous   oppressive or troublesome; burdensome

Ornate   elaborately or excessively decorated

Oscillate   to swing back and forth or to waver, as if between two conflicting courses of action; vacillate

Ostensibly   to all outward appearances; plausible rather than demonstrably true: *the ostensible purpose of the war*

Ostentatious   characterized by pretentious display that is meant to impress others; showy

Pacifism   the belief that disputes (such as between countries) can and should be settled peacefully, without war or violence

Palatable   acceptable or agreeable to eat

Palette   a board, which an artist can hold while painting, that is used to mix paint

Palliate   to make less intense or severe; mitigate

Palpable   capable of being touched or felt; tangible

Panacea   a cure-all; a remedy for everything

Paradigm   a philosophical or theoretical framework

Paragon   a model of excellence or perfection; a peerless example

Paramount   of highest importance or chief concern

Parched   dry; thirsty

Parody   an imitation done for comedy or ridicule

Parsimonious   excessively frugal or sparing

Partake   to take or be given a part of; to participate or share

Patently   in a unmistakable manner; openly, plainly, or clearly

Pathos   a quality that arouses emotions, especially pity or sorrow

Paucity   smallness of number; an insufficiency or dearth

Pejorative   disparaging; belittling

Pellucid   clear, allowing light to pass; transparent or translucent

Penchant   a strong liking or inclination

Penitence   the quality or state of being penitent; having sorrow or regret for wrongdoing

Pensive   deeply and often wistfully or dreamily thoughtful; often suggestive of melancholy thoughtfulness

Penultimate   next to last

Penury   an oppressive lack of resources; severe poverty or destitution

Perfidious   tending to betray; treacherous

Permeate   to spread or diffuse throughout; pervade

Pernicious   highly injurious or destructive; deadly

Perplex   to confuse or trouble with uncertainty or doubt

Perspicacity   acute mental vision, perception, or discernment; keen

Peruse   to examine with attention and in detail

Pervasive   having the quality of being diffused or permeated throughout: *a pervasive odor*

Petulant   unreasonably rude or irritable

Philanthropist   a person who makes charitable donations with the intent of increasing the well-being of humankind

Piety   the state or quality of being pious (religious devotion and reverence to God)

Pillage   to rob of goods by force or take as spoils; plunder

Pinnacle   the highest point; the culmination; summit

Pithy   concise and full of meaning

Pittance   a meager wage or monetary payment; a small amount

Placid   calm or quiet; undisturbed

Platitude   a banal or trite statement; cliché

Plaudits   enthusiastic approval or praise

Plebeian   characteristic of commoners

Plenitude   an abundance

Plethora   an overabundance or excess

Pliable   easily bent

Poignant   profoundly moving; touching

Polemic   a controversial argument, especially one attacking a specific opinion

Pompous   pretentious; characterized by exaggerated, lofty dignity and excessive self esteem

Pontificate   to talk or express opinions in a dogmatic or pompous manner

Portend   to serve as an omen or a warning of; presage, forecast

Portentous   foreboding; foreshadowing something bad

Potable   suitable for drinking

Pragmatic   practical, matter-of-fact

Precipice   a very steep or overhanging place

Preclude   to prevent or make impossible by an action taken in advance

Precocious   characterized by early development or maturity

Predilection   a partiality or disposition in favor of something; a preference

Premise   something assumed to be true and upon which an argument is based or conclusion drawn

Preponderance   a superiority in weight, importance, or strength

Prepossess   to preoccupy the mind to the exclusion of other thoughts

Presage   to warn of or indicate in advance; portend

Prescient   foreknowledge of events

Prescribe   to order the use of a medicine or remedy

Presumptuous   excessively forward; going beyond what is proper

Pretense   the act of pretending; a false appearance intended to deceive

Prevail   to prove superior; to triumph

Primeval   having existed since the beginning or earliest stage; original

Privation   a state of extreme poverty

Privy   informed about something not generally known

Probity   complete and confirmed integrity; uprightness

Proclivity   a natural propensity or inclination, especially a strong inherent inclination toward something objectionable

Procure   to get by special effort; obtain

Prodigal   marked by wasteful extravagance

Prodigious   impressively great in size; enormous

Profane   coarse or vulgar; characterized by profanity or cursing

Profess   to affirm openly; declare or claim

Profligate   recklessly wasteful; wildly extravagant

Profuse   produced or growing in great abundance

Propensity   an innate inclination or tendency; predilection

Prophecy   a prediction of something to come in the future

Propitious   presenting favorable circumstances; auspicious

Propriety   the quality of being correct, appropriate, or proper

Prosaic   lacking in imagination and spirit; dull

Proscribe   to condemn as forbidden; prohibit

Proselytize   to induce someone to join one's religion, cause, or party

Protean   exhibiting a great variety or diversity

Provident   providing carefully for the future

Prowess   extraordinary ability, superior skill

Prudent   marked by wisdom in handling practical affairs; exercising good judgment or common sense

Prurient   an inordinate interest in sex; lustful: *prurient thoughts*

Puerile   childish, juvenile, silly

Pugnacious   combative and quarrelsome in nature; truculent

Pulchritude   great physical beauty and appeal

Punctilious   strictly attentive to minute details of form in action or conduct; meticulous

Pungent   affecting the organs of taste or smell with a sharp, acrid, or irritating sensation

Punitive   inflicting or involving punishment: *punitive damages*

Putrid   being in a state of putrefaction; rotten

Quagmire   a difficult or precarious position; a predicament

Quaint   charmingly odd or unusual, especially in an old-fashioned way

Quandary   an unpleasant or trying situation from which extrication is difficult

Quell   to pacify, quiet

Quiescent   being quiet or at rest; inactive

Quintessential   a perfect or most typical example

Quixotic   foolishly impractical in the pursuit of noble deeds and idealistic goals

Quotidian   everyday, commonplace: *a quotidian routine*

Radical   departing markedly from the usual or customary; extreme

Rail   to express objections or scold in bitter, harsh, or abusive language

Rampant   occurring unchecked and frequently or widely

Rancid   having a foul smell or taste

Rant   to speak or write in a angry or violent manner

Rapport   relationship, especially one of harmony, accord, and emotional affinity

Rarefied   belonging to a small, select group

Rash   characterized by reckless haste

Rational   based on reason; logical

Raucous   disagreeably harsh, loud, or rough sounding: *a raucous party*

Ravenous   extremely hungry

Raze   to demolish or tear down to the ground

Rebuke   to scold or criticize sharply; reprimand

Rebuttal   the act of refuting by offering a contrary argument

Recant   to formally retract or renounce a or previously held belief or statement

Recapitulate   to summarize or repeat in concise form

Reciprocate   to give in response or return

Reckoning   a settling of accounts

Reclusive   providing seclusion or isolation

Reconcile   to settle or resolve

Reconciliation   the act of reestablishing a close relationship

Reconnaissance   an exploration or survey to gain information, especially military information about an enemy

Rectitude   moral uprightness

Redoubtable   worthy of respect or honor; illustrious, eminent

Refute   to deny the accuracy or truth of: *he refuted the allegations*

Regurgitate   to rush or pour back

Relegate   to assign to an obscure place, position, or condition

Relish   to take keen pleasure in

Reminiscent   tending to recall or suggest something in the past

Renown   a state of being widely acclaimed and highly honored; famous

Repentant   having remorse for misdeeds; penitent

Replete   abundantly supplied or filled

Repose   the act of resting

Reprehensible   deserving of blame, censure, or rebuke; blameworthy

Reprieve   temporary relief, as from danger or pain

Reproach   to express disapproval or criticism of; admonish

Reprobate   one who is morally unprincipled

Reprove   to convey disapproval of

Repudiate   to reject an obligation or to refuse to acknowledge or pay

Repugnant   causing disgust or aversion; offensive

Repulsive   causing aversion or repugnance; disgusting

Reputable   having a good reputation; honorable

Requisition   a formal written request for something needed

Rescind   to take back; cancel

Reservoir   a natural or artificial pond or lake used for the storage of water

Resilient   marked by the ability to recover readily, as from misfortune or change

Resolve   to make a firm decision about

Respite   a short interval of rest or relief

Resplendent   splendid or dazzling in appearance; brilliant

Restitution   the act of compensating for loss, damage, or injury

Restive   a feeling of impatience or uneasiness, usually as a result of external restriction or coercion

Retract   to take back

Retribution   a justly deserved penalty

Revel   to take intense pleasure, delight, or satisfaction

Reverence   a feeling of profound respect and awe; veneration

Reverie   lost in thought; daydreaming

Revoke   to void or annul by recalling, withdrawing, or reversing; rescind

Rhetoric   language that is pretentious, insincere, or intellectually vacuous

Ribald   vulgar, lewd humor

Rife   abundant or numerous

Righteousness   adhering to moral principles

Ruminate   to reflect on over and over again

Ruse   a deceptive maneuver designed to deceive or surprise an enemy

Sagacity   having good judgment; wisdom

Sage   marked by wisdom and good judgment

Salacious   appealing to sexual desire; lascivious

Salient   very conspicuous; prominent, noticeable

Salutation   a polite expression or gesture of greeting

Salvage   to extract something as valuable from garbage or wreckage; or to save something from destruction: *goods salvaged from the sinking ship*

Salve   something that soothes or heals; a balm

Sanctimonious   feigning piety or righteousness

Sanguine   cheerfully confident, optimistic

Satiate   to satisfy a need or desire fully or to excess

Savory   appetizing to the taste or smell

Scathing harshly critical or injurious: *a scathing review*

Scintillating animated and brilliant: *scintillating conversation*

Scion an heir or descendant

Scourge a source of widespread suffering and devastation; ravage

Scrupulously conscientious and exact; painstaking, meticulous

Scrutinize to examine closely and minutely

Scurrilous vulgar or coarse language

Scurry to go with light running steps; scamper

Sedentary characterized by a lack of physical activity and a lot of sitting

Semaphore a device used for visual signaling with lights, flags, or mechanically moving arms, such as is used on the railroad

Sensual relating to gratification of the physical and especially the sexual appetites

Sentiment a thought or attitude, especially one based primarily on emotion rather than reason

Sentinel a guard

Sequester to remove or set apart; segregate, isolate

Serendipitous finding valuable or agreeable things not sought for: *serendipitous discoveries*

Serene without disturbance; calm

Servile relating to or suitable for a slave or servant

Simulate to take on the appearance of; imitate

Sobriety the state of being sober, refraining from alcohol and drugs

Solicitous anxious concern or care: *a solicitous mother*

Soluble something that can be dissolved to form a solution

Solvent   a liquid, in which a substance can be dissolved, forming a solution

Somnolent   drowsy, sleepy

Sophomoric   exhibiting great immaturity and lack of judgment

Soporific   tending to induce sleep

Speculation   a conclusion based on insufficient evidence; conjecture

Spurious   lacking authenticity or validity; false

Staid   characterized by sedate dignity and often a prim sense of propriety

Staunch   firm and steadfast in loyalty or principle

Stealthy   acting with quiet, caution, and secrecy intended to avoid notice

Stoic   seemingly indifferent to pleasure, pain, or grief

Stolid   revealing little emotion or sensibility; impassive

Strenuous   requiring great exertion or effort

Strident   sounds that are loud, grating, or shrill; discordant

Stupefy   to amaze; astonish

Sublime   inspiring awe; impressive, supreme

Succinct   characterized by clear, precise expression in few words; concise and terse

Succumbed   to yield or submit to an overpowering desire or force

Sully   to mar the cleanliness of; taint, stain, or soil

Supercilious   arrogant superiority, haughty disdain

Superfluous   beyond what is required or sufficient

Supine   lying on the back or having the face upward

Surmise   to infer something without sufficiently conclusive evidence

Surreptitious   marked by stealth; secret, clandestine

Surrogate   one who takes the place of another; a substitute

Swagger   to walk or conduct oneself with a proud, arrogant air; strut

Swarthy   having a dark complexion or color

Sycophant   a servile self-seeker who attempts to win favor by flattering influential people

Tacit   expressed without words or speech

Taciturn   temperamentally disinclined to talk; uncommunicative

Taint   to affect with a tinge of something reprehensible, such as a disease or decay; contaminate

Tantamount   equivalent in value, significance, or effect; being essentially equal to something

Tedious   tiresome by reason of dullness, length, or slowness; boring

Temerity   foolhardy disregard for danger; recklessness, rashness

Temperance   moderation and restraint in behavior

Tenable   rationally defensible; capable of being defended in argument: *a tenable hypothesis*

Tenuous   lacking strength or substance; flimsy

Terrestrial   living on land; not aquatic

Theoretically   based on theory

Threadbare   frayed, worn, or shabby

Timorous   full of apprehensiveness; timid, fearful

Tirade   a long angry or violent speech

Toady   a person who flatters or defers to others for self-serving reasons; a sycophant

Tome   a book, especially a large or scholarly one

Torpor   the dormant, inactive state of a hibernating animal

Torrid   scorching hot, burning

Tortuous   having repeated bends, twists, or turns; winding

Traipse   to walk or tramp about

Trajectory   the path of a moving body through space

Tranquility   the quality or state of being tranquil (free from disturbance, agitation, or turmoil)

Transgression   the act of overstepping a boundary or violating a law

Travesty   a debased, distorted, or grotesque imitation; parody: *a travesty of justice*

Trenchant   forceful, penetrating, and effective

Trepidation   a state of alarm, fear, apprehension, or dread

Trite   boring from overuse; not fresh or original; hackneyed

Trivialize   to make appear trivial or insignificant

Truculent   disposed to violence; fierce

Trudge   to walk in a laborious, heavy-footed way; plod

Truncate   terminating abruptly, as if cut off

Turpitude   lacking moral standards; depravity, baseness

Ubiquitous   being or seeming to be everywhere at the same time; omnipresent

Umbrage   Shadow or shade (can also be used to indicate resentment or offense: *she took umbrage at his insult*)

Unabated   sustaining at the original intensity or force with no decrease

Unctuous   characterized by affected, exaggerated, or insincere earnestness (can also mean oily or slippery)

Undermine   to weaken at the foundation; to impair or hinder

Undulate   to rise and fall in volume or pitch as if in waves

Unethical   not conforming to approved standards of social or professional behavior; dishonorable

Unfettered   free of shackles, chains, or other restrictions

Unfounded   not based on solid evidence or fact

Ungainly   lacking grace or ease of movement; clumsy

Uninhibited   free, open, and unrestrained

Unkempt   deficient in order or neatness

Unnerve   to deprive of strength or vigor and the capacity to act

Unorthodox   not adhering to what is commonly accepted or traditional; independent in behavior

Unpretentious   lacking pretension or ostentatious affectation; modest

Unscathed   not harmed, damaged, or injured

Unswerving   constant; steady and unfaltering

Unwieldy   difficult to manage or carry because of size or shape

Unwitting   not knowing; unaware

Upbraid   to scold severely or sharply; reproach

Usurp   to wrongfully seize someone else's place, authority, or possession

Utilitarian   having utility, often to the exclusion of other values; practical

Utopia   an imaginary and ideally perfect place

Vacillate   to swing indecisively from one opinion to another

Vacuous   lacking serious purpose, intelligence, or substance

Validate   to establish the soundness or validity of; confirm

Vapid   lacking liveliness, animation, or interest

Vaporize   to convert into a vapor (gaseous state); to vanish as if vaporized

Vehement   forcefulness of expression or extreme intensity of emotions or convictions

Veracity   adherence or devotion to the truth; truthfulness

Verbose   using an excessive number of words; wordy

Verdant   green with vegetation

Vex   to bring distress to; plague, afflict, or annoy

Viable   capable of being done; practicable: *a viable plan*

Vicarious   feeling the experience of someone else as if it were you: *the mother felt her daughter's pain vicariously*

Vicissitude   one of the sudden or unexpected changes or hardships encountered in one's life, activities, or surroundings

Vigilant   carefully observant and on the alert

Vigilante   one who takes law enforcement into his or her own hands

Vilify   to make vicious and slanderous statements about; malign, defame

Vindicate   to clear of blame or suspicion with supporting arguments or proof

Vindictive   involving revenge; spiteful

Virtuoso   exhibiting the fine skill, masterful technique, and ability similar to that of a master musician

Virulent   extremely infectious or poisonous; capable of causing disease

Viscous   having a high resistance to flow; thick and sticky, syrupy

Vitriolic   bitter, harsh, or scathing

Vituperate   to scold or criticize harshly or with abusive language; berate

Vocation   a regular occupation, especially one for which a person is particularly suited or qualified

Vociferous   marked by noisy and vehement outcry

Volition   the act of choosing or determining

Wallow   indolent or clumsy rolling around, as if in water, snow, or mud: *pigs wallowing in the mud*

Wane   to gradually decrease

Wanton   being without check or limitation; undisciplined, unrestrained

Wary   cautious, on guard, watchful

Winsome   charming, often in a childlike or naive way

Wistful   full of wishful yearning or desire, often tinged with melancholy

Witticism   a witty remark; often clever, ironic, or funny

Wizened   shriveled, withered, dried up

Wrath   intense anger

Zeal   enthusiastic devotion to a goal and tireless diligence in its pursuit

Zenith   the highest point above the observer's horizon attained by a celestial body

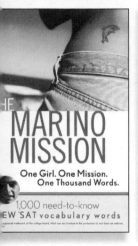